Towards the Abolition
of Whiteness

THE HAYMARKET SERIES

Editors: Mike Davis and Michael Sprinker

The Haymarket Series offers original studies in politics, history and culture, with a focus on North America. Representing views across the American left on a wide range of subjects, the series will be of interest to socialists both in the USA and throughout the world. A century after the first May Day, the American left remains in the shadow of those martyrs whom the Haymarket Series honors and commemorates. These studies testify to the living legacy of political activism and commitment for which they gave their lives.

Towards the Abolition of Whiteness

Essays on Race, Politics, and Working Class History

DAVID R. ROEDIGER

VERSO
London · New York

First published by Verso 1994
© David R. Roediger 1994
All rights reserved

Verso
UK: 6 Meard Street, London W1V 3HR
USA: 29 West 35th Street, New York, NY 10001-2291

Verso is the imprint of New Left Books

ISBN 0-86091-438-0
ISBN 0-86091-658-8 (pbk)

British Library Cataloguing in Publication Data
A catalogue record for this book is available from the British Library

Library of Congress Cataloging-in-Publication Data
A catalog record for this book is available from the Library of Congress

Typeset in Janson by NorthStar, San Francisco, California
Printed and bound in Great Britain by Biddles Ltd, Guilford and King's Lynn

To Anna Mae, Brendan and Donovan

Contents

Preface

When President William Clinton withdrew the nomination of the civil rights lawyer Lani Guinier for assistant attorney general, Guinier both expressed sharp disappointment at not having the opportunity to defend her views and added her agreement that a 'divisive debate' over race was the 'last thing' the nation could now afford. In taking the latter position, though not in her larger views, Guinier typified the current stance of most American liberals and much of the left by implying that the Democratic Party's hesitantly progressive politics is such a fragile flower that it cannot survive even the frank disucssion of racism, let alone the pursuit of 'race-specific' reform initiatives. The essays collected in this volume argue that the history of US labor sharply calls into question the proposition that those who seek to address class oppression in the US should hesitate to raise the issue of race. The essays suggest that race and class are so imbricated in the consciousness of working-class Americans that we do not 'get' class if we do not 'get' race. Indeed the refusal to engage the complexities of race can result in the 'retreat from class' just as surely as can a reductive obsession with race as a transhistorical, essentialist category. Moreover, the whiteness of white workers, far from being natural and unchallengeable, is highly conflicted, burdensome and even inhuman. To address not only racial oppression, but also class exploitation and even militarism, the idea that it is desirable or unavoidable to be white must be exploded.

These essays are offered as political, as well as historical, interventions with considerable modesty. Many are contributions to debates still in the initial stages of definition. By themselves, and even in combination with my *The Wages of Whiteness: Race and the Making of the American Working Class* (Verso, 1991), they represent only the beginnings of a reconceptualization of US labor history. Moreover, to claim a place for revising labor history in mapping the renewal of left politics is bound to seem like special pleading for a discipline currently much regarded as less than relevant and in decline. It is part of the burden of this volume to show that the 'crisis of labor history' is not only closely connected to crises in the larger society, but also that a working-class history that takes race and gender seriously can speak tellingly to such crises. In that sense and, I hope, in others these essays echo W. E. B. Du Bois's insistence in *Black Reconstruction in America* (1935) that replotting US history with African American workers and racially privileged, but also burdened, white workers at its center is a political act that opens dramas in the past and the present.

Many people shared their ideas, their reactions to drafts of these essays, their own not-yet-published research and even their research notes as this book took shape. I am grateful to Laura Edwards, Donna Gabaccia, Julie Willett, Caroline Waldron, Philip S. Foner, Bonnie Stepenoff, Randy McBee, Patrick Huber, Eric Arnesen, Roger Horowitz, Nancy Hewitt, Herbert Hill, Lawrence Glickman, LeeAnn Whites, Noel Ignatiev, Jean Allman, Susan Porter Benson, Steve Watts, Robin D. G. Kelley, Steve Rosswurm, Barry Goldberg, Archie Green, John Kuo Wei Tchen, Franklin Rosemont, Rose Feurer, Sundiata Cha-Jua, Tera Hunter, Yvette Huginnie, George Lipsitz, Paul Garon, Rick Halpern, Abra Quinn, Aldon Morris, Bruce Nichols and Paul Taillon for such assistance. Barrett and Whites in particular provided detailed suggestions and searching commentary to which the revision process has not done full justice. The more that I discover how much I have to learn about race in the US, the more that I appreciate how brilliantly I was taught about race by George Fredrickson and Sterling Stuckey in graduate school at Northwestern University. Talks before audiences at the Newberry Library (Chicago), the *New Left Review* Lecture Series, the Southern Labor History Conference, Iowa State University, University of Chicago, University of California at San Diego, University of Michigan, the United Auto Workers New Directions Summer School, Purdue University's American Studies Symposium, the University of the Western Cape (South Africa) Marxist Theory Seminar, and meetings of the Missouri Conference on History, Organization of American Historians and American Studies Association afforded opportunities to test ideas in this book. Thanks are also due to the Newberry Library's Lloyd Lewis Fellowship (funded in part by the National Endowment for the Humanities) and the University of Missouri Research Council. Library staff at the Newberry and at the University of Missouri's Western Historical Manuscript Collections were immensely helpful. Research assistance from Shuang Hu, Brett Rogers, and Amanda Bishop made the writing go much faster than it otherwise could have as did typing and editorial assistance from Patricia Eggleston. Mike Davis and Mike

Sprinker, as series editors, provided their customary perfect mixture of patience and prodding.

This collection mixes in about equal parts new essays and reprinted ones. Citations to the original publication are included in the first note of each reprinted essay. Thanks are in order to the editors of *Monthly Review, The Year Left* (Verso Books), *New Left Review, Labour/Le Travail, Journal of Social History, New Politics, American Quarterly* and the Charles H. Kerr Publishing Company for permission to reprint articles originally appearing in their pages and to *International Review of Social History* (Cambridge University Press) for permission to reprint portions of an article. In the case of the reprinted articles few changes have been made beyond the correction of small errors, mostly typographical or stylistic. The articles, which follow a previously unpublished introduction on the political implications of studies of the historical and social construction of race, are arranged chronologically in the order of their appearance and are grouped under two headings. The first includes largely historiographical articles on the new labor history and race, while the second gathers mostly new essays addressing the possibility of studies in whiteness and the replotting of US working class history.

' . . . the only whitey is system and ideology.'

Amiri Baraka (1991)

'As long as you think you are white, there's no hope for you.'

James Baldwin
The Price of the Ticket (1985)

INTRODUCTION

From the Social Construction of Race to the Abolition of Whiteness

A telling joke that has made the rounds among African American scholars comments on the distance between academic trends in writing on
race and life in the 'real world'. 'I have noticed', the joke laments, 'that
my research demonstrating that race is merely a social and ideological
construction helps little in getting taxis to pick me up late at night.' The
humor here is sufficiently ironic that the joke does not signal a rejection
of the idea that the social construction of race is worth talking and writing about, but it does focus attention on the fact that race may be more
easily demystified on paper than disarmed in everyday life.

The problem raised by the 'taxi joke' is a part of the broader questioning of recent critical scholarship on the grounds that its professed attempts to be popular and political have not yielded results that have
proven useful in stemming the tide of reaction in the US. Among the
most sweeping critics of the 'new scholarship', there is a tendency to regard its lack of immediate political impact as proof that not only postmodernist studies, but also scholarly works emphasizing race and gender, are
at best frivolously apolitical and at worst obscenely hypocritical in their
radicalism. Such attacks demand an answer, both because they at times
score effectively in criticisms of the hyper-academicized jargon filling recent writing and because radical intellectuals should want to be held to a
standard of political engagement. It would be easy to show that the critics
of the new scholarship themselves often lack any coherent politics beyond
a vague populism or a longing for a kind of Marxism that is unlikely to
survive in a world in which women and people of color increasingly form
the core of both the working class and the left. Similarly, it would be easy
to argue that it is unfair to expect a small number of university teachers to
influence the habits of America's cabdrivers. What is harder, but neces-

1

sary, is for those of us who believe that recent scholarship does make some modest contribution to radical change to be far more specific about how this is so and about the political implications of our work.

In taking up this challenge, I want to focus here particularly on the political implications of the idea that race is given meaning through the agency of human beings in concrete historical and social contexts, and is not a biological or natural category. The development of this insight constitutes a major achievement of recent scholarship and one broadly established across disciplinary lines. Students might learn this lesson in biology through the writings of Stephen Jay Gould or Donna Haraway; in history via Alexander Saxton's and Edmund Morgan's penetrating studies or Barbara Fields's seminal essays; in sociology from Richard Williams; in literature courses from the works of Toni Morrison or Hazel Carby; in women's studies from bell hooks or Vron Ware; in religious studies from Cornel West; or in African American studies by reading Sterling Stuckey's indispensable *Slave Culture*. Poststructuralist theory has enriched the work of some of these scholars and more fully informed the studies by Eric Lott, Colette Gullaumin, and Coco Fusco, all of which open important dimensions in the 'denaturing' of race.

Students who come to understand that race is given meaning within human society rather than within DNA codes are thus often putting together what they have learned in a number of areas. It often takes a good while for the insight to click. Even among left-inclined students, the idea that race is natural is so ingrained that there is an assumption that liberal and even radical education must be trying to teach that race is not very important, but nonetheless is a material reality. When students do 'get it', they are often tremendously enthusiastic. Seeing race as a category constantly being struggled over and remade, they sense that the possibilities of political action in particular and human agency in general are vastly larger than they had thought. They reflect on the manner in which structures of social oppression have contributed to the tragic ways that race has been given meaning. They often come to indict those structures. To the limited, but important, extent to which these things happen, one small corner of the extravagant *Reader's Digest/New Republic* nightmares regarding what goes on in 'politically correct' American higher education is happily made flesh.

But as important as this transformation is, it sometimes proves more satisfying as a guide to making a way through seminars than through the rest of the day. As the joke that begins this chapter suggests, for all its insubstantiality race is a very powerful ideology. If students hope that the potency of race will give way simply because they can offer a strong intellectual demystification of the concept, they will quickly be disappointed. More important, the insight that race is socially constructed is so sweeping that by itself it implies few specific political conclusions. In the absence of a large student movement or class movement in which they might test directions to proceed from general insight to specific actions, students whose eyes have been opened concerning race may turn up in the Clinton campaign, with its emphasis on bringing all Americans together. They may end up in small socialist sects, whose general acceptance of race as a natural category is balanced by an eager insistence that race is also manipulated and given prominence by employers and politicians seeking to divide workers – an insistence that makes for an argument that sounds like a thorough demystification of race based on the understanding of class. On campus, students who have been enlightened regarding race may be found agitating for the expansion of African American studies, because they appreciate the ways that racial ideology has conditioned history and daily life. Conversely, they may argue that anything race-specific is illusory and dangerous. Or those challenging the existence of race as a natural category may argue a hodge-podge of political positions. *Newsweek's* special section on the Los Angeles rebellions of 1992, for example, takes the enlightened view that the 'very concept of race' may be 'a relic', which is 'scientifically spurious' since 'there is no such thing as "black"', and 'white ... does not define a race.' The article then more or less randomly offers a thoroughly familiar and confused set of remedies for the urban crisis, emphasizing tax incentives to business, workfare, free enterprise zones, self-help, family values and beefed up police forces.

Obviously, no amount of writing by radical intellectuals can stand in for a freedom movement in which ideas can be tested. But it nonetheless is incumbent on those of us who have argued that seeing race as socially constructed is a vital intellectual breakthrough to suggest where we think that breakthrough may lead politically. This introduction begins with a short travelogue of examples from England and Africa. This section is designed to show that the idea that race is socially constructed broadly 'works', by helping powerfully to clarify important issues, but that it does not, by itself, settle the question of what political direction to take in matters of race and class. Returning to the US, the chapter critiques attempts to minimize emphasis on allegedly 'divisive' on 'illusory' racial issues in American political struggles. It argues that the central political implication arising from the insight that race is socially constructed is the specific need to attack *whiteness* as a destructive ideology rather than to attack the concept of race abstractly. While acknowledging a tragic past and significant roadblocks to the creation of working class nonwhiteness, the essay concludes that consciousness of whiteness also contains elements of a critique of that consciousness and that we should encourage the growth of a politics based on hopeful signs of a popular giving up on whiteness.

3

Transatlantic Notes on the Social Construction of Race

It is not possible to travel far without encountering vivid evidence that race is a socially constructed ideology rather than a biologically determined category. In Ghana's Ashanti Region, where this is being written, we are greeted on the streets by children who chant, '*Oburoni koko maakye.*' English-speaking Ashantis often translate this as 'Red white man, good morning.' Similarly, *oburoni wawu*, the term for used Western clothing, is charmingly translated as 'the white men, they have died.' However, *oburoni* derives from *Aburokyere*, the Akan word for 'from across the waters', and is thus not the equivalent of Euro-American usages of *white*. The many Chinese, Koreans and Japanese now in Ghana are generally also termed *oburoni*. But in discussing translation Ashantis will point out that this is not just because they are 'from across the sea' but because they 'are white' – that is, they are perceived as looking and acting like Europeans and Americans. African American visitors present an intriguing case because they literally have crossed the waters to reach Ashanti. In most cases today only the fairest of such visitors would be called *oburoni*. But in the recent past there apparently was some tendency to apply the term to them according to its original derivation. Thus it is intriguing in a number of ways that British listeners to Malcolm X's talks in Ghana on his celebrated pilgrimage to Mecca tell me that Ghanaians expressed surprise to them that an *oburoni* could say such things. Indeed one listener recalls hearing Malcolm described as a *white man* with astonishing ideas. Whatever strong elements of playfulness run through such characterizations, they ought to alert us to the complexity and the reality of the social construction of race.

Other transatlantic experiences demonstrate the ways the social construction of race enters politics. In 1984, when we lived in the London borough of Brent, immigrants and descendants of immigrants of many nationalities often called themselves 'Blacks', because that 'racial' category came close to becoming what A. Sivanandan's brilliant work has characterized as a 'political colour' of the oppressed. Asian Indians, Pakistanis, Malaysians, Turks, Chinese, Bangladeshis, Arabs and even Cypriots and some Irish so identified themselves. While on a movement-approved speaking tour in South Africa in 1989, we noted how consistently opponents of apartheid exposed the government-created 'mixed race' category of *coloureds* as an ideological creation, by always taking care to use the term 'so-called coloureds'. Many among the 'so-called coloured' population insisted that they were in fact *Africans*. On the same visit to South Africa, the son of an African laborer in the Cape Town harbor told a story that further wonderfully illustrates how race is a created, and recreated, ideology. 'WHITES ONLY' signs, according to the father, appeared historically on the Cape Town waterfront only after literally minded white US seamen avoided 'EUROPEANS ONLY' facilities.

Each of these examples is valuable in showing that the insight that race is socially constructed is apt and important. But they are also useful in pushing our discussions toward the complexities of how such knowledge might be applied politically. If extended, or probed, each example raises its own problems. For instance, we need to reflect on the fact that since the early 1980s the initiatives towards building a pan-Black identity among the British oppressed have been stalled and even dismantled, amidst a sharp resurgence of ethnic particularism. How should political activists, armed with the knowledge that race is a mutable, ideological category, evaluate this change? Was it the inevitable result of trying to build resistance based on the 'illusion' of 'political colour'? Is ethnic particularism, a more historic if not more 'real' identity, bound to outlast an invented tradition of common Blackness? Or, as Sivanandan forcefully maintains, was the real possibility of unifying the exploited around the class- and race-based consciousness of 'political colour' subverted by deliberate state policy and by opportunism among ethnic leaders?

Similar problems attend the South African example. In my early talks there, I eagerly attempted to extend the phrase 'so-called coloured' to all racial constructions, and spoke of 'so-called whites' and 'so-called Blacks'. As a way to force consideration of the fact that these were also historically created categories this was perhaps a justifiable strategy. As a contribution to political debate in the freedom movement in South Africa it was less apposite. The best militants there were arguing for thorough programs of affirmative action in the schools, the movement structures and the larger society, holding that the way to nonracialism includes a consideration of race. I offered a formulation that could comfort those who thought that a nonracial future could be created by dismissing race-based politics and even discussion of race as unnecessary and counterproductive. Powerful as it is, the insight that race is socially constructed does not magically inform us with strategies for overcoming race-class oppression.

The twist on the Ghanaian example only appears to be more mundane. As we walk in Kumasi, especially in neighborhoods we have not been in before, residents sometimes cheerfully shout, in English, 'Hey, you are white!' This struck me as being a puzzling, as well as a spectacular, example of non sequitur until I realized that you almost never see whites walking more than a short distance there. The full thought was, 'Hey, you are white and out walking around!' or 'Hey, you are white and ought to have a car!' While the comment seemed purely 'about color' or 'about race', it was in fact about a behavior that made color worth commenting upon. Thus, while race is ideologically constructed, it is constructed from real, predictable, repeated patterns of life. Indeed, as Barbara Fields and Walter

Rodney point out, it is this *connection* to reality that gives race such a powerful ideological appeal. Whites are not biologically programmed to have a car or motorbike, but in Ghana they seldom lack one, and this makes race seem very much to matter in a hot, hilly, dusty place where walking is work. To announce that what 'really' predicts vehicle ownership are income, ties to multinational corporations and roles in organized relief operations, missionary projects or academic research would hardly dissolve the perceived connections of car and color. As Rodney's magnificent *History of Guyanese Working People* observes, perceptions of the world in terms of race have thrived because they have 'seemed reasonably consistent with aspects of people's life experiences'. Race is thus both unreal and a seeming reality. Its demystification cannot be accomplished by even an airtight intellectual case, but only by hard and immensely complicated cultural and political struggle.

Why Keep Talking about Race?

The stateside evidence that race is socially constructed, ideologically powerful and fraught with complexity is more familiar but equally compelling. Electorally, as Thomas and Mary Edsall and others have shown, whiteness has become, to use Sivanandan's phrase, a 'political colour' that binds a disparate New Right coalition together and allows it to attract enough votes from fearful and embittered middle class and working class whites to rule. From the completion of mid-1960s civil rights legislation through 1992, only one Democrat occupied the White House, and he after a particularly astute bow to the importance of 'ethnic purity'. From 'benign neglect' to Willie Horton, even the lukewarm Democratic commitment to civil rights has left the party so vulnerable to suspicions of being 'soft on race' that its leadership has engaged for eight years in a more-or-less open search for an unassailably white candidate in what has been called a Southern strategy but is better understood as a suburban one.

Whiteness exercises such political force despite its thorough discrediting as a 'cultural color', despite its having become the fair game of standup comics who reflect on the vacuity of 'white culture' in a nation in which so much that is new, stirring, excellent and genuinely popular – in music, fashion, oratory, dance, vernacular speech, sport and increasingly in literature, film, and nonfiction writing – comes from African American, Asian American and Latino communities. We face, in short, a mad and maddening situation in which the appeals of whiteness are at their most pitifully meager and the effectiveness of appeals to whiteness – from Howard Beach to Simi Valley to the ballot boxes – are at a terrible height.

The great American writer Ralph Ellison saw it coming over a decade ago, and framed a question which goes to the heart of modern US politics and culture with merciless precision:

> What, by the way, is one to make of a white youngster who, with a transistor radio, screaming a Stevie Wonder tune, glued to his ear, shouts racial epithets at black youngsters trying to swim at a public beach – and this in the name of the ethnic sanctity of what has been declared a neighborhood turf?

Unable to answer this question and understandably tired after a long period of racially based reactionary rule, there is every temptation for us to move from the insight that race is an ideological construct to the conclusion that it's high time to denounce it as both snare and delusion and to return to a populist politics of economic reform. Dwelling on race, or advocating 'race-specific' remedies, is on this view suspected as counterproductive and even malicious. Thus Barbara Fields's staunchly materialist *New Left Review* article on the origins of US racism ends with an astonishingly idealist castigation of a mother who asks her four-year-old if a playmate is 'black' and then laughs when the child answers that he is 'brown'. 'The young woman's benevolent laughter was for the innocence of youth too soon corrupted', Fields writes, 'but for all its benevolence, her laughter hastened the corruption.' Fields argues that the woman, and radical intellectuals who emphasize race as a 'tragic flaw' in the US, give reality to race. She rather harshly suggests that in so doing they are like the Ku Klux Klan and the white murderers of the Black teenager Yusef Hawkins. Others hold that we should refrain from the discussion of racial issues on the practical grounds that only economic issues can generate electoral success. The concrete proposals vary widely as to what should be emphasized instead of race. Fields proposes the interesting, but constitutionally fanciful, strategy of affirmative action based on class, while for William Julius Wilson and the many influential policy thinkers around the liberal journal *American Prospect*, the issues capable of disarming race are those in which the white middle class has a direct interest, especially jobs and health care.

Such strategies closely fit the chastened and disspirited mood of contemporary American liberalism, and they have some mass appeal among African American voters ready for anything but Reaganism (and albeit on low turnouts and with little alternative, therefore generally supportive of Bill Clinton's candidacy). Nonetheless, in my view initiatives avoiding discussion of race have little chance of success, even on their own limited terms. The absence of a liberal labor vote – both because so few workers are now organized and because a majority of those in white households containing a union member have voted for Reagan and Bush over the last three elections – makes prospects for an ongoing mildly progressive, class-based alliance inauspicious. Nor can Democrats be much more thorough at shutting up about racial justice than they already have been in recent campaigns. Clinton's reticence in offering comment on the Los Angeles rebellions is standard operating procedure (excepting the Jackson campaigns) regarding race for post-1972 Democratic presidential politics, not a new departure. The strategy of ignoring race has in that sense been well and truly tried.

For that matter, neither do the Republicans engage in much open discussion of race. They couch their appeals for a 'white vote' in terms of welfare reform, neighborhood schools, toughness on crime and 'illegitimate' births. In the 1991 Mississippi governor's race, the rightwing Republican victor, Kirk Fordice, ended an antiwelfare campaign commercial with a still photograph of a Black woman and her baby. He literally invited white Mississippians to vote against African American people, but did so without directly discussing race. In the wake of the Los Angeles rebellion of 1992, Bush's most vital soundbite ran, 'For anyone who cares about our young people it is painful that in 1960 the percentage of births to unwed mothers was 5 percent – and now it is 27 percent.' As the London *Observer*'s US correspondent Andrew Stephen keenly observed, 'To the millions of Americans who saw the all-important soundbite, what he was really saying was "I'm talking about blacks, of course."' Even the celebrated Willie Horton ad of the 1988 Bush campaign did not *say* anything about race. During the 1992 campaign Dan Quayle managed to play on hostilities toward Black welfare mothers by talking about, of all things, white sitcom character Murphy Brown. Serious attention to race is already absent from US politics, and it is the right that benefits.

But might the positive content of economic reform programs wean white voters away from race-based politics, opening the way for experience in campaigns that cross racial lines to nurture the insight that race ought not divide working people? Such a strategy has undergirded much of the white American left's approach to race and class over the last century and more. Unions in particular have seemed such a promising venue for the gradual teaching of white workers that their real economic interests coincided with those of African Americans that endangering their organization by 'premature' assaults on racism has been seen as running counter to the interests of not only class justice but also of racial equality.

To the extent that we argue that whiteness and various kinds of 'white ethnicity' are reactions to alienation, an interesting modern case for this long-established strategy of overcoming white supremacy via an emphasis on class can be made. We may emphasize, as my *Wages of Whiteness* does, the role of powerlessness at work in opening people to settling for the fiction that they are 'white workers'. Or we may follow Frederic Jameson's

'Reification and Utopia in Mass Culture' in stressing the ways alienation produced by bureaucratic structures and commercialized culture helps to undergird ersatz ethnicity among whites. In either case, it would seem that participation in authentic struggles against oppression and powerlessness could be a useful antidote to whiteness. When, for example, a 'white rights' supporter of David Duke's 1991 gubernatorial bid in Louisiana stopped her litany of 'blacks on welfare' myths ('They get new cars every year ...') in an interview with *USA Today*, she added, 'The state won't take care of me.' Perhaps if there were a large, militant movement for decent health care, that woman might join it, press demands on the state, gain a sense of power and, in the course of struggle alongside the Black poor, question the myths she now recites.

It would be hard to imagine a successful assault on white supremacy that did not include millions of such small miracles, and that did not include a rallying around pressing class grievances. But far more problematic is the tendency to assume that a rediscovered emphasis on economic issues clarifies all, or even most, questions of political strategy where either race or class is concerned. The historical record of antiracist achievements of coalitions for economic reform is quite modest. From the National Labor Union through the Populists to the CIO, whatever we wish might have been and whatever their other accomplishments, such coalitions did not dramatically deliver the goods where racial justice was concerned. Nor does the record show that common struggles necessarily 'teach' common humanity lastingly. The Tom Watson wing of the Populists spectacularly learned the lesson of Black–white unity and more spectacularly forgot it. The experience of defeat – and there is no guarantee that class movements will win – particularly led to recrudescence of white supremacy. The dying convention of the National Labor Union respectfully entertained proposals by the Southern racist intellectual Hinton Rowan Helper to forcibly remove Blacks from the US, while the Knights of Labor, so brilliantly egalitarian at its height, actually came in its declining days to approve a resolution to colonize African Americans in order to help 'white labor'. Why there are prospects for a better outcome in a new effort at economic-oriented reform that minimizes immediate emphasis on racial justice remains unclear, especially given that the substance of the tepid reforms on offer from neoliberals who spearhead the call for economic-based strategies is hardly the stuff great transformations of consciousness are made from.

Advocates of increasing the weight placed on economic reformist appeals and of continuing the silence surrounding race sometimes have internalized a kind of Marxism that wants to emphasize the objective reality of class relationships as against the ideology of race. I have no quarrel with that distinction, but in applying it we need to avoid imagining that workers objectively view the world through their class experience in one part of their brain and subjectively through the distorting filter of race in another. At the level of consciousness, class is anything but a faithful reflection of objective reality. Moreover, the subjective way in which white workers perceive and define class is thoroughly shaped in the US by their whiteness. Two recent studies of contemporary New Jersey workers make this rather airy point concrete. In David Halle's excellent sociological study of chemical workers there, white male workers identify themselves as 'working men' and as 'middle class'. They tend to see their white neighbors as being like them in class terms whether or not those neighbors are wage workers. They see Black workers in jobs like theirs – workers more likely than the white neighbors to share AFL-CIO membership with the white chemical workers – as different in class terms, as 'loafers' and 'intruders'. Even more striking is Katherine Newman's recent study of industrial decline, based on interviews with white former factory workers whose plant has closed in Elizabeth, New Jersey. Many of the workers process this stark class experience by arguing that the employer was forced to leave because it was impossible to turn profits while being forced to employ Blacks and Hispanics. A movement that seeks to outflank a David Duke simply by popularizing the kind of unemployment and healthcare plans that would benefit the hard-hit whites who form a large part of his constituency runs head-on into the problem that many of the white poor, including not a few on relief, cast the welfare state as a scheme to benefit 'those people'. As an influential study quoted by the Edsalls puts it, for a key sector of the white electorate 'virtually all progressive symbols and themes have been redefined in racial and pejorative terms.' In such situations, one could as easily argue that attacking racism in a precondition for class-based reform as that class-based reform is a precondition for attacking racism.

Nearly half a century ago, C. L. R. James critiqued traditional left strategy on race and class by writing, '"Black and White, Unite and Fight" is unimpeachable in principle. ... But it is often misleading and sometimes even offensive in the face of the infinitely varied, tumultuous, passionate and often murderous reality of race relations in the United States.' Many of those advocating single-minded emphasis on common economic grievances today might shy away from words like 'Fight', from the mention of race in their slogans and even from slogans altogether. But we should still share James's unease with any political strategy that supposes that class grievances in the US can be addressed without full attention to race.

The British theorist Terry Eagleton has held that gender and nation, like class, are socially constructed identities based on an alienation that 'cancel[s] the particularity of an individual life into collective anonymity.' But he has refused to follow 'some contemporary poststructuralist theory' in concluding that we should therefore suppose that we can 'go around' any of these identities rather than go 'all the way through' them. He has argued practically that 'because the truth remains that women are oppressed *as women* – that such categories, ontologically empty though they may be, continue to exert an implacable force' – we must struggle over (and talk about) gender. We must pursue a political strategy 'caught up in the very metaphysical categories it hopes finally to abolish.' I would suggest that race is another such 'ontologically empty' and 'metaphysical' category that we must confront to abolish. Many leftists and liberals would perhaps grant the truth of at least parts of this critique of economism, but would still argue that, like it or not, 'race-specific' politics have in practice simply been discredited as unworkable. In making a serious effort to locate 'the left wing of the possible', they point to demographic realities and white voting patterns and emphasize the dangers of minorities 'going it alone' by continuing to organize around particularistic grievances. Indeed the Edsalls and other recent writers who champion economistic strategies do so not out of a dismissal of the importance of white supremacy but – like the great early exemplar of such strategies, Bayard Rustin – out of a very grim appreciation of racism's influence. In an important public exchange with Democratic North Carolina politician Harvey Gantt, the victim of Jesse Helms's race-baiting in a recent Senate election, the populist historian Lawrence Goodwyn argues for economic reform as the only viable Democratic strategy because he doesn't 'see any other way to cope with the racism of the American electorate'.

In opposing such economism, we must be humble enough to admit that it has triumphed as a strategy against reaction because existing alternatives to it have proven less than attractive. A liberalism based on half-hearted pursuit of affirmative action has not proven more popular than a liberalism based on half-hearted pursuit of job creation and health insurance. Attempts to combine and transcend the two approaches within a Rainbow Coalition have largely stalled. Initiatives to unite workers around revolutionary, rather than reformist, economic demands have had far less mass resonance than the appeals of a David Duke. In trying to stop a Duke, or a George Bush, opponents of reaction gravitate towards economic reformism almost by default. Supporting the pale populism of Eddie Edwards in Louisiana or Bill Clinton nationally is not so much the politics of lesser evil as one of last resort.

But as understandable as such 'last resortism' is, it remains a dead end. The strategy generally fails, even on its own terms, by not keeping the Helmses, Bushes and Reagans from victory (nor even keeping Duke from winning a majority of the 'white vote'). More seriously, the caution and the fear of open discussion of race bred by constant attention to the immediate electorally 'possible' blinds us to the real tensions within white supremacy. It leaves us unable to appreciate the ways in which a sharp questioning of whiteness within American culture opens the opportunity to win people to far more effective opposition to both race and class oppression. To take advantage of such possibilities requires that we not only continue to talk about race but that we pay attention to the most neglected aspects of race in America, the questions of why people think they are white and of whether they might quit thinking so.

Towards a Withering Away of Whiteness

When residents of the US talk about race, they too often talk only about African Americans, Native Americans, Hispanic Americans, and Asian Americans. If whites come into the discussion, it is only because they have 'attitudes' towards nonwhites. Whites are assumed not to 'have race', though they might be racists. Many of the most critical advances of recent scholarship on the social construction of race have come precisely because writers have challenged the assumption that we only need to explain why people come to be considered Black, Asian, Native American or Hispanic and not attend to what Theodore Allen has marvelously termed the 'invention of the white race'. Coco Fusco sums up this central insight and its political import, writing, 'Racial identities are not only Black, Latino, Asian, Native American and so on; they are also white. To ignore white ethnicity is to redouble its hegemony by naturalizing it.'

To make its fullest possible contribution to the growth of a new society, activism that draws on ideas regarding the social construction of race must focus its political energies on exposing, demystifying and demeaning the particular ideology of whiteness, rather than on calling into question the concept of race generally. In defending this position, three points deserve elaboration. The first is that, while neither whiteness nor Blackness is a scientific (or natural) racial category, the former is infinitely more false, and precisely because of that falsity, more dangerous, than the latter. The second is that in attacking the notion that whiteness and Blackness are 'the same', we specifically undermine what has become, via the notion of 'reverse racism', a major prop underpinning the popular refusal among whites to face both racism and themselves. The last is that whiteness is now a particularly brittle and fragile form of social identity and that it can be fought.

By far the most penetrating modern analysis of whiteness comes in the unlikely form of an essay of a mere two pages in a 'lifestyle' magazine. Writing in *Essence* in 1984, James Baldwin reflected 'On Being "White" and Other Lies' and immediately put his finger on what sets whiteness apart as an American social phenomenon. 'The crisis of leadership in the white community is remarkable – and terrifying – ' Baldwin began, 'because there is, in fact, no white community.' It is not merely that whiteness is oppressive and false; it is that whiteness is *nothing but* oppressive and false. We speak of African American culture and community, and rightly so. Indeed the making of disparate African ethnic groups into an African American people, so lucidly described by Sterling Stuckey, is a genuine story of an American melting pot. In her passionate attacks on both the concept of an African American race and that of a white race, Barbara Fields characterizes African Americans as a 'nation'. Whites are clearly not that. There is an American culture, but it is thoroughly 'mulatto', to borrow Albert Murray's fine description. If there is a Southern culture, it is still more thoroughly mulatto than the broader American one. There are Irish American songs, Italian American neighborhoods, Slavic American traditions, German American villages, and so on. But such specific ethnic cultures always stand in danger of being swallowed by the lie of whiteness. Whiteness describes, from Little Big Horn to Simi Valley, not a culture but precisely the absence of culture. It is the empty and therefore terrifying attempt to build an identity based on what one isn't and on whom one can hold back.

Almost no left initiatives have challenged white workers to critique, much less to abandon, whiteness. Baldwin's wonderful comment in the film *The Price of the Ticket*, that 'As long as you think you're white, there's no hope for you', seems more poetic than political to radicals who have so long confined their struggles to encouraging whites to unite with Blacks, and who have found it difficult to disarm racism, much less to think of abolishing whiteness. But a highly poetic politics is exactly what is required in a situation in which workers who identify themselves as white are *bound* to retreat from genuine class unity and meaningful antiracism. In a fascinating 1974 essay, outlining the preconditions for the emergence of united labor struggles, the great London-based theorist A. Sivanandan defied usual formulations of the relationship between race and class, writing that 'in recovering its sense of oppression, both from technological alienation and [from] a white-oriented culture [the white working class must] arrive at a consciousness of racial oppression.' On this view, the rejection of racial oppression by white workers must arise not just out of common participation in class, or even antiracist, struggles alongside Blacks, but also out of a critique of the empty culture of whiteness itself. Rejection of whiteness is then part of a process that gives rise to both attacks on racism and to the very recovery of 'sense of oppression' among white workers.

If it does not involve a critique of whiteness, the questioning of racism often proves shallow and limited. Indeed, at this horrifying juncture in race relations, most whites describe themselves as 'not racists'. Even David Duke packages white supremacy as a National Association for the Advancement of White People, allowing supporters to feel that, as one of them told *USA Today*, they are only doing the 'same thing' as Blacks in the NAACP. Even open Klan members now at times describe their organizations 'not racist'. In St Louis, young whites call Blacks 'nigger' on the 'nonracist' ground that they are describing behavior, not genetics. 'Black guys are nice and polite', they reason, 'but niggers are pests.' It is easy to regard such rationales as rank hypocrisy, especially in David Duke's mouth, but we should also face the fact that many whites genuinely feel absolved from being what they would call 'bigots' or 'racists'. To most white students these terms imply being an 'extremist', being 'violent' or being 'worse than average'. Most students are sure that they are none of those.

The destructive term 'reverse racism' grows out of this assurance among whites that they have transcended race. They are sure that they see the world based on merit, while multiculturalists, affirmative action officers, Native American fishermen, Black nationalists and pointy-headed liberals 'bring in race'. An analysis that simply demystifies all conceptions of race without concentrating on critiquing whiteness runs the risk of reinforcing such widely and sincerely held notions.

The whole struggle against the concept of 'reverse racism' is in fact terribly difficult when we fail to question whiteness and instead stay on the terrain of politics as usual. Conservatives creepily quote Martin Luther King, obscuring the fact that he himself was an advocate of affirmative action, as they hold that they are the true believers in raceless standards based on the 'content of one's character'. We try to argue from history to an audience not especially inclined towards the longer view. We hold that racism implies the systematic power to dominate and that since people of color lack such power, reverse racism is not a useful term. This perfectly valid point falls on deaf ears to the extent that the firmest believers in the reality of 'reverse racism' are often precisely those whites most convinced of their own powerlessness. Our last despairing comments often begin with 'But you refuse to see. ...'

But those feeling victimized by 'reverse racism' do see. They see in just the way, with just the blindnesses, that their assurance that they are 'white' (but not racist) and have 'white' interests demands that they see. In the Simi Valley trial they saw Rodney King, down and being kicked, but as one juror put it, somehow still in 'control' of the situation and menacing the white police. When Bill Clinton signalled his whiteness by using his appearance before the Rainbow Coalition to attack the rapper Sister Souljah, he hoped to appeal to the way many whites see. Or perhaps he just sees that way. He railed against Sister Souljah's comment that it is unremarkable that Black youth in South Central Los Angeles who attack and kill each other all year, would consider doing the same to whites for a week. Souljah's comment itself is no more than an exercise in introductory sociology, but Clinton offered a soundbite comparing Sister Souljah to David Duke. His demand that listeners imagine that the situation were reversed and that Duke made a statement like Souljah's was on one level absolutely perfect nonsense. What would the 'reverse' be? Would Duke go to Simi Valley or Beverly Hills, and say that it is unremarkable that whites who attack each other all year would attack Blacks for a week? The situation hasn't a reverse. Police do not single out whites for racial harassment and brutality. Hundreds of white youths are not killed in crack wars and gangbanging. Only whites could take Clinton's comment seriously. And they do.

But the Sister Souljah incident also ought to alert us to the fact that we need not just capitulate to whiteness. The Rainbow Coalition, before which Clinton spoke, mobilized tens of thousands of whites not only around its social democratic politics but around the idea that the fight against Reaganism should include people of color as central constituencies and as leaders. The Rainbow's most striking success in moving young white workers to act on the perception that the fighting style of the Black freedom movement was more appropriate to their plight than anything in 'white' politics – its mobilizing of Midwestern autoworkers in impressive 1988 rallies – did not, it is true, always translate into votes. The Rainbow's disorganization, lack of democracy and timidity combined with the continuing power of race-thinking among whites to limit the extent to which white workers entered politics as nonwhites, but the possibility that they could do so within an organization agitating on both class and race issues was clearly present.

We may suspect, moreover, that many white young people strongly appreciate hiphop artists like Sister Souljah far more than they do Bill Clinton. The tremendous popularity of hiphop music and style among white youth has been written off as a fascination with violence and sexism among very young white suburban males; but the attraction is much broader than that. Rappers with varying messages appeal to male and female middle class and working class whites from grade school to adulthood. Unlike rock, which brought whites to African American music but quickly diluted the Black influence and threw up white performers as the most celebrated stars, hiphop is embraced by whites without any sharp tendency to expropriate it. In this it more nearly parallels white working class attraction to soul music in the 1960s and 1970s (and still, see – by all means – *The Commitments*) and perhaps to reggae. Hiphop offers white youth not only the spontaneity, experimentation, humor, danger, sexuality, physical movement and rebellion absent from what passes as white culture but it also offers an explicit, often harsh, critique of whiteness.

Of course it would be ridiculous to claim that every white hiphop fan is finding a way out of whiteness, let alone of racism. There will be no simple fix for the white problem in America and it is well to emphasize limits as well as possibilities. The 'guido' subculture in Italian American New York City, well described in the recent writings of Donald Tricarico, stands as an ambiguous example of both those possibilities and limits. Guidos have much adopted hiphop and asserted a distinctive Italian American identity as against white American 'wannabes'. They refer to themselves as 'Guineas', turning that anti-Italian, anti-Black slur into a badge of honor. But the break with whiteness and racism on New York's streets is less than complete. As Tricarico nicely understates it, in many ways Guidos 'resist identification with Black youth' and 'bite the hand that feeds them style'.

Historically, the use of an (often distorted) image of African American life to express criticisms of 'white culture', or longings for a different way of life, has hardly been an antidote to racism. The minstrel show expressed such longings beneath blackface while still holding African Americans in contempt in a perfect illustration of Herman Melville's wise observation that '… envy and antipathy, passions irreconcilable in reason, nevertheless may spring conjoined … in one birth.' In some ways the greater the longing has been, the greater the need to reassert whiteness and white supremacy. Nor, as Norman Mailer showed, largely unwittingly, in 'The White Negro', has the use of African American culture to critique whiteness come without superficiality, fatuity and paternalism. Loss of whiteness can have the beauty it does in a film like John Waters's *Hairspray* or the vapidity and arrogance it does in a film like *Soul Man*. And these extremes exist not just among, but within, individual whites. Finally, there is a sense in which whites cannot fully renounce whiteness even if they want to. The Italian American heroine (in many ways, I think) of Spike Lee's *Jungle Fever* is as exemplary a race traitor as any seen on the big screen within memory: but when the police come, she is still white.

Even given all these problems, we cannot afford to ignore the political implications of the mass questioning of whiteness as a trend and a possibility in the US. In a variety of settings, including even the Duke campaign, whites are confessing their confusion about whether it is really worth the effort to be white. We need to say that it is not worth it and that many of us do not want to do it. Initiatives against a Duke, or a Bush, should not only be class-oriented and antiracist, but also in a sense explicitly antiwhite, with a central focus on exposing how whiteness is used to make whites settle for hopelessness in politics and misery in everyday life. When a Clinton panders to whiteness, we should not let him off the hook on the grounds that his comments are only arguably 'racist' as currently defined. Our opposition should focus on contrasting the bankruptcy of white politics with the possibilities of nonwhiteness. We should point out not just that whites and people of color often have common economic interests but that people of color currently act on those interests far more consistently – in politics, at the workplace, and increasingly in community-based environmental struggles – precisely because they are not burdened by whiteness. We should transform 'reverse racism' from a curse to an injunction (Reverse racism!), campaigning for expanded affirmative action on the grounds of both justice and the need to remove the privileges that tragically reproduce whiteness. Coalitions for economic reform need to be considered not only as vehicles for class mobilization and for the disarming of racism but also as places where whites learn that people of color currently make more close connections between class and community than whites do and therefore of course assume a central place in insurgent movements. If even MTV realizes that there is a mass audience for the critique of whiteness, we cannot fail to attempt to rally, and to learn from, a constituency committed to its abolition.

NOTE: This article is based on a keynote address given during Socialist Week at Iowa State University in the fall of 1992 before the presidential election of that year.

PART I

The New Labor History and Race

'The reality, the depth, and the persistence of the delusion of white supremacy in this country causes any real concept of education to be as remote, and as much to be feared, as change or freedom itself.

What Black men here have always known is now beginning to be clear to the world. Whatever it is that white Americans want, it is not free-dom – neither for themselves nor for others.

"'It's you who'll have the blues", Langston Hughes said, "not me. Just wait and see."'

James Baldwin
The Price of the Ticket (1985)

'Despite the fact that the nineteenth century saw an upsurge in the power of the laboring classes and a flight toward economic equality and political democracy, this movement ... lagged far behind the accumulation of wealth, because in popular opinion labor was fundamentally degrading and the just burden of inferior peoples. ... It was bad enough to have the consequences of [racist] thought fall upon colored people the world over; but in the end it was even worse when one considers what this attitude did to the European worker. His aim and ideal was distorted. ... He began to want not comfort for all men but power over other men. ... He did not love humanity and he hated "niggers".'

W. E. B. Du Bois
The World and Africa (1946)

1

'Labor in White Skin': Race and Working Class History

'Labor in white skin cannot emancipate itself where the black skin is branded.'[1] That line from an 1866 letter to François Lafargue, and repeated in *Capital*, is perhaps the most quoted of Karl Marx's observations about the United States. But the work of our labor historians, past or present, has done little to illuminate why Marx's aphorism not only has the ring of truth but that of a ringing truth.

The scholarship which most ambitiously attempts to conceptualize the history of workers in the United States continues to ignore Black workers and, as critically, to ignore the effect of attitudes towards Blacks (and towards Indians, Chinese and Latinos) on the consciousness of white workers. George Rawick's call for a history that recognizes slavery as 'a fundamental part of the history of the whole American people',[2] was pioneered by W. E. B. Du Bois[3] and is continued today by Alexander Saxton, Herbert Hill, Richard Slotkin, Gwen Mink, Manning Marable, Peter Rachleff, Mike Davis and a few others.[4] But in the structuring of the debates that most preoccupy labor historians, race moves quickly and decidedly to the wings.

Criticisms abound of lack of attention to race and slavery in US labor history in particular, and in Western scholarship generally, with such leading scholars as Eugene Genovese, Immanuel Wallerstein and David Montgomery all sounding warnings in recent review essays.[5] And the many recent studies by sociologists, political scientists and even occupational folklorists showing the staying power of racism as a pole around which white workers' consciousness takes shape give added urgency to the comprehension of these themes in history as, of course, do the starkly contrasting patterns of white and Black working class voting in the 1980 and 1984 elections.[6]

21

Nonetheless, the new labor history has yet to find an approach worthy of the problems being examined or even to acknowledge that such problems must be consistently examined. The recent comments on Sean Wilentz's *Chants Democratic* by the historian Christopher Clark are instructive on this score:

> While Wilentz does not ignore women or Black workers, they are not central to his notion of a New York working-class movement, which at times ... achieved heights of class consciousness and even insurrectionary potential ... he has not written a thorough history of New York workers, but only of the most prominent and perhaps the most class conscious. Future studies will have to assess how far this slants his conclusions.[7]

This assessment comes in a review of a book which, while it ignores Black workers and the national context of slavery even more than Clark allows, is still of great value. But the assumption remains, even as the issue of race is raised, that the Black worker enters the story of American labor as an actor in a subplot that can be left on the cutting-room floor, probably without vitiating the main story. What if race is instead part of the very lens through which labor's story must be filmed?

The Old Labor History: Problems Right and Left

The original seminal works of labor history shared the racism of most scholarship on America written in the early twentieth century. The approach of the Wisconsin School of John R. Commons and his pioneering associates betrayed what Melvyn Dubofsky recently termed 'evident' measures of 'chauvinism and racism'.[8] Alongside the more active racism of Commons and his associates was the benign neglect typified by Werner Sombart's influential 1906 essays collected as *Why Is There No Socialism in the United States?*

Sombart does not discuss Black labor at all in a chapter entitled 'Politics and Race', in which he uses *race* to refer to ethnicity. The same silence characterizes the entire study despite Sombert's rather extreme and flat assertion, never pursued, that the 'Negro question has directly removed any class character from each of the two parties. ... '[9] But the most durable heritage of the original masterworks, especially from the Wisconsin School, has been the idea that in the normal course of things class alone, rather than race and class together, ought to be at the center of labor history in the United States. In an extravagant passage on Chinese exclusion, for example, the Wisconsin School's *History of Labor in the United States* holds:

The anti-Chinese agitation in California, culminating as it did in the exclusion Law of 1882, doubtless was the most important single factor in the history of America labor, for without it the entire country might have been overrun by Mongolian labor, and the labor movement might have become a conflict of races instead of one of classes.[10]

Rare is the modern labor historian who does not recoil from regarding Chinese exclusion as *the* historic victory of the American working class or from the image of the 'overrunning' Chinese. But almost as rare are historians who would focus their objections on the final words in the quoted passage and emphasize how often the struggles of labor were about both race and class and how thoroughly racism shaped and narrowed the conceptions of class of some unionists recently celebrated for their 'Americanism'.[11] In practice, neither the Marxism of the Old Left nor the populism and neo-Marxism of the new labor historians has managed to sustain a sharp break from the Commons tradition where race and class are concerned. Indeed in many ways the traditions of labor history in the last twenty-five years have reinforced the Commons approach.

By a long distance, the Old Left scholarship of Philip S. Foner comes nearer to an effective synthetic treatment of race and labor than any other of today's labor historians. Even Melvyn Dubofsky, whose 'Give Me That Old Time Labor History' is an almost relentlessly hostile review of Foner's work, allows that in his writings, 'one can ... find ... as nowhere else, the full story of the nation's minority and oppressed peoples.' Foner, whether in books specifically on race, labor and radicalism or in his general history of US labor, never misses a chance to narrate fully the story of Black workers or to detail instances in which racism undermined strikes and, more rarely, labor political action. Nor, as is so often charged, is his work 'mere narration'. As Harold Cruse, certainly no ideological friend to Foner, has observed, *American Socialism and Black Americans* breaks exciting new ground not just in its narration but in terms of Foner's method and the framing of questions.[12] Much the same could be said about *Organized Labor and the Black Worker*, especially in its insistence that Black self-organization, far from balkanizing the labor movement, was often the precondition for united struggle.

If, in the aphorism that begins this article, Marx had meant just that white labor would be oppressed by virtue of Black labor's remaining branded *because labor unity would therefore be breached and strikes undermined*, Foner's work could be considered a full history drawing on the analytic and predictive powers of Marx's brief words. Foner's stance is spelled out in his approving quotation of an 1865 editorial in the *Boston Daily Evening Voice* in the preface to *Organized Labor and the Black Worker*, as an illustration of the 'crippling effects of racism on organized labor'. The editorial compares cooperation of Black and white workers with that between 'the clerk [and] the coal heaver'. It adds that if any element in the labor force stands aloof 'there is the end of hope for the labor movement'. Commenting specifically on the recent emancipation of four million slaves, the editorial warns it would be 'blind and suicidal' to fail to make common cause with the freedman because lack of unity would make 'the Black man ... our competitor. He will underwork us to get employment and we have no choice but to underwork him in return.' Foner traces the bleak scenario of Black–white disunity and recounts the rarer and inspiring instances when the slogan which graces a placard on the book's cover became real: BLACK AND WHITE/UNITE AND FIGHT![13] He has found a large and important theme, I would argue, but one less grand than that suggested by Marx's aphorism or by the words of Du Bois and Baldwin which open Part I.

In that passage on the deleterious effects on white workers of the 'branding' of Blacks, Marx might have had in mind cracks in the front of labor unity, but that could hardly have been his foremost consideration. At about the same time Marx wrote to Lafargue, he and Engels apparently still thought that ex-slaves 'will probably become small squatters, as in Jamaica', and thus would not be a great force in the industrial labor market. Moreover, Marx's famous comment came in the context not of an assessment of trade union possibilities but of praise for Northern white workers who had helped to defeat *politically* President Andrew Johnson's forces in Congressional elections.

Most important, the passage links the overcoming of the branding of Black workers with no mere piecemeal gains in either the trade union or political realm, but with the possibility that labor might 'emancipate itself', that most broadly visionary of Marx's prophecies. This and other evidence, including Marx's 1869 comment that the Civil War and emancipation 'gave to [the working] class [a] moral impetus', suggests that Marx, at least for a time, saw the stakes in the battle over racial oppression as involving matters quite beyond trade-union unity.[14] Only Du Bois, with his brilliant framing of Black–white unity within the broader issue of white labor's willingness to sacrifice its possibilities for the spurious public and psychological wage of petty and not-so-petty racial privileges, begins to develop fully an approach that transcends the narrow parameters of 'Black and white/unite and fight.[15]

The point is obviously not that Marx knew best about America or that Foner has led us away from the truths laid down by the great teacher. Marx's own follow-up of the insights in his aphorism proved quite uncertain in the years after 1866. And in any case, Foner's approach, essentially that of Popular Front Communism with some sympathy for Black nationalism, has few followers among the new labor historians.[16] But few have managed to improve on this approach.

Class and Race: Base and Superstructure Revisited

Curiously, another aspect of Old Left Marxism – overemphasis on the point that class and not race is the central consideration in the history of white and Black workers – has found a place in the new labor history, with not entirely happy results. The privileging of class over race, which Foner largely abandons, was a consistent theme in early Socialist Party thought and is given more sophisticated expression in Barbara J. Fields's recent and sometimes scintillating essay 'Ideology and Race in American History'.[17] Fields reminds readers that race is not a biological fact but a social construct and argues that it is therefore an 'ideological' category in a way that class is not. Though she makes the invaluable points that racism is not 'transhistorical' and not, at a given time, understood in the same way by different classes, her essay is open to caveats and serious criticisms.

While it is true that racism evolves in a context of class relations, class is also defined by workers in partly racial terms. Thus David Halle's recent work on white New Jersey chemical workers describes men who, as David Montgomery has observed, cherish the notion that 'whites are "working men", while Blacks who live 'in nearby Elizabeth [and] are far more likely to be members of the AFL-CIO than the neighbors of the white chemical workers' are counted as 'intruders'.[18] In addition, Fields treats the formation of a 'Black' racial category almost exclusively as a process occurring among whites and underplays the extent to which it reflected a process of nation-building by the various African ethnic groups undergoing forced emigration. A full discussion would have to organize itself around the categories of nation, race and class rather than only the latter two.[19]

But even if we grant in good orthodox Marxist fashion that class is a theoretical category more basic than race 'in the last instance', Fields's approach generates problems. The overall burden of the essay is to distance class from race by putting the former above (or in the older Marxist schema of base and superstructure, below) the latter in a design of historical causation. Thus, we are treated to flights of fancy like 'the reality of class can assert itself independently of people's consciousness'.[20] (Race, in Fields's essay, cannot; in the real world, neither can.)

Ironically, this emphasis on class comes very close to reproducing a version of Foner's 'Black and white/unite and fight' view of history. Fields finds those 'moments' of Black–white unity in the South, which she acknowledges to be 'rare', to be of signal importance in that they show class relations could be the 'solvent of some of the grosser illusions of racialism'. She then cites New Orleans in the late nineteenth and early twentieth centuries, with its alternation of impressive integrated strikes and racist violence, as proof that racial prejudice is sufficiently fluid and 'at home with contrariety to be able to precede and survive dramatic instances of interracial unity in action'.[21] Quite so, but whether outcroppings of strike unity could survive in an atmosphere of terror against Black workers is only one issue and one not more important than whether an impetus towards self-emancipation of the working class could so survive.

If we look at the words of a leader of the interracial New Orleans strikes, we find indications that race can perhaps not be distanced very far from class and that, although the city's waterfront labor movement displayed laudable unity on the picket line, it was perhaps far from challenging politically the racist order of the city. As Oscar Ameringer recounts the words of Dan Scully, the Irish American head of the longshoremen's union, testifying before a committee of the Louisiana legislature during a 1907 strike:

> I guess before long you'll call us nigger-lovers, too. Maybe you want to know next how I would like it if my sister married a nigger? ... I wasn't always a nigger-lover. I fought in every strike to keep Black labor off the dock. I fought until in the white-supremacy strike your white-supremacy governor sent his white-supremacy militia and shot us white-supremacy strikers full of holes. You talk about us conspiring with niggers. ... But let me tell you and your gang, there was a time when I wouldn't even work beside a nigger. ... You made me work with niggers, eat with niggers, sleep with niggers, drink out of the same water bucket with niggers, and finally got me to the point where if one of them ... blubbers something about more pay, I say, 'Come on, nigger, let's go after the white bastards.'[22]

Here racism and class feeling are utterly 'at home with contrariety', and as utterly bound up one with the other. Moreover, the white-supremacy strikes, strikebreaking by white supremacists and white attacks on Black communities in Louisiana during this period illustrate that what Fields acknowledges *could* happen did regularly happen: 'an ideological delusion [race] ... once acted upon ... may become as murderous as a fact'.[23] Racism, in its many varieties, often gave rise to actions murderous not only of Black workers but of the highest aspirations of labor. Its status as an ideological construct (though one reinforced by material facts like violence, job competition and segregation) therefore in no way disqualifies it, as Fields supposes it does, from being a 'tragic flaw' in the history of the South and the nation.[24]

Whatever the weaknesses of Fields's stance, her essay captures the logic that undergirds some of the best of the new labor history. In Wilentz's *Chants Democratic*, the murderous anti-Black, anti-draft New York City riots of 1863, which weave together so many strands in the book that they might have been a fit subject for its final chapter, receive five lines of attention in which we learn that the disturbance 'still manifested (with all its racism) the hatreds and collisions of class' before the paragraph turns to 'more disciplined' wartime trade union actions. Admittedly we are here dealing with a short summary of events beyond the scope of the book, but Du Bois's summary of the same event, which emphasizes that 'it was easy to transfer class hatred so that it fell on the Black worker', is significantly more exact and suggestive.[25]

Similarly, failure to treat the Black working class and its culture impoverishes the sections on working class culture generally in *Chants Democratic*. Wilentz's discussions of vital cultural forms sometimes tell us little more than that class was more important, and race less so, than we had ever thought. For example, the short section on minstrel shows begins from the premise that these mass entertainments 'took racism for granted'. Wilentz finds that 'the real object of scorn in these shows was less Jim Crow than the *arriviste*, would-be-aristo', and that the minstrels, 'turned from racist humor to mocking the arrogance, imitativeness and dimwittedness of the upper classes'.[26] But it is precisely the *coexistence* of racism and a partial class criticism that makes the minstrel shows, especially in the work of Alexander Saxton, such fascinating sources regarding the development of white working class consciousness, its assertiveness and its debasement. Although Wilentz cites Saxton in support of his position, the emphasis in the latter's 'Blackface Minstrelsy and Jacksonian Ideology' is different:

> The ideological impact of minstrelsy was programmed by its conventional blackface form. There is no possibility of escaping this relationship because the greater the interest, talent, complexity and *humanity* embodied in its content, the more irresistible was the racist message of the form. ... Blackface minstrelsy's dominance of popular entertainment amounted to half a century of inurement to the uses of white supremacy.[27]

Nor, in the absence of a full discussion of racism directed against Indians and Blacks, can Wilentz explore the rise of the penny press and its impact on New York City working class culture with the subtlety and brilliance characteristic of recent work by Alexander Saxton[28] and Richard Slotkin.[29]

Racism and Self-Activity

Wilentz's work is of special interest because it merges the Old Left privileging of class over race with the largely New Left passion, laudable in its origins, to avoid condescension towards working class subjects, to eschew determinism and to end the fruitless practice of preaching to people long deceased about what they should have done. Just as Wilentz, like many young historians, consciously models his work on Herbert Gutman's, Gutman consciously attempted to write history in which 'the essential question for study ... is not what has been done to men and women but what men and women do with what is done to them.'[30] This emphasis, drawing variously on anti-Stalinist Marxism, a populist emphasis on the role of the people in making history and, perhaps, elements of modern liberalism, may also gain adherents because, as Eric Hobsbawm has put it, 'historians ... are naturally more concerned with what actually happened ... than they are with what ought really to happen.'[32] The result, as Montgomery has recently observed, has been that many of the best new labor historians have chosen to dwell upon 'working men and women as agents of historical change' rather than 'the structures of social power that have historically divided workers, frustrated their collective undertaking, limited their objectives and secured the hegemony of capital.'[32]

Some of the writing that stresses the self-activity of American workers has emphasized, from a more-or-less revolutionary socialist position, the radical potential which can be glimpsed in such activity at certain junctures. Influenced by C. L. R. James, those arguing for this view have praised the ability of 'workers in motion' to take actions which transcend the possibilities envisioned by union leaders, which lay aside past prejudices of the workers themselves and which express the alternative, resistant culture present in daily working life – indeed, born of experiences at work.[33]

More frequently, especially recently, the emphasis on workers 'making their own history' has had a distinct reformist spin in its ideological stance and its political implications. Such scholarship has reflected what Geoff Eley calls, in a comment on recent European historiography, 'the scaled-down defensive expectations resulting from ... the world economic recession and the rightward political shift in Britain, the US and other capitalist countries.'[34] In this context it is the capacity for survival with dignity, for limited political influence, for compromise and for giving a twist to hegemonic ideas, which occupies center stage. There is little sense that the class expressions being described symbolize or presage greater things. Instead, especially in Wilentz, we find an increasingly shrill impatience with those 'essentialists' and 'American exceptionalists'

28

who expect too much from the working class and therefore miss the 'class perceptions that did exist' in the US.[35]

Obviously, much separates the revolutionary socialist approach to self-activity of workers from that of Wilentz and others, politically and otherwise. However, what is worth comment within the confines of this article is that both approaches reinforce tendencies to minimize the role of racism and of Black workers and can, therefore, leave their practitioners unable to penetrate some of the deepest problems their work raises. Deficiencies in each approach are best criticized through an examination of the body of scholarship they most thoroughly inform. In the case of the 'revolutionary socialist' perspective, that is the upsurge of American labor, often in wildcat strikes, in the 1940s. That upsurge is arguably the best-studied process in the twentieth-century history of US labor. It has attracted the attention principally of those interested in the revolutionary implications of rank-and-file action.[36]

Writing before much of this literature had been published, Joshua Freeman issued a challenge it has too often failed to meet. He observed that during World War II Black workers were often the victims of wildcat strikes, and argued that historians must not consider racially based strikes apart from strikes of other kinds. The week-long 1943 strike in Detroit at Packard Motors, making thousands of workers idle over the promotion of two black workers and the 1944 'hate strike' by white Philadelphia streetcar workers over Black employment were only, according to Freeman, two of the most famous of many such usually unauthorized strikes that occurred in the auto, armaments, aircraft, electrical, shipbuilding, rubber and transport industries during the war. In one three-month period of 1943, over 100,000 man-days of war production employment were lost to 'hate strikes'.[37] Freeman, having noted their prevalence, raised an urgent question about these racially motivated wildcats: 'Were the same workers, or types of workers, involved in the racial and non-racial strikes?'[38] One might ask further whether the racist wildcats set limits on the sweep of the goals of later unauthorized strikes? On their moral claims? On the participation of Black workers?

The newer studies take us very little distance towards answering these questions, but content themselves with observing that white workers sometimes overcame racism. Glaberman does not treat the hate strikes, except to say that Black workers were among wartime wildcat strikers in auto but did not, and this is hardly surprising, join walkouts to protest their own employment. In a footnote, Glaberman also underlines the fact that in 1945 the same Packard plant that witnessed the massive 1943 hate strike saw an unauthorized strike in which some whites supported a grievance of three Black workers.[39] Lichtenstein's shorter and more critical account of the wildcats emphasizes that racially motivated strikes declined in numbers later in the war as 'many white workers did accept Blacks as part of the factory work environment.'[40]

If we are to understand the joyous scene on the cover of Glaberman's book – in which Black workers, some in zootsuits, lead an integrated crowd starting a 1943 wildcat at Detroit Chevrolet, we need a far more penetrating discussion of race and shopfloor actions and, perhaps, of the complex connections between Black cultural radicalism and rank-and-file insurgencies. If we are to account for the pattern of wildcats in those plants, in which, as George Lipsitz has noted, separate white and Black wildcats occurred, sometimes in response to each other, we obviously need to look deeply at racial issues. Similar study is necessary if we are to account for the failure of the wildcats to develop a lasting insurgent movement in the unions, or in politics.[41]

If we are to place the auto wildcats in the context of race relations in Detroit during the war – and to determine why sometimes neighborhoods and sometimes (though decreasingly) workplaces served as sites of racial violence – full discussion of the hate strikes must be on the agenda.[42] The more we are attentive to all of these costs and complexities, the less we can assume that the subjective views of white workers are unimportant, that 'the question is not what this or that proletarian, or even the whole of the proletariat, *considers* its aim. The question is *what the proletariat is*, and what, consequent on that being, it will be compelled to do.'[43]

In contrast to the lines quoted above, in most of new labor history workers are not seen as 'compelled' to do anything by capital, by the state or by their class experience and destiny. But healthy as the push against determinism begun by Gutman and others has proven in some ways, it cannot be said to have given rise to a body of literature that has addressed the issues of class and race in a new, penetrating or even a sustained way. Indeed, if we look at the scholarship that perhaps represents the most sophisticated expression of what I have called the 'reformist' approach to working class self-activity – the best works on labor and republicanism in the nineteenth century and especially those of Sean Wilentz and Steven J. Ross – we find silence or extreme caution where vital issues such as the impact of slavery, racism and settler colonialism are concerned.[44] To the extent that such gaps help keep these meticulously crafted local studies from placing the processes they describe fully in the context of the best historiography on republicanism, free labor, popular culture and national politics, they keep labor history isolated and unable to nurture works of broad synthesis.

It is a tribute to the ambitious agendas of Wilentz and Ross that they call to mind the finest insights regarding republicanism and the meaning of the American experiment. But insufficient attention to race makes comparisons of their work unfavorable when it is set alongside that of our best novelists and historians. Wilentz, for example, invokes Herman Melville. But while Melville's work constantly reminds us that people of color were central to the culture of those who worked on or near water in nineteenth-century America, New York City's Black workers – during part of the period discussed one New Yorker in eleven was Black – appear twice in *Chants Democratic*, once in a footnote and once as victims of prejudice. The abolition of slavery in New York, and artisanal perceptions of abolition, are ignored. Nor does Ross give us much more than population figures for Cincinnati's Black community, small in size but important in the waterfront working class.

For Melville, a river between slave territory and the free states was an opportunity to explore the relationship between liberty and slavery (not just symbolically but referring concretely to Black slavery). Even when writing about Northern workers on dry land, he never let slip from view the national reality of slavery, and all the manifold comparisons which workers and others must have drawn. In the best of the new labor history the idea that white workers were 'wage slaves' is almost purely metaphor, connected not at all, or in only the simplest of ways, to the actual practice of slavery, present across the river from Cincinnati and in New York City through 1827. For Melville, the experiences of settler colonialism and the 'metaphysics of Indian-hating' were central to the development of an America 'intrepid, unprincipled, reckless, predatory, with boundless ambition, civilized in externals but a savage at heart – a country which may yet be the Paul Jones of nations.' Jacksonian Indian policies and the connection of Native Americans to the labor agitation over the land question are not broached in the studies of Ross and Wilentz.[45]

Of course, if we judged modern historians against the sweeping insights of Melville, none of us would get tenure. But if we adopt a somewhat less daunting standard, using the work of those historians offering the most challenging analyses of the growth of republican and free labor ideas as a yardstick, we would again note that sparse coverage and caution where racial matters are concerned keep even the best analyses of labor republicanism from drawing upon and enriching the debates begun by those outside the field of labor history.

For example, in his lengthy survey 'The Formation of the American Working Class', Wilentz observes: 'Of course, the history of proletarianization can be traced back to the first European settlements and to the confiscation of land and labor from the indigenous population. See, for a start, Edmund S. Morgan, *American Slavery, American Freedom*.' But he then adds: 'For simplicity's sake, I have concentrated here on the period of sustained growth of a "free labor" working class.' Several pages later slavery is also noted as being largely beyond the scope of the article.[46]

Whether Wilentz is right to concentrate on antebellum Northern urban workers, especially artisans, in writing the history of class formation in the US is an open question. If he is wrong, he makes an error reproduced in my own recent work. But allowing his choice of emphasis, can we understand the consciousness of that Northern urban working population, again especially artisans, without sustained reference to the existence of slavery as a national 'nightmare' that charged every debate over republicanism and the manly independence of craft workers? Morgan's work, though concerned with an earlier period and a Southern colony, is so replete with subtle connections between slavery and white popular consciousness that it suggests the need for extreme caution in deciding to achieve simplicity by foreshortening discussion of racial matters.[47]

Or, to take a problematic within the time period of Wilentz's and Ross's works, we might consider the debate initiated by David Brion Davis's monumental studies of antislavery thought. Davis argues that abolitionist critiques of chattel slavery 'unwittingly' bolstered capitalist hegemony by acting as 'selective response[s] to capitalist exploitation'. For Davis, the focus is on middle class reform leaders, but his arguments open a range of questions vital to labor historians. As Thomas L. Haskell has recently written:

> What remains unclear, in spite of much recent discussion of the relationship between abolitionism and the labor movement, is the exact basis of the labor critique [of abolitionism]. Did labor leaders work from a more advanced humanitarian perspective that really assigned equal importance to all varieties of exploitation, whether slave or free labor … ? Or did they simply assign a higher priority to the problems of wage laborers (nearby and racially similar) than to those of enslaved laborers (far away and racially different)? To what extent was the working man's criticism of abolitionism a pragmatic tactic for drawing attention to his own cause rather than a considered judgment of the equivalence of exploitation in the two cases?[48]

Haskell's questions are cast somewhat moralistically and will be refined by further research, but they are none the less vital. They must be supplemented by questions about whether many workers did not consider themselves 'free' largely in contrast to the Black and enslaved population to the South. In Davis's terms, if the existence of slavery served to justify wage labor to abolitionist reformers, did it also do so to workers at some times and in some ways? These are urgent questions not much addressed in existing treatments of labor republicanism.

Concretely, we ought to ask what was meant, for instance, in 1836, when New York City's journeymen tailors protested the conviction of their fellow-workers in a conspiracy case with a handbill featuring a coffin and declaring, 'The freemen of the North are now on a same level with the slaves of the South.' If, as Ross's and Wilentz's discussions of 'wage slavery' and similar constructions imply, the language was metaphoric, was it not also an extravagant metaphor and one given to collapsing upon itself at the first sign of amelioration? (In the 1836 incident, a more favorable court decision in a similar case came days later and, as Wilentz puts it, 'the journeymen's fury abated'.)[50] It is at least arguable that even in post-bellum years American labor rhetoric was impoverished rather than enriched by quick and easy invocations of 'slavery' as a metaphor not backed up by any thoroughgoing critique and therefore quickly abandoned.[51] We hear little these days, for example, about the Taft-Hartley 'Slave Labor Act', although its provisions still apply in ways little softened since organized labor fastened that epithet on it.

Similar issues pervade Wilentz's discussion of Mike Walsh, a central figure in *Chants Democratic* and the leader of antebellum New York City's 'shirtless democracy'. Walsh emerges as a tragic figure ('destined for the ignominy of a penny dreadful'), who between 1842 and 1846 developed 'a radical anti-capitalist republicanism' and took that philosophy 'out of the workshops and meeting halls and into the streets', but who so succumbed in the 1850s to the lures of office in Congress, to a Napoleonic fascination with his own flamboyant image, to alcohol and, above all, to such a fixation on proslavery politics that he lost contact with labor issues in his own district. But Walsh became a proslavery demagogue not in the 1850s, when his labor interests were waning, but in the 1840s, when his anti-capitalist rhetoric was reaching white heat. His critique of the 'slavery of wages' developed hard by his sympathies for pro-slavery Calhoun Democrats and, even in Wilentz's account, by the mid 1840s Black slavery was for Walsh already the dominant issue. Thus it seems overly generous to preface praises of Walsh's 'anti-capitalist variant of artisan republicanism' with 'If his radicalism did not extend to the question of slavery and race', as though the two were separate and racial egalitarianism might have been grafted onto his ideas. Rather, his racism, much like that of the minstrel stage, made possible extravagant criticisms of the North's aristocrats but simultaneously undercut those criticisms.[52]

The tragedy of Walsh's career should also give us pause before accepting all of Wilentz's passionately stated strictures against approaching US labor history from an 'essentialist' or an 'American exceptionalist' standpoint. Wilentz warns against 'essentialist reasoning – measuring American working-class ideas and actions against some abstract orthodox Marxist model of what would have been' and against idealizing the European working classes.[53] But Walsh need not be measured against the Paris Commune to be seen as lacking in the recoil against exploitation necessary to preach maturely the possibility of a thoroughly transformed America. It is enough to set his career against the finest American bourgeois radicals, such as William Lloyd Garrison or Wendell Phillips or Abraham

Lincoln, who were his contemporaries.

In fact, were race and slavery considered, Wilentz could not portray the 'essentialist/exceptionalist' framework with such sweeping caricature. If historians argue that the colonial settler experience in the US (and its attendant racism) and the singular experience of undergoing the 'making of a working class' at a time when the slave population nationally dwarfed that of wage workers (and again with the racism attendant) influenced class consciousness in the US in ways that discouraged the development of a revolutionary tradition, it is not clear why they should be charged with engaging in outmoded Marxist theology, as Wilentz would have it.

It would be more charitable to say that such historians are establishing the context for what Wilentz calls 'American class consciousness'. They are weighing from another angle the ways in which slavery was, as Eugene D. Genovese and Elizabeth Fox-Genovese put it, the 'world's burden', while adding that in the US that burden carried added dimensions and particular weight.[54] To explore how, whatever their racism, American workers made class-conscious choices within the parameters open to them, is of undoubted importance. To explore how racism shaped those parameters is also profitable. To join both concerns, or to realize that they are joined in a tragic history, is one of the key areas of unfinished business for the new labor history.

Notes

Thanks to Jean Allman, Eli Zaretsky, Herbert Hill, Steve Watts, Mike Davis, George Rawick and Robin Blackburn for comments on this article, which originally appeared in Mike Davis and Michael Sprinker, eds, *The Year Left 3: Reshaping the US Left*, London 1988.

1. As translated in Saul K. Padover, ed., *Karl Marx on America and the Civil War*, New York 1972, 275; Karl Marx, *Capital: A Critique of Political Economy*, New York 1967, 1:301.

2. George Rawick, *From Sundown to Sunup: The Making of the Black Community*, Westport, Conn. 1972, xiii.

3. See W. E. B. Du Bois, *The World and Africa: An Inquiry into the Part Which Africa Has Played in World History*, New York 1965, 18-21, and *Black Reconstruction in America, 1860–1880*, New York 1935, esp. 17–31, 125, 237; also 'Dives, Mob and Scab, Limited', *Crisis* 19 (March 1920).

4. See esp. Alexander Saxton, *The Indispensable Enemy: Labor and the Anti–Chinese Movement in California*, Berkeley, Calif. 1971; Saxton. 'George Wilkes: The Transformation of a Radical Ideology', *American Quarterly* 33 (Fall 1981): 437–58; Saxton, 'Blackface Minstrelsy and Jacksonian Ideology', *American Quarterly* 36 (1984): 211–35; Richard Slotkin, *The Fatal Environment: The Myth of the Frontier in the Age of Industrialization*, New York 1985; Herbert Hill, 'Race, Ethnicity and Organized Labor: The Opposition to Affirmative Action', *New Politics* 1 (Winter 1987): 31–82; *New Politics* 10 (Spring 1982): 5–78; Gwen Mink, 'The Alien Nation of American Labor' (Ph.D. dissertation, Cornell University, 1982); Peter Rachleff, 'Black, White and Gray: Race and Working-Class Activism in Richmond, Virginia, 1865–1890' (Ph.D. dissertation, University of Pittsburgh, 1981); Manning Marable, *How Capitalism Underdeveloped Black America*, Boston 1983; Mike Davis, *Prisoners of the American Dream*, London 1986. That Saxton is not widely recognized as among the most important of American

historians is a fair index of our backwardness in discussing race and class.

5. By far the sharpest criticism is found in Wallerstein's 'Basil Davidson's African Odyssey', *Third World Book Review* 1 (1985): 9, which contrasts Davidson's work with the otherwise dismal state of affairs. See also David Montgomery, 'America's Working Man', *Monthly Review* 37 (November 1985): 1–8; Eugene Genovese, 'Outgrowing Democracy', *Salmagundi*, no. 67, (Summer 1985): 203; and Michael Frisch, 'The Northern Illinois University NFH Conference', *International Labor and Working Class History (ILWCH)* 21 (Spring 1985): 102.

6. See, e.g. David Halle, *America's Working Man: Work, Home and Politics among Blue–Collar Property Owners*, Chicago 1981; Ira Katznelson, *City Trenches*, New York 1981, esp. 12; Edward Greer, 'Racism and US Steel' *Radical America* 10 (September–October 1976): esp. 60–63; Robert Emil Botsch, *We Shall Not Overcome: Populism and Southern Blue-Collar Workers*, Chapel Hill, N.C. 1980; Robert S. McCarl, 'You've Come a Long Way and Now Is Your Retirement: An Analysis of Performance in Fire Fighting Culture', *Journal of American Folklore* 97, 1984; Mike Davis, *Prisoners of the American Dream*, 256–300. The recent work by economists on segmented labor markets also sharply raises the question of race but does not much discuss the consciousness of white workers. Some attempts in that direction are found in David M. Gordon, Richard Edwards and Michael Reich, *Segmented Work, Divided Workers*, Cambridge 1982, esp. 206–14.

7. Christopher Clark, 'Politics, Language, and Class', *Radical History Review*, no. 34 (1986): 80.

8. Melvyn Dubofsky, 'Give Us That Old Time Labor History: Philip S. Foner and the American Workers', *Labor History* 26 (Winter 1985): 128.

9. Werner Sombart, *Why Is There No Socialism in the United States?*, New York 1976, 27–8, and 49.

10. John R. Commons et al., *History of Labor in the United States*, New York 1918–35, 2:252–3. The passage was written by Selig Perlman. For a good account of ethnicity, class and the making of the Wisconsin School, see Bari J. Watkins, 'The Professors and the Unions: American Academic Social Theory and Labor Reform, 1883–1915' (Ph.D. dissertation, Yale University, 1976).

11. Sean Wilentz, 'Against Exceptionalism', *ILWCH* 26 (Fall 1984): esp. 17–18; see also Wilentz's 'The Formation of the American Working Class: A Survey' (paper delivered at the National Endowment for the Humanities, The Future of Labor History Symposium, Northern Illinois University, 10–12 October 1984, esp. 63 and 71). Note the gingerly treatment of Samuel Gompers's racism in Nick Salvatore's introduction to his excellent abridgment of Gompers's *Seventy Years of Life and Labor*, Ithaca, N.Y. 1984, esp. xxiv. A mirror of the tendency of labor historians to minimize race and racism is J. Sakai's *The Mythology of the White Proletariat*, Chicago 1983, an unforgiving account of white working class racism, though ultimately unconvincing in its attempt to collapse class into race.

12. Melvyn Dubofsky, 'Old Time Labor History', 136 and passim; Cruse, 'Review', *Journal of Negro History* 63 (July 1978): 253–7, treating Philip S. Foner, *American Socialism and Black Americans*, Westport, Conn. 1977.

13. Philip S. Foner, *Organized Labor and the Black Worker*, x and passim.

14. In Saul K. Padover, ed., *Marx on America*, 274n1–275 and 244. The Marxological claims here are advanced quite modestly. They do not pretend to settle what Marx 'really thought' on these matters.

15. W. E. B. Du Bois, *Black Reconstruction*, 700–701 and passim.

16. But see Michael Honey, 'The Labor Movement and Racism in the South', in Marvin J. Berlowitz and Ronald S. Edari, eds, *Racism and the Denial of Human Rights*, Minneapolis, Minn. 1984; David R. Roediger, 'Racism, Reconstruction and the Labor Press', *Science and Society* 42 (Summer 1978): 156–78, and to some extent, Herbert Gutman, 'The Negro and the United Mine Workers of America', in Julius Jacobson, ed., *The Negro and the American Labor Movement*, Garden City, N.Y. 1968, 149–77. On Marx's later weaknesses in analyzing race and other matters in the US, see Mark Lause's forthcoming work on splits in the First International.

17. Foner dissects this overemphasis on class in *Black Americans and American Socialism*, xii–xiii and passim; see also Barbara J. Fields's 'Ideology and Race in American History', in J. Morgan Kousser and James M. McPherson, eds, *Region, Race and Reconstruction*, New York

1982, 143–78, esp. 150–6.

18. David Montgomery, 'America's Working Man'.

19. Barbara J. Fields, 'Ideology and Race', 44–5, broaches this dimension of the problem but in a very imprecise and foreshortened manner.

20. Ibid, 150. See Michael Burawoy, *The Politics of Production Factory Regimes under Capitalism and Socialism*, London 1985, 39.

21. Ibid., 159 and 174n37.

22. Oscar Ameringer, *If You Don't Weaken*, Norman, Okla. 1983, 218–19. See also David Bennett, 'Black and White Workers: New Orleans, 1880–1900' (Ph.D. dissertation, 1972) and Daniel Rosenberg, 'Race, Labor and Unionism: New Orleans Dockworkers, 1900–1910' (Ph.D. dissertation, CUNY, 1984). In the face of such very complex interaction between race and class, we may wish to review Eugene D. Genovese's excellent essay 'Black Experience, White Historian', in *In Red and Black*, Knoxville, Tenn. 1984, esp. 70: 'Racism in America has grown out of a complex conjunction of historical forces and cannot be viewed as a class question except in a special sense – namely, that its destruction demands the destruction of bourgeois hegemony over the American people.'

23. Fields, 'Ideology and Race', 159. See also Jeffrey Gould, 'Sugar War', *Southern Exposure* 12 (November–December 1984): 45–55; William Ivy Hair, *Bourbonism and Agrarian Protest*, Baton Rouge, La. 1969; Foner, *Organized Labor and the Black Worker*, 66–9, 88–92 and 113–14. Gould's article begins rather artificially by criticizing those who focus on racism in explaining the 1887 Sugar Strike and does succeed in showing how social relations in the industry influenced racism. But in his excellent narrative it can hardly be said that racism does not loom as the main factor in the defeat of the strike. His early formulation, 'If white workers were "racist", why did they join the [Knights of Labor], which admitted blacks and whites, and initially participate in the strike movement?' neatly illustrates the tendency to view willingness to cooperate in a union setting as proof against racism. In this instance trade union cooperation proved quite ephemeral and its end bloody.

24. Fields, 'Ideology and Race', 43 and passim.

25. Sean Wilentz, *Chants Democratic: New York City and the Rise of the American Working Class, 1788–1850*, Oxford 1984, 395; W. E. B. Du Bois, *Black Reconstruction*, 103.

26. Wilentz, *Chants Democratic*, 259.

27. Saxton, 'Blackface Minstrelsy', 27: see also p. 23. Emphasis original. For another view, see 'Irish Mornings and African Days on the Old Minstrel Stage: An Interview with Leni Sloan', *Callahan's Irish Quarterly* 2 (Spring 1982): 49–53. A penetrating discussion of race and popular culture in New York City in those years is Alessandra Lorini, 'Festive Crowds in Early Nineteenth Century New York: Republican Virtues in the Evil City' (unpublished paper presented at the Conference on Time and Space of Work and Leisure in Pre-Industrial America, University of Paris VII, June 1987).

28. Saxton, 'George Wilkes' and 'Problems of Class and Race', passim; Slotkin, *Fatal Environment*, 438ff.

29. Whether the work of David Montgomery and Eric Foner, perhaps the very best of the new labor historians, also overstresses the primacy of class over race and ends with thin discussions of racism, is open to question. I have hesitantly argued elsewhere that Montgomery's *Beyond Equality: Labor and the Radical Republican*, New York 1967, underplays working class racism in its discussion of the failure of labor–Radical Republican cooperation during Reconstruction; see David R. Roediger, 'Racism, Reconstruction and the Labor Press', *Science and Society* 42 (Summer 1978): 77–8. But the choice of a subject – indeed the opening up of the vital new subject of class and Radicalism – perhaps accounts for his emphasis. Foner's *Nothing but Freedom: Emancipation and Its Legacy*, Baton Rouge, La. 1983, has been both criticized and praised by reviewers for its reorientation of the debate over Reconstruction toward class and away from race. Compare Dan T. Carter, 'Politics and Power', *Reviews in American History* 12 (September 1984): 396, and Judith Stein's review in *In These Times*, 19–25 September 1984. My own view is that the brief essays in *Nothing but Freedom* show a line of thought and a debt to Du Bois, which in Foner's longer study of Reconstruction could underpin a set of arguments that consider both the racial and class dimensions.

30. Herbert Gutman, *Visions of History*, New York 1983, 203, paraphrasing Jean-Paul Sartre.

31. Eric Hobsbawm, 'Notes on Class Consciousness', in *Workers: Worlds of Labour*, New York 1984, 17.

32. Montgomery, 'Labor's Long Haul', *Nation*, 19–26 July 1986, 52.

33. See Martin Glaberman, *Wartime Strikes*, Detroit 1980; George Lipsitz, *Class and Culture in Cold War America*, South Hadley, Mass. 1982, esp. Chapters 1 and 6; Stan Weir, 'American Labor on the Defensive', *Radical America* 9 (July–August 1975): 163–85; C. L. R. James, Grace Lee and Pierre Chaulieu, *Facing Reality*, Detroit 1958.

34. 'Response to David Abraham's "Labor's Way"', *ILWCH* 28 (Fall 1985): 27.

35. Wilentz, *Chants Democratic*, esp. 15–16; 'Against Exceptionalism', esp. 1–4 and 17, and 'Wilentz Answers His Critics', *ILWCH* 28 (Fall 1985): esp. 53; see also Eric Foner, 'Why Is There No Socialism in America?', *History Workshop Journal*, no. 17 (Spring 1984): esp. 67.

36. Montgomery, 'Labor's Long Haul'; Ed Jennings, 'Wildcat! The Wartime Strike Wave in Auto', *Radical America* 9 (1975); Nelson Lichtenstein, *Labor's War at Home*, Cambridge, Mass. 1982, 121–35, 189–94 and 234–44. Not sharing this approach but giving a good narrative account are August Meier and Elliott Rudwick, *Black Detroit and the Rise of the UAW*, New York 1979, 162–74.

37. George Lipsitz, *Class and Culture*, 14–25; Philip S. Foner, *Organized Labor and the Black Worker*, 255–7 and 265–8; Joshua Freeman, 'Delivering the Goods: Industrial Unionism during World War Two', *Labor History* 19 (Fall 1978): 585–7. For a superb recent account of race, class and the CIO in the steel industry in Birmingham, see Robert J. Norrell, 'Caste in Steel: Jim Crow Careers in Birmingham Alabama', *Journal of American History* 73 (December 1986): 669–94.

38. Freeman, 'Delivering the Goods', 587.

39. Glaberman, *Wartime Strikes*, 32 and 57; cf. Lipsitz, *Class and Culture*, 20.

40. Lichtenstein, *War at Home*, 125–6.

41. Glaberman, *Wartime Strikes*, 126, and Lipsitz, *Class and Culture*, 20.

42. See Freeman, 'Delivering the Goods', 586–7, and Dominic J. Capeci, Jr, *Race Relations in Wartime Detroit*, Philadelphia 1984; Lipsitz *Class and Culture*, 14–29.

43. Glaberman, *Wartime Strikes*, 125, quoting Marx and Engels from *The Holy Family*, Moscow 1956, 53. See also *C. L. R. James: His Life and Work*, Chicago 1981, 79–80, and *Wartime Strikes*, 27 and 31, for Glaberman and Frank Marquart's interesting observations on Southern white immigrants as 'among the most militant' in the wartime auto industry and the failure to explore the interaction between racism and such militancy.

44. See Wilentz as cited in note 11 and, esp., *Chants Democratic*, passim. Steven J. Ross, *Workers on the Edge: Work, Leisure, and Politics in Industrializing Cincinnati, 1788–1890*, New York 1985.

45. Wilentz, 'Formation of the American Working Class', 1. On race and class in Melville, see Carolyn L. Karcher, *Shadows over the Promised Land*, Baton Rouge, La. 1980; Ron Takaki, *Iron Cages: Race and Culture in Nineteenth-Century America*, New York 1979; Michael Paul Rogin, *Subversive Genealogy: The Politics and Art of Herman Melville*, New York 1983; C. L. R. James, *Mariners, Renegades and Castaways*, Detroit 1953. For Wilentz and Ross on the issues discussed here, see *Chants Democratic*, 48a and 264ff (Black workers) and esp. 186 and 332–4 (wage and chattel slavery); also Ross, *Workers on the Edge*, 6, 72, 74, 197 (Black workers) and esp. 199 (wage and chattel slavery). Cf. Howard B. Rock, *Artisans of the New Republic: The Tradesmen of New York City in the Age of Jefferson*, New York 1979, esp. 311, for a more promising treatment. For an account of popular politics in antebellum New York City in which these issues disappear still more thoroughly, see Amy Bridges, *A City in the Republic: Antebellum New York and the Origins of Machine Politics*, Cambridge 1984. The Melville quote is from *Israel Potter*, New York 1974 (1855), 159. On Indians and Jacksonian politics, see Michael Paul Rogin, *Fathers and Children: Andrew Jackson and the Subjugation of the American Indian*, New York 1975.

46. Wilentz, 'Formation of the American Working Class', 63n3, 71n58.

47. Edward S. Morgan, *American Slavery, American Freedom: The Ordeal of Colonial Virginia*, New York 1976. I borrow 'nightmare' from F. Nwabueze Okoye's provocative extension of Morgan's arguments: 'Chattel Slavery as the Nightmare of American Revolutionaries', *William and Mary Quarterly* 37 (January 1980): 3–28; Ross, quoting Holt, *Workers on the Edge*, 199.

48. Thomas L. Haskell, 'Capitalism and the Origins of Humanitarian Sensibility, Part I', *American Historical Review* 90 (April 1985): 350n29 and passim; David Brion Davis, *The Problem of Slavery in the Age of Revolution, 1770–1823*, Ithaca, N.Y. 1975, esp. 251. See also William E. Forbath, 'The Ambiguities of Free Labor: Labor and Law in the Gilded Age', *Wisconsin Law Review*, 1985, 782ff.

49. Wilentz, *Chants Democratic*, 293 and 286–94 passim; Eric Foner, 'Workers and Slavery', in Paul Buhle and Alan Dawley, eds, *Working for Democracy*, Urbana, Ill. 1985, 22.

50. David R. Roediger, 'Ira Steward and the Antislavery Origins of American Eight-Hour Thought', *Labor History* 27 (Summer 1986): 410–26. For a consideration of this issue in psychohistorical terms, see the important observations of Joel Kovel, *White Racism: A Psychohistory*, New York 1970, 197.

51. On postbellum usages, see Barry Goldberg, 'Beyond Free Labor' (Ph.D. dissertation, Columbia University, 1978).

52. Wilentz, *Chants Democratic*, 334 and 327–35, 356.

53. Wilentz, 'Wilentz Answers His Critics', 53. For a brilliant brief treatment of the overblown 'essentialism' debate, see Cornel West, 'Rethinking Marxism', *Monthly Review* 38 (February 1987): 52–6.

54. Wilentz, 'Wilentz Answers His Critics', 53; Eugene Genovese and Elizabeth Fox-Genovese, 'Slavery: The World's Burden', in *Fruits of Merchant Capital*, New York 1983. For Wilentz's dismissal of racism, along with a laundry list of other factors, in shaping American working class consciousness, see his 'Against Exceptionalism', 2.

2

The Greatness of Herbert Gutman

Few eminent United States historians in the recent past have received such sharp and consistent criticism as the late Herbert Gutman. Eugene Genovese and Elizabeth Fox-Genovese, for example, found Gutman a 'bourgeois' writer 'occasionally referred to as a Marxist by people who could not possibly tell the difference.' His work on the Black family, according to Genovese and Fox-Genovese, 'embraces ... a self-generating black family ... worked out, as it were, after dark and in almost total abstraction from the labor process.' They further suggested that Gutman's massive book on the Black family could have been trimmed to 200 pages.[1] Lawrence T. McDonnell characterized Gutman's labor history as marked by a 'strange sentimentality' and added that it was a 'sentimentalism of the right'.[2] Michael Kazin, in a recent essay, dismisses McDonnell's criticisms of Gutman as examples of 'muscular Marxism' but adds that Gutman's writings suffered from a 'wistful conception of the past'.[3] The increasingly irrepressible John Patrick Diggins called Gutman, not flatteringly, a 'Parrington in overalls'.[4] Herbert Hill, in a significant forthcoming article, regards Gutman's work on race relations in the United Mine Workers as 'mythmaking' based on a 'romanticized vision of the working class'.[5]

None of these criticisms is wildly off the mark, but the harshest of them tend to collapse on themselves. If Gutman's work were mainly noteworthy as an example of leftish culturalist nostalgia, then what would be of interest is not so much a dissection of his errors as a political explanation of how he nonetheless came to be one of the two or three most influential historians of his generation.[6] How, specifically, did he come to inspire so many socialist historians?

I am not quite yet ready to argue, using the image offered by Fox-

Genovese and Genovese, that a whole generation of historians has sunk 'into a neo-antiquarian swamp'.[7] This essay therefore tries to come to grips with Gutman's substantial heritage by first looking to the strengths that make his work appeal to those wanting to understand and change the world. It argues that Gutman's work was not only better than most of his detractors allow, but also that it managed to transcend some of his own lapses and rhetorical excesses. Part of his success derived from Gutman's individual passion and genius but, I will argue, much of it also derived from his roots in the much-maligned Old Left.

Power and Culture provides an excellent opportunity to examine Gutman's contributions. It gathers a dozen of Gutman's articles, representing Gutman's interests in labor history, African American history, and public history. Celebrated essays like 'The Workers' Search for Power' (1963) appear alongside unpublished manuscripts and pieces previously published in other languages. The longest essay, almost a book in itself, is the previously unpublished 'Labor in the Land of Lincoln: Coal Miners on the Prairie', Gutman's most sustained study of the white working class in a given area. Materials not included in Gutman's classic *The Black Family in Slavery and Freedom, 1750–1925* (New York 1976) are published here for the first time. Especially important is 'Schools for Freedom: The Post-Emancipation Origins of Afro-American Education', an unpublished fragment edited for inclusion in *Power and Culture* by Eric Foner. 'Schools for Freedom' wonderfully captures what W. E. B. Du Bois called 'the rhythm of united effort' through which freed people sought 'to learn and know'.[8] 'Class Composition and the Development of the American Working Class, 1840–1890', co-authored by Gutman and Ira Berlin and published in English for the first time, provides abundant statistical support for Gutman's contention that the urban working class was largely remade through immigration in the late nineteenth century. A useful bibliography of Gutman's writings, compiled by Andrew Gyory, is appended to the collection.

Berlin, the editor of *Power and Culture*, also contributes a long and fascinating introduction, 'Herbert G. Gutman and the American Working Class'. That essay reflects its author's friendship with Gutman but also manages a fair portrayal of the academic quarrels in which Gutman came to be involved. Most of all, Berlin shows that at every turn Gutman's historical writings reflect a political commitment, though not a politics easily summarized or labeled. Berlin succumbs to occasional overstatements, as when he characterizes Gutman's *The Black Family* as a study of 'class formation', but the introduction as a whole is the best published appraisal of Gutman's writings.[9]

Berlin provides an excellent initial clue as to what set Gutman apart from, and above, most historians of US working class life: 'For Gutman,

... study of the Afro-American family was not a detour on the road to a history of the American working class, but the center lane on the main highway' (p. 46). With the exceptions of old leftists such as Herbert Hill, Philip S. Foner and George Rawick, few American historians have deeply researched both the white and Black working class.[10] Gutman's project was startlingly expansive and sophisticated. As Genovese wrote in 1970:

> Gutman has set out to reinterpret the history of the American working class and in doing so has come to emphasize the process by which various immigrant groups ... became acculturated, in the double sense of 'Americanized' and integrated into an advanced industrial economy. This concern has naturally led him toward a critical appraisal of the intersection of peasant migrations, the growth of the working class in its particular ethnic manifestations, and the black experience. This new approach to the history of the black and white working class points toward an appreciation of culture as politics.[11]

Perhaps predictably, Gutman only partially realized this full agenda. His work on Black workers and that on white workers, for example, generally remained separated. When he attempted to discuss race relations within the working class, a desire to recover antiracist traditions led to a straining of the evidence and an unwillingness to probe the extent of white working class racism. That Gutman lacked any sympathetic understanding of Black nationalism likewise left profound gaps in his work.[12] But he did argue for the fullest possible inclusiveness in working class studies, moving away from the profession's concentration on large urban workplaces and towards the small city, often in the Midwest, the artisan workshop, the plantation and the slave-holding farm. He pioneered in the study of workers off the job and his students made seminal contributions to the study of gender and labor. He studied railway workers, miners, plantation slaves, house slaves, industrial slaves, the unemployed, coopers, refinery workers, housewives, and more. And yet he did not 'disaggregate' the working class out of existence. His work was broad but also broadly focused – and the focus was on the making and reconstruction of the working class.

The second great virtue running through Gutman's work is an abundance of intellectual curiosity. He was clearly no master of theory – the most subtle insights of Raymond Williams and Sidney Mintz are quoted alongside ahistorical and idealist pronouncements from Clifford Geertz in Gutman's work and with little sense that different ways of looking at the world are being alluded to. But Gutman was enormously interested in, and adept at handling, evidence and ideas growing out of that evidence. In 'Labor in the Land of Lincoln', for example, he lingers over details in portraying working class life, providing even descriptions of footraces among the miners (p. 136). Gutman's writing in this regard much resembles Marx's *Ethnological Notebooks* and W. E. B. Du Bois's early sociological work.[13] Like these two, Gutman provides a wealth of ideas to go with the wealth of detail. Rereading 'The Workers' Search for Power', written by Gutman a quarter-century ago, one is struck not so much by its well-known thesis – that in smaller cities cross-class, pro-labor alliances developed more frequently than in large urban areas – but by the article's variety. The central thesis, as Gutman himself came to realize (pp. 16–17), has not survived intact. But the article survives because of the stories it tells and the fact that it contains a half-dozen subthemes, on topics ranging from republicanism to ethnicity, and develops those themes brilliantly. *The Black Family* similarly shows Gutman at his absolute best in interpreting sometimes fragmentary evidence.

Another of the tremendous strengths of Gutman's work is its attention to the timing of historical changes. His writings show a sharp concern for periodization, a concern not common among US labor historians. His groundbreaking essay, 'Work, Culture and Society in Industrializing America', not reprinted in *Power and Culture*, proposed a new periodization for working class history, and Gutman was quite disappointed that, though the essay won wide praise, it sparked little debate over periodization.[14] His 'Class Composition and the Development of the American Working Class, 1840–1890' (with Berlin), included in *Power and Culture*, returns to the issues of timing raised in 'Work, Culture and Society'. And, of course, *The Black Family* and related essays insist that history must be understood as a process, even as an unfolding drama. This emphasis on time and change grew not just from historical craftsmanship but also from a belief that showing a fluid past contributed to a sense of alternatives in the present and widened political possibilities for the future.[15] 'Twas not, Gutman emphasized, ever thus.

Sustaining Gutman's intellectual curiosity and his attention to change was his commitment to history as a democratic process. As the concluding essay in *Power and Culture*, 'Historical Consciousness in Contemporary America' makes clear, Gutman worked hard to make history accessible. Individually and through his American Working Class History Project (later, American Social History Project) he sought both to popularize history and to humanize it. As Berlin points out, part of the reason for his sharp attacks on Fogel and Engerman's *Time on the Cross* was that the book had been so thoroughly hyped as the triumph of high-tech, computerized history. Gutman believed, according to Berlin, that *Time on the Cross* had 'mystified a democratic art'.[16] He relished his position defending that 'democratic art' with but a pocket calculator, just as he enjoyed his role as a public historian attacking Daniel Patrick Moynihan and other scholar-policymakers in his writings on the Black family.

42

All of the above bears emphasis but it will be unexceptionable at least to Gutman's admirers. It argues that Gutman was a great historian because he was diligent, curious, broad-minded and committed. It suggests that to emulate Gutman we should be bright, meticulous and democratic. This is true enough, but in the balance of this essay I should like to advance one further, far more controversial, reason for Gutman's strengths – one that quite complicates the manner in which we envision taking up and extending Gutman's heritage. Gutman was successful, I would argue, in large measure because he was enough a product of the Old Left to maintain a focus on power and exploitation even as he moved toward a culturally based history.

Berlin provocatively titles this collection *Power and Culture* as an answer to those of Gutman's critics who branded Gutman soft, sentimental and nostalgic. Berlin maintains that:

> whatever else Herbert Gutman was, he was not 'soft'. Although he spoke in the language of culture, he was preoccupied with questions of power ... the relationship between the two – power and culture – was the central theme of his work. (*Power and Culture, viii*)

The individual essays in *Power and Culture* give some support to Berlin's assessment. 'The Workers' Search for Power' is, of course, about power, though it has little sense of the extent of ruling-class power at either the state or the national level. The same can be said of 'Joseph P. McDonell and the Workers' Struggle in Paterson, New Jersey', 'Labor in the Land of Lincoln' and the superb 'The Labor Policies of the Large Corporation in the Gilded Age: The Case of the Standard Oil Company': these are tough-minded assessments of workers' self-activity and of the power of companies and of the state. The material criticizing Fogel and Engerman, especially their use of statistics on whippings, tries to make a vital point regarding power, a point that perhaps never explicitly emerged in the debates with Genovese over *Time on the Cross*. Gutman argues, implicitly at least, that not short-term profit maximization but long-term labor and race control governed the logic of capital in the slave South.

But in other places Gutman does adopt loose and sentimental culturalist assumptions. His work on race relations within the working class, discussed above, is the worst example, but essays like 'A Note on Immigration History' and 'Labor History and the Sartre Question' show that these tendencies in Gutman's work were not confined to racial matters. In the valuable interview with Mike Merrill in *Power and Culture*, Gutman's confused discussion of republicanism and socialism would have been greatly enriched by attention to power. Similarly, in the same interview, in discussing 'essentialism' and what is of lasting value in Marxism,

43

Gutman rather softly settles for saying that Marx's theories provide 'some ... very useful questions' (p. 344).

The overall picture that emerges from Gutman's work is neither that he has the sure-handed ability to balance culture and power posited in Berlin's essay nor that he wears nostalgic blinders as charged by his critics. Instead Gutman's work, as a whole and in many individual instances, tends towards sentimentality and towards a hesitancy to confront ruling-class power – but it never quite succumbs. He complains rather wildly that historians have shown 'excessive interest' in high points of class struggle like 'the Haymarket riot ..., the great strikes of 1877, the Homestead lockout and the Pullman strike'. He laments that 'close attention has also focused on the small craft unions, the Knights of Labor and the early Socialists, excluding the great mass of workers who belonged to none of these groups' (p. 70). But Gutman constantly focused in his work on strikes and on organized workers. He wrote fine introductions to reprints of the International Working Peoples Association's *Alarm* and to *International Socialist Review*. Under his direction the American Social History Project began the making of an award-winning film, *1877*, about the great strikes of that year.

The best example of Gutman's flirting with unedifying formulations but then transcending them in practice lies in his frequent allusion to the 'Sartre question'. In *Power and Culture* Jean-Paul Sartre is frequently and most approvingly quoted or paraphrased as saying, 'The essential is not what "one" has done to man, but what man does with what "one" has done to him' (pp. 358 and also 58, 326–8, 346, 349). Though a clever phrasing, issues of gender and language aside, the quote shows Sartre at far from his best. Despite the way the 'Sartre question' inspired Gutman, it is not even a slightly useful formulation for historians. In order to portray what 'man does with what "one" has done to him', we must, of course, know what 'one' did. Thus putting the most charitable interpretation on it, the 'Sartre question' is but a convoluted and inferior phrasing of Marx's point that people make their own history but not under circumstances of their own choosing. The use of 'one' rather than 'exploiting class' in Sartre's maxim is problematic and, oddly enough, the maxim subverts its own populism by seeing the oppressed as reacting within ground rules set by 'one's' behavior.

But Gutman apparently extracted from the 'Sartre question' a way to balance emphases on power and on culture. He called Sartre's line a 'Thompsonian formulation', referring to the work of E. P. Thompson. Thompson has consistently studied class struggle and has reminded his readers that 'class entails a historical relationship' that cannot be portrayed except in writings which discuss both the exploiters and the exploited.[17] The first three historians Gutman mentions as being successful

at answering the 'Sartre question' are all Old Left Marxists, albeit monumentally subtle and creative ones. In praising W. E. B. Du Bois's approach
in *Black Reconstruction*, C. L. R. James's historical writings and the work of
George Rawick, Gutman singles out historians concerned with exploring
class conflict by analyzing workers' self-activity within class relationships.[18]

Gutman once said that much of the new labor history 'developed out
of the decomposition of classical Marxism' and that it came 'out of a politics broadly associated with the redefinition of socialism' (pp. 342–3). It
might be added that the best of recent historical writing – that of Rawick,
Genovese, Alexander Saxton, David Montgomery, and E. P. Thompson –
as succeeded because these writers retained, even internalized, Old Left
problematics regarding exploitation, resistance and class power as they
made creative advances. This pattern holds to a significant extent for Gutman, who grew up in a radical family, was immersed in Popular Front
causes while at Queens College, and was for a time a Communist. Berlin
is on the mark in calling Gutman 'very much a son of the Jewish Old Left'
(p. 7), and it may well be in this heritage as well as in his creative depar-
tures from it that Gutman's work gains its strength.

Notes

This review essay was written in tribute to Herbert Gutman after the posthumous publication
of his *Power and Culture: Essays on the American Working Class*, Ira Berlin, ed., New York 1987.
It is reprinted with the permission of the editor from *Labour/Le Travail*, 23 (Spring 1989):
255–61. © Committee on Canadian Labour History.

1. Elizabeth Fox-Genovese and Eugene D. Genovese, 'The Debate over *Time on the Cross*:
A Critique of Bourgeois Criticism' in *Fruits of Merchant Capital: Slavery and Bourgeois Property
in the Rise and Expansion of Capitalism*, Oxford 1983, pp. 143 and 426–7n3; 'Solidarity and
Servitude', *Times Literary Supplement*, 25 February 1977.

2. Lawrence T. McDonnell, '"You are Too Sentimental": Problems and Suggestions for
a New Labor History', *Journal of Social History* 17 (1984): 638 and 630.

3. Michael Kazin, 'The Historian as Populist', *New York Review of Books* 35 (12 May 1988):
48–50.

4. John Patrick Diggins, 'Comrades and Citizens: New Mythologies in American Historiography', *American Historical Review* 90 (1985): 625.

5. Herbert Hill, 'Myth-Making as Labor History: Herbert Gutman and the United Mine
Workers of America', *Politics, Culture and Society* 2 (1988): forthcoming.

6. Hill's article, cited above, does attempt to make political sense out of the influence of
Gutman's work, at least that part of his work on labor racism. He argues that Gutman's writing
reproduces the privileging of class over race found generally among US scholars, especially
radical scholars, and among American progressives generally.

7. Fox–Genovese and Genovese, 'The Political Crisis of Social History', in *Fruits of Merchant Capitalism*, 201.

8. W. E. B. Du Bois, *Black Reconstruction in America*, New York 1971 (1935), 637.

9. Berlin, ed., 'Gutman and the Working Class', in *Power and Culture*, 45. As Gutman's
own 'The Black Family in Slavery and Freedom: A Revised Perspective' in *Power and Culture*,

359–79, esp. 374, makes clear, the book version of the *The Black Family* is based primarily on nineteenth-century records, especially those covering 1830–60. By that time slaves had long since become a class. Nor do the intriguing short passages in the 'revised perspectives' (pp. 374–409) provide more than hints about slave class formation in the eighteenth century. Moreover, there is too little sense of the master class and slaves in conflict in *The Black Family* and too inconsistent interrogation of the relationship between kin networks and class consciousness for the book to qualify as a treatment of class formation. See George Fredrickson, 'The Historiography of Slavery', in *The Arrogance of Race: Historical Perspectives on Slavery, Racism and Social Inequality*, Middletown, Conn. 1988, 122.

10. See David R. Roediger, 'Labor in White Skin': Race and U.S. Working Class History', in Mike Davis and Michael Sprinker, eds, *Reshaping the U.S. Left*, London 1988, 287–308. Eric Foner is also exceptional in this regard.

11. Genovese, 'The Influence of the Black Power Movement on Historical Scholarship: Reflections of a White Historian', in *In Red and Black: Marxian Explorations in Southern and Afro–American History*, New York 1984, 245.

12. Hill, 'Myth-Making as Labor History'; see also the handling of evidence of possible violence and racism against Black workers by white Illinois miners in the 'Labor in the Land of Lincoln' article in *Power and Culture*, esp. 178–80, 189–90 and 202–5, and Herbert G. Gutman, 'Black Coal Miners and the Greenback-Labor Party in Redeemer Alabama, 1878–1879', *Labor History* 10 (1969): 506–35. On Black nationalism, see Gutman's mechanistic response to Manning Marable, 'Toward a Black Politics: Beyond the Race-Class Dilemma', *Nation*, 11 April 1981, 434, and Genovese and Fox-Genovese, 'Debate over *Time on the Cross*', in *Fruits of Merchant Capital*, 170–71.

13. See Franklin Rosemont's superb essay on Marx and the *Ethnological Notebooks*, forthcoming in *Arsenal*; Du Bois, *The Negro American Artisan*, Atlanta 1913; Du Bois, *The Philadelphia Negro: A Social Study*, Philadelphia 1899.

14. Gutman, 'Work, Culture and Society in Industrializing America, 1815–1919', *American Historical Review* 78 (1973): 531–88; Gutman, *Power and Culture*, 338–42.

15. See Gutman, 'Historical Consciousness in Contemporary America', in Berlin, ed., *Power and Culture*, 411.

16. Berlin, ed., 'Gutman and the Working Class', in *Power and Culture*, 54. Parts of Gutman's criticisms of *Time on the Cross* are reprinted in *Power and Culture* as 'Enslaved Afro-Americans and the "Protestant" Work Ethic', 298–325.

17. E. P. Thompson, *The Making of the English Working Class*, New York 1966, 9 and passim.

18. On self-activity and power, see esp. George Rawick's comments in 'Symposium on Herbert Gutman's *The Black Family in Slavery and Freedom*', *Radical History Review* 4 (Spring-Summer 1977): 87–8 and passim.

3

Precapitalism in One Confederacy: A Note on Genovese, Politics and the Slave South

In a recent issue of *Commentary*, historian Eugene D. Genovese says goodbye to socialism and to Marxism in three rambling pages. The farewell to socialism is straightforward. 'But surely the 80's', Genovese writes, 'will be remembered as the decade in which socialism met its Waterloo.' It failed, Genovese adds, 'for reasons that ... Ludwig von Mises, among other right-wingers, long ago identified.' 'Private property' must now hold sway, not just for the foreseeable future but as a transcendent truth, though perhaps it can be placed 'in the context of a corporatism [that] makes it subject to social control and the guidelines of a national moral consensus.' For Genovese, not socialists but 'traditionalists and especially the Southern traditionalists' now hold the key to political wisdom.[1]

The abandonment of Marxism is more hedged. Fugitive phrases suggest that 'once marxist' ideas might have some merit, if they could be combined with 'traditional' ones and reclaimed from the majority of the Left, which got 'drunk on the anarchism of the 60's'. Nonetheless Marx has not, for Genovese, simply been dragged down by traducers. He is himself culpable in that 'the Left has carried Marx's utopian view of human nature to its logical – and, ironically ultra-individualist – conclusion and embraced every mutually exclusive call for personal as well as group liberation.'[2] Genovese's political defection is of slight consequence. It may in fact be good that the belittling of gay liberation and abortion rights and the calls for capital punishment in his article are not identified with Marxism. In any case, Genovese never was known mainly as a political thinker or as a theorist. Certainly few radicals searched through *National Review*, *Commentary*, *New Republic* and other conservative journals to follow twists in Genovese's soured-on-the-left Marxism in recent years.

However, Genovese is deservedly important among American histori-ans. After C. Vann Woodward he is probably the most important historian of the US South.[3] His distinctive and learned interpretations of slavery in the South as a precapitalist social system have influenced a generation of students of the American past and have exercised a particular attraction to radical historians in that they represent perhaps the most ambitious and surely the most celebrated application of Marxism to US history.[4] The value of looking at Genovese's exit from the left therefore lies in its clear expression of the specific politics of history he is abandoning and to some extent clings to. Indeed so vividly are those politics spelled out that it becomes easier to see how intimately connected Genovese's historical work has always been to a specific brand of Marxism, a variety that unfor-tunately has too often been seen by American intellectuals as the only possible one.

In leaving Marxism, Genovese manages to preserve his longstanding critical respect for Stalinism. He would take this as no slur and perhaps as a compliment. His writings and talks have consistently emphasized an ap-preciation of Stalin.[5] In pointing to his continued affinity for Stalinism, I do not refer to Genovese's use of invective and overstatement in argu-ment, as in his wild recent charge that those who wish to open the literary canon to works by women and writers of color are really 'attacking West-ern Civilization ... , and dishonestly.'[6] Hideous as such a charge is, it finds an echo in the words of so many neoconservatives formerly on the anti-Stalinist left that it is dangerous to overemphasize the habit of 'Stalinist methods'. What instead identifies Genovese as retaining elements of a Stalinist approach is his specific equation of the possibility of socialism with Stalinist attempts to build 'socialism in one country' and, later, in several underdeveloped countries.

As recently as 1983, in the *Fruits of Merchant Capital*, Genovese wrote with mixed but tremendous admiration for Stalin, 'that great and fero-cious warlord' who brilliantly predicted in 1931, 'Either we close the gap in ten years or they crush us.' This prediction, Genovese thought as late as 1983, captured the reality of global class war and pointed to '... the essential content of the revolutionary fires that are engulfing the earth.'[7] Today, for Genovese, those fires are out. But his analysis of the present retains an admirable, if misplaced, consistency. He still sees our century as a death battle between Soviet-style socialism, the 'only socialism we have had', and its opponents.[8]

Now, however, we have a winner. The result for Genovese shows not the folly of Stalinism but the impossibility of socialism: 'No amount of blather about the collapse of Communism's having opened the way to "real" and democratic socialism will serve.' Nor can the 'radical, Left day-dream' of workers' control help salvage any of Marxism, which for

Genovese was grounded in claims of superior productivity, not on visions of freedom, and has now been defeated on the battleground of production.[9] Genovese in fact makes the unlikely argument that Stalinism has not been harsh and closed enough – that the 'central contradiction in the socialist countries has been the vain attempt to combine an unrealizable goal of personal liberation with a form of social organization that, above all, required maximum social discipline.'[10]

This sense that distinct capitalist and socialist systems fought it out in the twentieth century is mirrored by Genovese's view of the nineteenth-century United States, in which a distinctly 'prebourgeois' South challenged the capitalist North. In both cases, it is granted that capitalism is the dominant system of the world economy, but it is freely supposed that ruling classes in enclaves like the American South or the Soviet Union can attempt to compete indefinitely in a capitalist world without coming to see extraction of surplus value from laboring people as the key to their fortunes. At the least, Genovese has held, even after slaveholders 'adapted to capitalist norms' in order to survive, the 'property foundation' of their system 'pulled them out of that [capitalist] orbit' and toward 'prebourgeois' psychology, ideology and material interest.[11] Genovese's view proved exceedingly popular among historians, in part I would argue, because it appeared during the hottest years of the Cold War, a time when the idea of stark opposition between totally different political economies was a staple of American media, popular culture and intellectual life.

Marx and Engels generally thought about the South differently. They credited ascendent capitalism with considerably broader impact than Genovese has. Thus the *Communist Manifesto* – in a passage that Jurgen Habermas has recently observed may have as much relevance to the precariousness of 'postcapitalist' as to that of 'precapitalist' social formations – argues that capitalism

> ... compels all nations, on pain of extinction, to adopt the bourgeois mode of production; it compels them to introduce what it calls civilization into their midst, that is, to become bourgeois themselves. In one word, it creates a world after its own image.[12]

However schematic, overstated and even problematic such a passage is, it does carry clear and important implications for any consideration of the slaveholding American South. Marx did not shrink from such implications. He wrote (with Engels) of the Civil War as 'a struggle between two social systems, the system of slavery and the system of free labor.' But this did not imply that one social system was capitalist and the other not. While the *form* of appropriation of surplus value made a vital difference, the logic of both systems was, for Marx, capitalist: 'That fact that we not only call the plantation owners in America capitalists, but that they *are* capitalists', he explained, 'is based on their existence as anomalies within a world market based on free labor.'[13] For Marx, in *Capital*, the question of the political economy of the South was a historical one based on relation to the world capitalist system. The Southern economy 'preserved something of a patriarchal character, so long as production was chiefly directed to immediate local consumption.' However, integration into the capitalist world economy as a cotton exporting area changed all that: 'It was no longer a question of obtaining from [the plantation worker] a certain quantity of useful products. It was now a question of the production of surplus labor itself.'[14]

In contrast, Genovese argues that the 'prebourgeois' status of the South derived from the internal dynamics of the master–slave relationship, which imparted a paternalism to the system. The paternalism, like socialism in one country, was not only able to survive in a hostile world but to develop a coherent noncapitalist ideology. In making this case, Genovese strongly attacks Marx and Engels, but never on the central issue of the political economy of the South. His 'Marxian Intepretations of the Slave South' begins with Alfred North Whitehead's admonition that 'a science which hesitates to forget its founders is lost.' It holds that there is little worth remembering in the writings of Marx and Engels on US slavery. Maintaining, not quite accurately, that Marx and Engels 'restricted themselves to journalistic pieces on the secession crisis and never attempted that kind of analysis which we have come to call Marxian', he traces subsequent Marxist failures to discuss the South intelligently to the 'sins' of 'our fathers'.[15]

The sins are many: largely ignorant of the South, he writes, Marx and Engels let pro-Union partisanship erode their judgement. They engaged in 'politically expedient fabrications' and gave in to a 'dangerous tendency toward economic determinism in their own thought.' Genovese also charges, in a long section of small relevance to the South, that Marx and Engels alternated between idealizing and savaging the Lincoln government and between romanticizing and judging harshly British working class support of the Union.[16] However, the most serious accusation is that they did not regard slaveholding Southern leaders as moral and worthy adversaries. They failed to see that 'Judah P. Benjamin, Jefferson Davis and J. H. Hammond [were] class conscious, socially responsible and personally honorable' representatives of a distinct, paternalistic and 'antibourgeois' Southern ruling class. Marx and Engels, Genovese complains, refused to see Southern rulers as 'neither cynical nor hypocritical but honest.' They withheld 'full respect and admiration' from the slaveholders and were 'blind' to 'everything ... virtuous, honorable, decent and selfless' in 'the best elements of the slaveholding class.'[17]

Nowhere in the essay does Genovese give any sense of the *reason* that Marx and Engels did not accord admiration to the Southern ruling class. He implies that they were functioning as moralists and opportunists and then moves on to a discussion of the highly problematic view of the Second International popular historian, Algie M. Simons, that the antebellum South was somehow 'semi-feudal'. Genovese loosely likens Simons to Marx and Engels and then easily demolishes the notions of Simons and others regarding Southern 'feudalism'.[18] He does not point out that Marx's own views were even more critical of the 'feudalist' position than his own. For Marx, the South was not feudal but distinctly bourgeois. And it is exactly for that reason that Marx refused to regard the paternalist and patriarchal claims of the planters as worthy of respect and admiration. He saw such ideology as cant, posturing and hypocrisy because he disagreed with Genovese on the issue of whether the Southern elite was 'antibourgeois'. Marx, to use Genovese's phrases, persisted in a 'denial of Southern legitimacy' and refused to see a 'War for Southern Independence', because Marx believed that 'the South ... is neither a territory strictly detached from the North ... nor a moral unity ... not a country, but a battle cry.' For Marx, the South was a dissenting but bourgeois part of a bourgeois republic. For Genovese, it was the one 'serious, internal opposition' to the 'powerful, confident bourgeoisie' in US history.[19]

I do not propose here to discuss whether Marx or Genovese had the better of this argument. My view is that Marx did, but neither analysis wholly settles a hornet's nest of theoretical and historical issues. What does deserve comment is that Genovese could undertake, in that long article and in a long career as a Marxist, to explore his differences with Marx while not identifying the roots of those differences. Clearly Genovese was being honest and not hypocritical. He did not seek to muddy Marx's position but sincerely did not see how Marx could believe that the North and South had different property forms and labor markets (and thus different 'systems, the system of slavery and the system of free labor') but still share one capitalist political economy with the rest of the bourgeois world. Indeed Genovese's 1983 (with Elizabeth Fox-Genovese) return to a consideration of Marx's work on slavery, though much closer to acknowledging Marx's position, still minimizes the importance of Marx's contention that the slaveholder had developed a capitalist 'personality' in his relation to labor. Moreover, it tends to attribute Marx's position to ignorance and 'contradictory' logic and ultimately to conclude that Marx could not have been making an important point.[20]

A reconsideration of Genovese's Marxism as he himself abandons socialism illuminates how closely intertwined history is with politics and helps us appreciate some of the subtle and immense changes brought about by the collapse of Communism. On the former score, it is not

Genovese alone whose perceptions have been limited by Cold War politics. My own rather embattled anti-Stalinism has, over the years, tended to make me think of Genovese's treatment of Marx's writing on the South as a deliberate obfuscation. Looking at the same historical works by Genovese in a new political context such a charge appears ridiculous. His sharing in a Cold War consensus that, East and West, divided the world in two based on property forms now seems a much better explanation for his skewed presentations of Marx's view. That the Soviet bloc has given up, largely without a fight, on what it had called socialism, has opened tremendous intellectual space as well as political space. As the turn to the right by Genovese shows, such openings do not mean that there will be automatic movement towards left positions critical of Stalinism. But the openings do give us an unprecedented opportunity to rethink the past, present and future.

Notes

This article originally appeared in *New Politics*, no. 11 (Summer 1991): 90–95.

1. Genovese in 'The American 80's: Disaster or Triumph, A Symposium', *Commentary* 90 (September 1990): 48, 49 and 50.
2. Genovese, 'American 80's', 48–50. Cf. Genovese, 'Introduction to the New Edition', *In Red and Black: Marxian Explorations in Southern and Afro-American History*, Knoxville, Tenn. 1984, vii–li, for similar arguments less dismissively made.
3. See *AHA Perspectives* (February 1990): 8.
4. Genovese's work may be followed in his *The Political Economy of Slavery: Studies in the Society and Economy of the Slave South*, New York 1965; *The World the Slaveholders Made: Two Essays in Interpretation*, New York 1969; *From Rebellion to Revolution: Afro-American Slave Revolts in the Making of the New World*, New York 1979; *Roll, Jordan, Roll: The World the Slaves Made*, New York 1976; and Elizabeth Fox-Genovese and Eugene D. Genovese, *Fruits of Merchant Capital: Slavery and Bourgeois Property in the Rise and Expansion of Capitalism*, New York 1983.
5. See especially Fox-Genovese and Genovese, *Fruits of Merchant Capital*, 412–13 and 150; Genovese, *Red and Black*, xxiii–iv, xx and 14.
6. Genovese, 'The Arrogance of History', *New Republic*, 13 August 1990, 35.
7. Fox-Genovese and Genovese, *Fruits of Merchant Capital*, 413.
8. Genovese, 'American 80's', 48.
9. Ibid., 48–9.
10. Ibid.
11. For some of Genovese's attempts to characterize the political economy of the South, see *Political Economy of Slavery*, 28–31 and passim; *World the Slaveholders Made*, 16–20 and 95–9; Fox-Genovese and Genovese, *Fruits of Merchant Capital*, 20, 148–9 and 160.
12. Cited in Habermas, 'What Does Socialism Mean Today?' *New Left Review*, no. 183 (September-October 1990): 9.
13. Marx and Engels, *The Civil War in the United States*, Richard Enmale, ed., New York 1937, 81; Marx, *Grundrisse*, New York 1973, 513 (Marx's emphasis). The pamphlet 'Marx on American Slavery', by Ken Lawrence, Tougaloo, Miss. c. 1976, remains a valuable summary of Marx's briefly sketched formulations in this area.
14. Karl Marx, *Capital*, Chicago 1906, 1:260; cf. Marx, *Theories of Surplus Value*, Part II, Moscow 1971, 302–3.

15. Genovese, *Red and Black*, 315, 321 and passim.

16. Ibid., 319–36; cf. Fox-Genovese and Genovese, *Fruits of Merchant Capital*, 19–25.

17. Genovese, *Red and Black*, 325–6 and 342.

18. Ibid., 335–7.

19. Ibid., 325–7; Marx and Engels, *Civil War*, 72.

20. Fox-Genovese and Genovese, *Fruits of Merchant Capital*, 18–24. See also *World the Slaveholders Made*, 16–20. Clearly the emphasis in *Fruits of Merchant Capital* on the conservative nature of merchant capital is meant as a reply to the argument that the capitalist world economy was bound to have transformed the South. However, after a brief introduction the reply is seldom made directly. Much of the case for noncapitalism in the South made in the book consists of true but not relevant points, such as the fact – carried by a reference to Stalin's writing – that the ancient world was not capitalist though it produced and traded commodities. Commodity production, needless to say, was not what Marx thought made the South capitalist. See *Fruits of Merchant Capital*, 7 and 15–24. Moreover, the book takes the easy road of criticizing non-Marxists' views of the South as capitalist (for example, pp. 125–7 and 148–9) while leaving to 'another time and place' the consideration of differences with Marxist opponents on this score (p. 427n8).

4

Where Communism Was Black

Liberal columnists at the Johannesburg *Weekly Mail* gently mock South Africa's Communist Party by placing 'World's Last' before its name in editorials. But the joke does not so much succeed in dismissing the importance of that nation's Communists as in raising sharply their achievements in remaining, as nowhere else in the world, a key part of a mass freedom movement. One might explain this achievement by following South African Communist Party (SACP) leader Joe Slovo's argument that his party in effect had developed a 'premature Gorbachevism' – a concern for democracy and human rights and a spirit of independence that made it more capable of critical thinking and less subservient to Moscow than its sister parties elsewhere. However, as African National Congress education officer Z. Pallo Jordan shows in a brilliant reply to Slovo, it is dangerous to overemphasize the extent of the SACP's break with the stultifying traditions of Stalinism.[1] If it is admitted that the SACP has historically functioned at the national level less democratically and independently than some other Communist parties (such as Italy's), we might have to look elsewhere for the source of its strengths. Perhaps, in providing a forum for local resistance to an apartheid police state, the Communists offered to Black South Africans new ways of looking at the world, and of imagining and carrying out self-organization and resistance, even while laboring under the dead weight of Stalinism.

Robin D. G. Kelley's superbly crafted *Hammer and Hoe* explores the history of Communism in another apartheid police state, Alabama in the 1930s. Indeed, Kelley originally set out to write a comparative history of Communism in South Africa and in the American South. His emphasis helps to make sense of the historical appeal of South African Communism. Kelley asks not whether the Communist Party was good (or correct or independent), but how the party came to attract a substantial number of African American workers in Alabama and to energize their struggles. Or, more exactly, he asks how these Black workers could embrace and use the Communist Party as a vehicle for organizing themselves. He insists on measuring radicalism not by its idelogical purity but by its ability to interact with a received culture to generate bold class organization. In so doing, *Hammer and Hoe* closely resembles, ironically enough, Roman Laba's recent fine but fiercely anti-Communist study of Polish Solidarity in its approach.[2]

The result is a story that is fresh in every way. Although we have two wonderful oral memoirs by Alabama Communists – in Share Croppers' Union (SCU) leader Ned Cobb's *All God's Dangers* (told to Theodore Rosengarten) and in Birmingham labor leader Hosea Hudson's *Narrative* (told to Nell Irvin Painter) – nothing like so full an analytical account of the Communist Party (CP) in Alabama or any other Southern state exists.[3] Moreover, Kelley establishes Alabama's important place not so much as a microcosm but as a cauldron holding currents vital for understanding the twentieth-century South and modern America. Quasi-feudal oppression in the countryside persisted alongside Birmingham's highly, though recently, developed iron and steel industries. Jim Crow and lynch law poisoned the state's political culture but existed alongside traditions of biracial labor unity, an African American culture of opposition and a fragile presence of white liberalism.

Equally fresh are Kelley's interpretations, which do nothing short of turn much of the current wisdom regarding the history of Communism squarely on its head. For example, most scholarship that has offered a critical defense of the Communist Party in the thirties and forties has tended to hold its Popular Front policies in high regard, emphasizing attempts under Earl Browder's leadership to draw on American democratic political traditions, and to enter into meaningful political alliances with liberal political forces.[4] While this is an understandable viewpoint among engaged historians searching for models of left-center unity, for ways to 'Americanize' radical ideas, and even for precursors of Eurocommunism or *perestroika*, Kelley's interest is in African American agency in Depression-era Alabama. From that point of view, the Popular Front appears as much less of a blessing.

Kelley in fact argues that the wild, often ultra-Stalinist and sectarian Third Period that preceded the Popular Front better undergirded Black organization among tenant farmers and industrial workers. The extreme confrontational rhetoric of the Third Period Communists was not taken seriously by Alabama's early Black party members, who avoided posturing and suicidal confrontations whenever possible. But on another level, rhetoric regarding a 'new world', which probably appeared extravagant to other working class audiences, resonated among African Americans, whose traditions emphasized both a struggle for survival and the transcendant hope of deliverance. Help from a powerful ally, even one as far away as Moscow, could seem a source of power and possibility, especially when poor communications and the unfamiliarity with the South on the part of white party leaders from the North ensured that party discipline remained largely a local matter. Kelley regards the belief of at least one Black rural activist that 'all the leaflets, handbills, and newspapers he distributed were printed in Russia' (p. 100) as neither sad nor shameful. He sees it instead as a logical reaction to the 'centrality of Russia in popular notions of Communism', to the Third Period emphasis on Soviet achievements and, most of all, to the desire to believe that a powerful nation would support African Americans in a second Civil War by a people whose 'collective memory' of the first one was intense. The role of the Communist-led International Labor Defense in mobilizing around the world against lynch law in the Scottsboro case and other Alabama miscarriages of justice helped to establish the Communist Party's image as such an ally.

Kelley is at his subtle best in describing the role of race consciousness in making Communism appealing to significant numbers of Black Alabamans in the early 1930s. Eschewing a narrowly idelogical approach, Kelley does not place much emphasis on the Communist Party's distinctive call for self-determination for a 'Negro nation' in the Black Belt during these years. Sticking closely to the evidence, he finds that such a position was not nearly so important to rank-and-file party members in their organizing activities as it has been to modern historians of Communism.[5] Nor does he find grass-roots interest in pan-African struggles to have been overwhelming. While the Soviet Union was at times termed the 'new Ethiopia', the Birmingham campaign to defend the real Ethiopia against invasion by Italy was undramatic.

But Kelley is too shrewd to suppose that absence of grand expressions of nationalist sentiment meant that race was unimportant to Black Communists. In effect, the decision to recruit African Americans into the movement made sure that working class whites could easily be race-baited away. 'Thus two separate parties were formed', Kelley writes, 'a large, broad-based organization of Southern Blacks and a tiny cadre of Northern whites' (p. 30). Therefore, Communism offered an opportunity for race-conscious as well as class-conscious mobilization. Moreover, it became a vehicle for pursuing what Kelley calls 'intraracial class conflict', providing its working class cadre with resources, a sense of power, and training useful in challenging entrenched and cautious Black elites.

The culture of early Alabama Communism was therefore the culture of Birmingham's African American industrial working class and of the rural poor of the SCU. Indeed, it is noteworthy that *Hammer and Hoe* may be our most sophisticated study of Communism and culture but that it does not analyze socialist realism or the other much-debated cultural theories of international Communism. Instead, Kelley writes brilliantly on the folk traditions of resistance through cunning that made SCU members 'act humble' even as they assembled what Black Communist Harry Haywood would later call a 'small arsenal' of weapons (p. 45). 'Rural Blacks in and around the Party', according to Kelley, 'transformed popular spirituals into political songs', making 'Give Me That Old Time Religion' end 'It was good enough for Lenin, and it's good enough for me.' Third Period anti-religious propaganda enjoyed little currency in Alabama, where 'most black Communists ... continued to attend services regularly' (p. 115), even as they drew on a rich vein of African American folklore skewering opportunistic ministers to attack conservative preachers. For many members, even outside of organized churches, 'the Bible was as much a guide to class struggle as [the] *Communist Manifesto.*'

The Popular Front period saw Black participation in the Communist Party of Alabama decline both absolutely and relatively. A retreat from attacks on 'white chauvinism' and a tendency 'to deemphasize, however slightly ... involvement in local black issue-oriented politics' made the Communist Party seem less an instrument of deliverance. The former change, undertaken in an atmosphere in which white party members were capable of using 'comrage nigger' (p. 137) to refer to Black Communists, failed to attract many of the relatively liberal, but still segregationist, Southern progressives to the movement. However, enough whites did come in to make Alabama Communism less a vehicle for race-conscious African American mobilization. The shift to a Southern white leadership probably lessened room for local African American initiatives. An increasing cautiousness born of a desire to appeal to moderates doubtless made the party less of a clear alternative in intraracial class conflicts. Nor did building an open, above-ground party necessarily seem wholly desirable or possible to Black workers.

Even so, Kelley is far from claiming that the change to a Popular Front line was the sole reason for the decline of African American Communism in Alabama, or that the agency of Black workers proved entirely useless in the longer run. Intense repression, popularly supported with special zeal because Communism was associated with 'social equality' and 'nigger unions', made organization difficult no matter what the line. The Popular Front initially appealed to Birmingham's Black Communists because it seemed to open new strategies for blunting repression in a state where opponents at times professed a desire to 'lynch Russia', but settled for victims nearer at hand. Kelley's rounded portrait of the decline of the SCU emphasizes not the absence of a 'correct line' but the presence of factional battles with Socialist-led unions, of terror, and of agricultural transformations caused by market changes and federal intervention.

Kelley is also eager to demonstrate the continuing positive actions of ex-Communists, especially in the Congress of Industrial Organization (CIO) but also the modern civil rights movement. Daniel Singer's recent jest that ex-Communists constitute the largest political tendency in France may have literally applied in Black Alabama by 1940.[6] Even if the movement never had more than several hundred African American members in the state at any one time, it ran through members rapidly and the institutional presence of other political parties in Black Alabama was slight. Kelley argues that, absent the fierce factional infighting and purges that often characterized the Communist Party elsewhere, Alabama's Black members often drifted from the organization without bitterness and without a backlash against radical politics. In particular, the many who left to devote their full energies to CIO organizing saw the union as a force for deliverance, as they had seen the Communist Party some years before.

Much else deserves mention regarding this groundbreaking and beautifully designed book. Especially noteworthy is the sustained consideration of gender, both in probing the experience of Communist women and in nuanced consideration of the role played by manhood in the construction of both Communist and anti-Communist worldviews. For this reason and a host of others, Kelley's lyrical prose and rigorous analysis deserve the widest possible readership.

Notes

This review of Robin D. G. Kelley's *Hammer and Hoe: Alabama Communists during the Great Depression*, Chapel Hill, N.C. 1990, was first published in *American Quarterly*, vol. 44, no. 1 (March 1992). © 1992 American Studies Association.

1. Joe Slovo, *Has Socialism Failed?*, London 1990; Z. Pallo Jordan, 'The Crisis of Conscience in the SACP', *Transformation* 11 (1990): 75–89.

2. Roman Laba, *The Roots of Solidarity*, Princeton, N.J. 1991; among studies of US Communists, Mark Naison's *Communists in Harlem during the Depression*, Urbana, Ill. 1983, is probably nearest in approach to Kelley.

3. Theodore Rosengarten, *All God's Dangers: The Life of Nate Shaw*, New York 1974; Nell Irvin Painter, *The Narrative of Hosea Hudson: His Life as a Negro Communist in the South*, Cambridge, Mass. 1979.

4. Fraser M. Ottanelli, *The Communist Party of the United States: From the Depression to World War II*, New Brunswick, N.J. 1991, is the most recent and one of the most thorough and valuable studies reflecting this point of view. For recent debates on the history of Communism, see the article by Theodore Draper and responses by Paul Buhle, James R. Barrett, Mark Naison, Rob Ruck, Al Richmond, Maurice Isserman and others in *New York Review of Books*, 9 May, 30 May, and 15 August 1985.

5. Kelley may overstate this point. Communists attracted by the nationalism of the party probably left it sooner and are less likely to be identified by oral historians.

6. Daniel Singer, 'The Treason of the New Intellectuals', *Nation*, 19 April 1991, 560.

5

Notes on Working Class Racism

The west seems to suffer deep anxieties about the precariousness of its civilization and to have a need for constant reassurance by comparison with Africa. ... Africa is a carrier on to whom the master unloads his physical and moral deformities so that he may go forward, erect and immaculate. – *Chinua Achebe*

The work culture of university students enjoins against the dicussion of the final chapters of assigned books. Some students will have read the whole assignment but in solidarity with the majority who have not, discussants generally concentrate on the early pages. As it is in so many other ways, George Rawick's *From Sundown to Sunup: The Making of the Black Community* is exceptional in this regard. Each year my students react sharply to its final two chapters, which provide a wide-ranging discussion of relationships among slavery, racism, capitalism, repression and the American past.

They passionately take up the arguments in those brief chapters – the very ones most ignored by historians. The students are right in sensing that the closing pages of *Sundown* are full of meanings, past and present. The historians are wrong. Near the beginning of *Sundown*, Rawick observes that 'slavery was a fundamental part of the history of the American people.' In the final two chapters, he attempts to connect slavery and racism with that broader history and with the development of Western capitalism generally. The themes are obviously far too broad to be tackled in the thirty pages Rawick devotes to them. The chapters are episodic, skipping about in place and time. Periodization is quite loose. References to the racism of 'Englishmen' and of 'Northerners' are offered with insufficient attention to how class differences and ethnic divisions shaped racial

61

attitudes among whites.

All that granted, it still seems to me that Rawick's brief chapters on racism, slavery and capitalism in *Sundown* are indispensable for any analysis of the themes he addresses. They have a place alongside the writings of Edmund Morgan, W. E. B. Du Bois, Oliver Cromwell Cox, Walter Rodney and C. L. R. James as the truly seminal work in this area. They succeed in part because of Rawick's sheer force in generating ideas and connections. The argument that white working class disaffection with the Civil War effort helped cause Lincoln's emancipation of the slaves is brilliant, intriguing and ironic. The contention that 'racism took its strongest hold among those people who most thoroughly participated in the new, revolutionary developments of the modern world' ought to be the subject of volumes by students of comparative history.

But Rawick's chapters do more than generate intriguing hypotheses. They provide a framework that can be expanded to illuminate the political tragedy of white racism and particularly of white working class racism. They begin a discussion of the relationship between such racism and white workers' self-activity. In building on Rawick's framework, we can go in different directions. No attempt is made to implicate Rawick in the conclusions drawn here except to say that he inspired me and to note, in three separate sections, how his specific insights in *Sundown* might inform future work.

I

Rawick offers the best available short summary of efforts at Black–white unity in the US labor movement. 'Such efforts', he writes, 'were not successful often enough.' This is a painful truth for us as leftists who rightly admire those who risked much to take egalitarian positions within the labor movement. Nor will Rawick allow us to romanticize by supposing that working class organizations fell victim to racism as the result of misleadership that subverted the good intentions of the membership. He specifically addresses the cases of the National Labor Union and the American Railway Union, which maintained racist policies despite pleas by their very forceful leaders, William Sylvis and Eugene Debs, respectively. Rawick then discusses Populism, as a movement characterized first by Black–white unity, and then by a relapse into white supremacy. We are reminded that the lessons of class unity were unlearned as well as learned.

Recent work by US historians underlines the extent to which white antiracism was a weak trend in the labor movement. Even high points of Black–white unity, like the 1886 Richmond convention of the Knights of

Labor, so brilliantly explored in Peter Rachleff's work, contained serious compromises with racist opinion. Nor was the sole problem vacillation on the part of Terence Powderly and other leaders of the Knights. Rank-and-file racism also flourished. The fine studies of anti-Black and especially of anti-Chinese racism by Alexander Saxton reinforce the point that racism was *popular* and even a force encouraging white working class unity.

Herbert Hill's detailed studies of trade union racism take the tragic story of breaches in Black–white unity – even in progressive industrial unions – into the modern era. Accounts of the Louisiana Sugar Wars of the 1880s remind us how quickly unity could give way to murderous vigilante violence. Herbert Shapiro's and David Carlton's writings show white American workers in textiles and railroading using direct action to enforce color bars and maintain white workers' control. 'Hate strikes' against the employment of minority workers have been a recurring feature of US labor history, and have often involved white self-activity on behalf of workers' control, narrowly defined. My own work suggests that even Albert Parsons – hanged a century ago for his staunch advocacy of working class self-activity – could wholly forget the special oppression of Black workers despite his background as a Radical Republican antiracist.

Of course some factors have favored the growth of egalitarian working class organization. Industrial unions have been 'better' than craft unions; revolutionary unions or unions with strong radical contingents have been 'better' than conservative unions; democratic unions have been 'better' than bureaucratic and dictatorial unions; industries with large numbers of Black workers already present have given rise to more examples of Black–white unity than ones with lesser numbers of Black employees. The antiracist activities of two unions, the Southern Tenant Farmers Union and the Industrial Workers of the World, typify such trends. All these patterns matter, but they should not wholly divert our attention from the broad pattern of Black–white unity being 'not successful often enough' to undergird a workers' struggle against either racism or class rule.

II

In explaining why white workers accepted and even deepened American racism, Rawick argues that in a split labor market white workers gained or thought they gained certain advantages in avoiding misery and even in avoiding proletarianization. He allows that 'there was much illusion in their belief'. This is not the place to debate the extent of material benefits derived from white skin privileges. Clearly some material gains accrued and just as clearly white workers were often settling for what Du Bois called a higher 'public and psychological wage'. Rawick's greatest contribution lies in helping us understand the circumstances under which white workers would accept such tradeoffs. He proposes a framework that can make white working class racism both more understandable and more tragic. That framework moves beyond labor market–based explanations.

Rawick connects racism with the various losses of humanity required during the transition to capitalism. The separation of work from the rest of life, the bridling of sexuality, the loss of contact with nature, the timing of labor by clocks rather than by sun and season, the injunction to save by postponing gratification – all these were monumental, and monumentally painful, changes. Rawick suggests that in complex ways and especially for profit-minded Englishmen, such changes intensified racism during the years of American settlement. Racism served to justify slavery, but it also did more than that. Racists still longed for older ways, and even still practiced older styles of life, guiltily. All of the old habits and styles of life so recently discarded by whites in the process of adopting capitalist values came to be fastened on Blacks. As Rawick wonderfully puts it, Englishmen and profit-minded settlers in America 'met the West African as a reformed sinner meets a comrade of his previous debaucheries.' The racist, like the reformed sinner, creates a 'pornography of his former life. ... In order to ensure that he will not slip back into the old ways or act out half-suppressed fantasies, he must see a tremendous difference between his reformed self and those whom he formerly resembled.' Blackness and whiteness are thus created together.

Although Rawick does not apply this framework to the development of working class racism in the US, it works astonishingly well in that connection. Modern urban working class racism took shape alongside the imposition of time discipline, the bastardization of crafts, the attacks on holidays, and the attempts to control sexuality and drinking characteristic of capitalist development in the second quarter of the nineteenth century. Significantly, integrated and Black-led amusements were often singled out for attack. The banning of Negro Election Day in 1831 in Massachusetts is the best-studied example, thanks to Paul Faler and others. But Alessandra Lorini's work on New York City shows similar state repression of Black–white crowds. A poem in tribute to Negro Election Day, written after its demise, shows how much more than interracial mixing was under attack when the holiday was ended:

> And is Election Day no more?
> Good Old 'Lection ...
> No more shall we go up
> To see old Willis!
> He has hung up his fiddle

On the last peg.
The days of old 'Lection are over,
The glorious days of 'Landee John!'
When 'Gid' used to hustle coppers,
And the niggers play 'paw-paw,'
On Boston Common.
No more shall we eat 'Lection cake,'
Or drink muddy beer,
Misnomered 'ale,'
At 'Old Bly's.'
The days of dancing 'Suke' are done,
And Fat 'Bet' shall shake her jolly sides no more
To the merry winding about
Of linked sweetness, long drawn out,
From old 'Pompey's fiddle.'

III

Thirty years later urban workers in the United States would be flocking to minstrel shows. By that time many of them had painfully adapted to various forms of repression in a world not of their own making. The early minstrel stage, as the Black choreographer Leni Sloan has recently observed, often featured Irish immigrants beneath the blackface. Irish also took their places in the audience. Thus those most acutely experiencing the wrenching adaptation to urban wage labor helped to organize white working class longings, fantasies and dreams as projections upon supposedly oversexed, lazy and naive Black characters. That these adjectives fit the negative stereotyping of the Irish only made for greater psychic investment in minstrelsy's illusion of white supremacy.

Similarly, the late antebellum period sees the coining of the word *coon* as a racial slur and Zip Coon becomes a stock minstrel charcter. Before then, variations of *coon* had applied to rural whites, especially those trying to be clever. The transition to urban industrial life became no less painful for whites by virtue of their transferring the epithet and its negative connotations to Blacks. But perhaps that transition and its pains became more deniable, at least for those who did not read Herman Melville's fierce punning on the term *coon* in describing a racially indeterminate rural character in *The Confidence Man.*

The ways in which this tragic drama played itself out in US history are extremely diverse and complex. Allow me one personal example. I grew up in an Illinois family when Florida vacations were becoming possible for many workers. As my relatives and my parents' friends made the trip, a steady stream of their 'pickaninny' postcards from the South made their way back to Illinois. An extended and expensive Florida vaction violated the values of steady work and sacrifice that workers had internalized. Nonetheless, the cards reassured, it was Southern Blacks and not the vacationers who were taking it easy.

IV

'The pressure of Blacks for equality', Rawick concludes in *Sundown*, 'intensifies all social conflicts in the United States.' That hopeful statement, echoing Marx, provides a happy contrast to the bleakness of much of the American experience emphasized in this chapter so far. Revolutionaries can take small comfort from my argument that working class racism has not automatically given way even in moments of self-organization among workers. Nor is it a cheering thought that such racism has deep, unconscious roots in patterns of repression and is therefore quite irrational. Nonetheless, we know that history bears Rawick out: from the eighthour struggles after the Civil War to the rebellions in the auto industry in the 1960s and 1970s, as the walls of racial oppression tumbled, class rule was also shaken. Of course this doubly liberating potential comes in part because a united working class can fight more effectively than a divided one. But Rawick's analysis of racism would suggest that far more is involved than strategic unity. The stakes in discussing this question are very high, as Marx's formulation, quoted by Rawick, indicates: 'Labour cannot emancipate itself in the white skin where in the black it is branded.' Antiracism, in this reading, is not just linked with improving the prospects for success in this strike or that election but with the *self-emancipation of the working class*.

We cannot explain this historic connection of antiracism and self-emancipation on purely structural grounds. We cannot simply observe that Blacks constitute a key strategic sector of the working class. They did not constitute such a sector when Marx wrote. Any full explanation must therefore include, even emphasize, cultural and ideological factors. In particular, it must consider, after Rawick, the extent to which white workrers defined themselves by negation – as not Black and not Chinese. They were free laborers because they were not slaves. They considered themselves manly/respectable/Americanized/mature/middle class because they were not allegedly degraded and dissolute people of color.

But the process is two-sided. White workers have also historically longed for those values they imputed to Black culture: leisure, joy, expressiveness and community, for example. Even the minstrel show, in its own perverse way, expresses this hankering. The embrace of zoot suits, of rhythm and blues, and most recently, of rap and Tracy Chapman's music by white working class youth, indicates that longing more directly. George Lipsitz's evocation of the search of American workers for a 'rainbow at midnight' in the post–World War II US suggests how Black cultural forms have inspired white workers, how Blackness is linked with more than degradation in white workers' minds.

Indeed, as Rawick has argued, we may be living in a world in which large numbers of people who do not trace their roots to the African diaspora come to embrace the label *Black*. Non-African ethnic minorities in Britain, including Indians, Pakistanis, and even Cypriots call themselves Black in many cases. In South Africa, those designated 'coloured' often choose to call themselves Black. In France, SOS Racisme, the most important new social movement in the country, is Black-led and its white members largely adopt Black fashions. And whatever the political significance of the Jackson campaign in the United States, it at least showed that substantial numbers of white workers are willing to pair blackness and positive change, even liberation, in their conscious thoughts as well as in their subconscious.

It would be a wonderful irony if white notions concerning blackness – notions developed to rationalize both slavery and repression of white desires – gave way, even partially, to a sense among young workers that to be Black is to be more human and more able to resist the alienating aspects of late capitalist life. The idea of sharply different Black and white races is, of course, a social creation. So far the social definition of race has buttressed white supremacy and class rule. If an opposite process is now to take place, or even is already taking place, we can still expect no easy resolutions to the acute racial and class contradictions in the US. White attempts to embrace Black culture and Black modes of resistance will often be condescending. They will sometimes be silly. They will, if the history of white appropriation of jazz and rhythm and blues is any guide, frequently be shot through with racism.

But for all of that, radicals cannot afford to ignore the halting steps with which some white workers are not only dropping some racist assumptions, culturally and politically, but are negating those assumptions and recovering repressed parts of themselves. In the largest sense such cultural activity will be as vital as point-of-production struggles in any possible remaking of the working class. In the wonderful picture that graces the cover of Martin Glaberman's excellent *Wartime Strikes*, cultural and workplace activities merge as Black zoot suiters lead a celebration of largely white wildcat strikers outside an auto plant. Styles will change and there will be many problems, but I have the feeling we have not seen the end of such pictures.

NOTE: This essay was first published in *New Politics*, no. 7 (Summer 1989): 61–6.

6

The Crisis in Labor History:
Race, Gender and the Replotting of
the Working Class Past in the
United States

For at least a decade, labor history in the United States has proclaimed
itself in disarray. However, until recently the fretting has been pleasant
enough. The discipline seemed able to have what one commentator on
academic trends has called a 'fashionable crisis'.[1] It anguished eloquently
in rather prominent publications, bemoaning its own inability to achieve
a full synthesis of the proliferating studies of labor in various cities and
trades, studies which were widely and rightly regarded as important and
intelligent. Only in the last five years has the mood turned markedly
gloomier, with increasing worrying aloud that labor history is, as one
academic press editor puts it, a 'declining subfield'.

The sharpening concern with the future direction of labor history is an
international one – but the forces feeding that concern are perhaps distinctive in the US case. The so-called 'death of socialism', registered most
dramatically in the fall of the Soviet Union and of the Warsaw Pact regimes but also in the electoral misfortunes and decreased emphasis on
social transformation among Western European working class parties, has
obviously played a large part in generating a sense of crisis among labor
historians internationally. But the resonance of the 'death of socialism' in
causing a rethinking of US labor's past is less great. Writing about a nation long without a socialist left of any consequence in the unions or in
politics, Marxist US labor historians have long had to premise arguments
for the use of historical materialism on the grounds that class analysis
illuminates societies in which socialist movements are weak as well as
those in which such movements are strong.[2] Indeed US historians ought
to be especially well-placed to resist the increasing vogue of sliding tran-
sitions which hold that the Soviet Union = socialism = Marxism = any
challenge to capitalist hegemony.

On the other hand, the decline of organized labor has been far more wrenching in the US than in any other industrialized country, with union density cut in half from its post–World War II peak. This decline has obviously called into particular question many of the assumptions of the institutionally based 'old labor history', whose leading figure, Philip Taft, wrote in 1966 that 'American organized labor has succeeded in devising protections for itself unequalled in any other country.'[3] But in a broader sense it has challenged all of US labor history. From its inception as a subdiscipline within economics in the US nearly a century ago, labor history has benefitted from the presence of the 'labor problem'. Its promises to guide trade unionists, to inform the arguments of reformers and to promote class peace gained meaning in proportion to the perceived strength (and threat) of organized and organizing labor.[4] But with union membership now covering only one worker in six, with the labor vote small and split, and with strikes rare, defensive and often ill-fated, the labor problem commands less attention from institutions and from the public. Moreover, the internationalization of capital and the tendency of US-based corporations to relocate rather than to confront organized labor have tended to redefine the labor problem as one to be solved in space (by moving) rather than in time (by responding to labor's demands).

That the 'new labor history' emerged in the US in the late 1960s professing a determination to write the history of workers rather than unions has not prevented the decline of unionism from having a profoundly disorienting impact on new labor historians. Many of us who became interested in working class history in the late 1960s and early 1970s were quite critical of existing unions. But we still assumed that organized workers would be audiences for (and, in the inspired initiatives of Staughton Lynd and others, participants in) efforts to rethink labor history.[5] We also assumed that rank-and-file upsurges, especially in the highly unionized automobile sector, would continue to give urgency to research on the history of the labor process and of shopfloor militancy.

The lack of a labor audience and of a militant labor movement was especially troubling because trade unions continued to a surprising extent to be the subjects of the new history. Despite their substantial innovations, the new labor historians often ended using the history of unions, radical parties and strikes to tell the story of workers. This was of course true of the first such historians, most prominently David Montgomery, David Brody and Herbert Gutman, who had roots in Old Left and/or institutional approaches to labor history that emphasized organized labor.[6] But it has also continued to be true through a quarter-century in the works of Daniel Walkowitz, Shelton Stromquist, John Cumbler, Alan Dawley, Peter Friedlander, Robert Zieger, Michael Kazin, Patricia Cooper, Meredith Tax, Ronald Schatz, Mary Blewett, Thomas Dublin, James Barrett, Joshua

Freeman, Leon Fink, Ava Baron, Vicki Ruiz, Peter Rachleff, David Corbin, Joe William Trotter, Richard Ostreicher, Nancy Gabin, Susan Levine, Eric Arnesen, Nelson Lichtenstein, both Bruce Nelsons and even Sean Wilentz, among many others. Far from lapsing into what Howard Kimeldorf has criticized as a 'peripheralization of unions', the new labor history has made organized labor central to its attempts to capture the working class past.[7]

The fear voiced by critics of two decades ago was that the new labor history would be dominated by culturalists who would write the histories of bowling teams rather than of unions. Such fears persist, but with little basis in what has actually been published. When David Brody recently proposed that a new synthesis of US labor history might profitably begin by assuming that 'organizations can be taken as institutional manifestations of the consciousness of workers', he captured the trajectory of the new labor history, which set out to write the history of workers rather than of unions and often ended by writing the history of workers through the history of unions.[8] To identify that trajectory is not to ridicule it. The study of workers' consciousness partly through their responses to trade unionism has often yielded brilliant results, especially when combined with study of the labor process and study of gender. Moreover, there are still gaping holes in the history of organized labor. But in a society in which trade unions are increasingly marginal not only in national life but in shaping the consciousness of their members, a labor history identified largely with studies of the unions is bound to be susceptible to crises.

The crisis of the labor movement need not, of course, necessarily consign labor history to antiquarianism. It may be that a revival of working class organization is at hand. Brody is undoubtedly right to reject the recent arguments that hold that management has a 'new face [which] is not a replay of history' and that therefore 'not much can be learned from labor's past.'[9] But even if the unions do revive, it seems to me that the research agenda that has begun to mature in the latest stages of the long period of decline of US labor organization still deserves to be pursued. The record of pro-Republican voting by the white working class in the 1980, 1984 and 1988 elections, for example, has raised the critical historical issues of working class conservatism and working class racism in sharp relief.[10] Reflection on the assault on the labor movement by the state has encouraged rich studies of the legal history of labor and important accounts of labor and politics.[11] The many scholars sent by the recent past to the study of the impact of the Cold War in isolating trade union radicals are producing very significant work.[12] Studies that place US labor in the context of international relations and of the relocation of workers and industries have, not surprisingly, also developed impressively.[13]

Most important, the idea that white males, identified simply as workers, must be at the center of any synthesis of US labor history has come under sharp question as the labor force has become increasingly nonwhite and female and as white male trade union membership has plummetted. (As recent works by Michael Goldfield and Mike Davis show, African Americans are now considerably more supportive of trade unionism than whites and far more receptive to what might be called social democratic politics, American-style.)[14] The roles of working women and, to a lesser extent, of workers of color have understandably received greater emphasis from labor historians in the very recent past, as have the male gender identity and, again to a lesser extent, the white racial identity of white male workers.

Historians have, in this atmosphere of trade union decline, also become much more aware of the ways that a focus on organized labor can slight the histories of working class women, African Americans and others who historically were often excluded from unions. While agreeing that we need far more study of workers not in unions, I would take this point further and in a slightly different direction: Just as the question of whether organized labor in the US has a future is fully tied up with labor's ability to draw on the energies and critiques of such so-called 'new social movements' as feminism and antiracism, so too is the future of trade union history based on its ability to situate the past of labor organization within the dynamics of racial and gender formation.

Towards the Study of Race in Labor History

The best session at a superb labor history conference held recently in Detroit centered on slavery, emancipation and the transition to free labor in the US South. The convener of the session remarked at the outset that it had initially been difficult to put a panel together because some scholars working his field considered a labor history conference less than an appropriate venue for the discussion of their work. My mind immediately raced back to W. E. B. Du Bois's conclusion to his classic *Black Reconstruction* (1935). In one of the very few passages from a history book that I ever more-or-less managed to commit to memory, Du Bois wrote:

> The most magnificent drama in the last thousand years of human history is the transportation of ten million human beings out of the dark beauty of their mother continent into the new-found Eldorado of the West. They descended into Hell; and in the third century they arose from the dead, in the finest effort to achieve democracy for the working millions which this world had ever seen. It [post–Civil War Reconstruction in the US] was a tragedy that beggared the Greek; it was an upheaval of humanity like the Reformation and the French

Revolution. Yet we are blind and led by the blind. We discern in it no part of our labor movement. ...[15]

That, in 1992, the convener's remark to labor historians could recall Du Bois's 1935 indictment of American historians generally is decidedly less than a hopeful sign. However, the session did occur, with incisive, challenging papers given before a large and enthusiastic audience. One could argue a case for either hope or despair as to whether the new labor history at last is about to take up fully the question of racial identities within the working class. Though making the case for hope, I would stress that grounds for hope have been present before but not fully realized. I would also emphasize the tremendous stakes involved, stakes strikingly captured by the way in which Du Bois frames the issue in terms of drama. The ability of labor historians to convincingly cast their research in terms of dramatic issues like emancipation and independence depends in large measure on extending to the discussion of race the same sort of tough-minded analysis that has matured more quickly where the study of class and gender is concerned.

The tardiness of US labor historians in making the study of slavery and race central to their work is as ironic as it is regrettable. The very project of a 'new labor history' initially gained its appreciation for the fact that masses of working people make their own history not so much through witnessing significant trade union insurgencies as through the example of the Black freedom movement. The leading figures in early attempts to rewrite working class history were profoundly influenced by Du Bois and by the Black Trinidadian historian C. L. R. James. Herbert Gutman set out a research agenda which, as Ira Berlin has written, made 'study of the Afro-American family ... not a detour on the road to a history of the American working class, but the center lane on the main highway.'[16] Such scholars as Gutman, Harold Baron, Paul Worthman and James Green produced pathbreaking analyses of race and labor. Above all, Alexander Saxton published *The Indispensable Enemy: Labor and the Anti-Chinese Movement in California* in 1971.[17] Saxton's work, itself indispensable and unsurpassed, fully raised the question of the impact of white racial identity on unions and on white workers themselves at that early date.

Nonetheless, scholarship on race and labor failed to flower. Saxton and George Rawick did not come to be considered central figures in the new labor history as Brody, Montgomery and Gutman did. Fascinating studies of race and white workers, such as those by Mary Ellen Freifeld and Barry Goldberg, remained unpublished and underappreciated. Eric Foner, Sean Wilentz and David Montgomery brilliantly and convincingly restored the centrality of the sectional controversy, the Civil War and Reconstruction to working class US history, but they did so largely without the same emphasis Du Bois placed on the self-activity of Black workers and on the white racial identity of white workers.[18]

Herbert Hill may be partly correct in attributing the new labor history's failure to fully engage the questions of racial identity and racism to an excessively zealous search for a usable and inspiring past.[19] However, other factors also mattered greatly. The nearly total isolation of Communist historians from the new labor history deprived younger scholars of associations with Philip S. Foner and Herbert Aptheker, two of the most knowledgeable students of race, antiracism and labor.[20] The strong influence of Eugene Genovese's weighty studies of slavery as a precapitalist political economy tended to isolate the history of slavery from the history of wage labor.[21] Moreover, the very strength of the new history's emphasis on daily life made it less-than-quick to understand the symbolic and political importance of whiteness even to white workers who did not regularly encounter workers of different racial identities.[22]

Several recent developments open the possibility that the new labor history will at long last realize its early promise with regard to providing a full consideration of race and a critique of working class whiteness. The novelist and critic Toni Morrison has recently observed that studies of gender relations and identity have cleared the ground for the reconsideration of racial identity within cultural studies generally.[23] Her point applies with specific force to the study of labor's past. In the last decade, gendered studies of the working class past have proven far and away the most dramatic contributions to labor history. Studying not only women workers but the masculinity of male craft workers and trade unionists, historians have reinvigorated scholarship on unorganized workers, pioneered in sophisticated research on labor in the service industries, and convincingly connected the work experience with ideology, family, consumption and leisure.[24] Many of these historians, including Joanne Meyerowitz, Evelyn Nakono Glenn, Nancy Hewitt, Dolores Janiewski, Vicki Ruiz, Dana Frank, Patricia Cooper and Tera Hunter, have been enormously attentive to the dynamics of race as well as to class and gender.[25]

But even when they have not discussed race extensively, historians of labor and gender have made a decisive contribution to the study of race and class. They have demonstrated, particularly in the recent work of Joy Parr, Elizabeth Faue, and Jeanne Boydston, that the consideration of class and gender is not a zero-sum game in which an increasing emphasis on one 'variable' leads inexorably to a diminished emphasis on the other.[26] Instead class identity and gender identity are so thoroughly interpenetrating that intellectual excitement and understanding come precisely when both are stressed. This example has strongly encouraged a moving away from dead-end debates about whether to give priority to race or class identity in the study of labor as well, and have engendered a move toward the difficult, rewarding task of showing how racial identity and class identity have shaped each other. Moreover, in giving attention to masculine as well as feminine gender identity, recent labor history has set a vital precedent that can lead to full interrogation of the racial identity of the dominant racial group as well as of the subordinate ones.

The recent outpouring of work on African American, Asian American and Latino labor history further signals the possibility that a consideration of race will structure, and not just appear episodically in, new attempts at synthesis in US working class history. Workers of color occupy prominent places in recent studies of race relations in the unions and among the working class generally, with major contributions made by such scholars as Iver Bernstein, Bruce Nelson, Barbara Griffith, Rick Halpern, Peter Rachleff, Nelson Lichtenstein, Robert Korstad, Robert Norrell, Eric Arnesen, Michael Honey, Roger Horowitz and Nancy Quam Wickham.[27] Much of the finest work in labor history in the past five years has been the result of the partial democratization of the universities. Ronald Takaki, Earl Lewis, Joe William Trotter, Vicki Ruiz, Robin D. G. Kelley and Tera Hunter have written powerful studies that open the possibility that the best of labor history research in the near future will in large part be by, as well as about, 'nonwhite' Americans. Indeed the very recent scholarship by Kelley and Hunter comes closer to making real the new labor history's vision of connecting work, community, daily life, consciousness and resistance than do any other American studies written during the last decade.[28]

Finally, during a period in which every major election has provided reminders that finding a usable past necessitates confronting the issue of white racial identity, scholars have succeeded in raising the questions of when, why and with what results so-called 'white people' have come to identify themselves as white. Making whiteness, rather than simply white racism, the focus of study has had the effect of throwing into sharp relief the impact that the dominant racial identity in the US has had not only on the treatment of racial 'others' but also on the ways that whites think of themselves, of power, of pleasure, and of gender. Labor historians cannot claim to have pioneered in this problematizing of the notion of whiteness. That honor belongs to figures in literary and cultural studies, including bell hooks, Coco Fusco, Toni Morrison and a host of others who sometimes write with rather more postmodernist jargon than we would prefer.[29] But labor historians do have a distinctive and critical contribution to make by historicizing discussions of whiteness and by showing the ways that what Du Bois brilliantly termed the 'public and psychological wage' of white racial identity varied over time, place and class location. Moreover, insofar as the new labor history has consistently stressed the role of workers as creators of their own culture, it is particularly well positioned to understand that white identity is not merely the product of elites or of discourses. If some of the most deeply historical work on whiteness and class continues to emerge from English and political science departments, labor historians can at least point with pride to the fact that one of their number, Alexander Saxton, has written the most sweeping and provocative account yet of the pivotal role of whiteness in American politics and American culture in his remarkable *Rise and Fall of the White Republic*.[30]

It would stretch optimism too far to suppose that the study of race, or even of gender, has already established a claim to be central in any revivifying of labor history. Scholarship on race, class and gender remains in its early stages and deserves the searching criticism it is sure to receive. The theoretical sophistication of the new scholarship, for example, is at this point far from imposing. New approaches face practical problems in writing and conceptualization that are so daunting as to seem at times insurmountable. Discussing the triad of race, class and gender would be difficult enough, but that is just the tip of the iceberg. Writing about a single workplace or working class community might involve analysis of masculine and feminine gender identities formed in concrete material circumstances among workers holding, or developing, or being seen as having, white, African American, and Chinese 'racial' identities. Once we acknowledge that the class identity of, say, an African American woman worker is influenced not only by her own race and gender identities but also by social relationships with, say, Chinese males (and vice versa), we see the practical difficulties associated with treating race, class and gender in what Tera Hunter brilliantly terms their 'simultaneity'.[31] Too often, and here my own work holds out a revealing negative example, authors settle for treating complex identities in manageable dyads, treating white racial identity and class in one work, for example, and leaving class and gender for a later book, or a later section of the book. In addition, when scholarship on white racial identity focuses, as it sometimes must, on the broad political and cultural forces promoting whiteness, it exists in some tension with studies that take day-to-day relations between white and nonwhite workers or the self-activity of African American workers as their points of departure. Though such tension is potentially exciting and productive, we should not be blind to the threat of a worst-case scenario in which research on white racial identity and male gender identity becomes yet another way to arrogate to white men the center stage in an untextured labor history.[32]

But as crying as the need is for serious critiques of race, class and gender approaches, labor history has not been well-served by recent dismissive broadsides, which verge on branding as fraudulent the entire effort to see class consciousness as part of a set of interpenetrating and historically constructed identities. In a recent article in the prestigious *American Quarterly*, for example, Steven Watts characterizes race, class and gender analyses of American history and culture as merely fashionable 'incantations'. Within labor history, Judith Stein's essay on the work of Joe William Trotter and Robin Kelley sets an equally harsh tone. After perceptively noting that Trotter and Kelley pay substantial attention to gender in their studies of race and class, Stein criticizes their emphases on both race and gender as ahistorical exercises driven by 'current political sensibilities'. She charges that by imposing categories and judgements from the present onto the past, Kelley and Trotter lose sight of the relations of class power that shaped the lives and consciousness of both Black and white workers. Stein does not very much bother to claim, as more venerable Marxist formulations might, that class relations at the base shaped race and gender relations in the superstructure. Instead she seems to ignore the considerable extent to which white male workers themselves raised the issues of race and gender in fashioning a class identity and to assume that because it is supposedly derived from direct experience in production, class is a more timeless category.[33]

Stein's questionable judgement in choosing to single out for caricature two of the most closely documented and deeply historicized books yet produced by historians attentive to issues of race, gender and class obviously limits the appeal of her critique. Nor is there much possibility for wide embrace of the chaotic combination of wistful populism with hints of a prolier-than-thou Marxism that runs through the essays of both Watts and Stein when they argue that consideration of gender and race detracts from the study of class and power. Nonetheless, and especially insofar as they speak as part of a wider attack on multicultural scholarship, Watts and Stein do succeed in framing issues in a way which historians committed to the development of scholarship on race, class and gender ignore at their peril. The accusations of fashionability and of present-mindedness must in particular be met head-on if we are to avoid apologizing for our successes in producing work that is 'trendy' in the highly positive sense that it grows out of and engages real trends in the recomposition of the labor force and the labor movement in a way that more nostalgic formulations do not. This need not imply a moralistic lecturing of the dead for their failure to live up to current ideals of egalitarianism. The point of historical studies of racial identities in the working class in such groundbreaking books as Du Bois's *Black Reconstruction* and Saxton's *Indispensable Enemy* has never been to mount a facile indictment of white workers as simply racist. Rather it has been and is now to understand how historicized racial identities dramatically shaped what workers could do and dream in their lifetimes and how better deeds and dreams can be made possible in ours.

Notes

1. Karl Galinsky, in Peter Monaghan, 'Beleaguered Classicists Debate Strategies for Survival', *Chronicle of Higher Education* (6 January 1993): A–10.
2. See Eric Foner, 'Why Is There No Socialism in the US?' *History Workshop Journal*, no. 17 (Spring 1984): 57–80.
3. Philip Taft, 'Labor History and the Labor Movement Today', *Labor History* 7 (Winter 1966): 71. On the decline of the US labor movement in international perspective, see David Brody, 'The Breakdown of the Social Contract', *Dissent* (Winter 1992): 32–41
4. John R. Commons, 'Is Class Struggle in America Growing and Inevitable?' *American Journal of Sociology* 13 (1908): 756–66; Paul J. McNutty, 'Labor Problems and Labor Economics', *Labor History* 9 (Spring 1968): 239–61; Leon Fink, '"Intellectuals" versus "Workers": Academic Requirements and the Creation of Labor History', *American Historical Review* 96 (April 1991): 395–421.
5. Alice and Staughton Lynd, *Rank and File*, Boston 1973.
6. David R. Roediger, 'What Was So Great about Herbert Gutman', *Labor/Le Travail* 23 (Spring 1989), reprinted as the second essay in this section; David Brody, 'The New Labor History', in Eileen Boris and Nelson Lichtenstein, eds, *Major Problems in the History of American Workers*, Lexington, Mass. 1991, 3–9; 'Dave Roediger Interviews George Rawick' in Don Fitz and Roediger, eds, *Within the Shell of the Old*, Chicago 1990; Brody, 'The Old Labor History and the New: In Search of the American Working Class' in Daniel J. Leab, ed., *The Labor History Reader*, Urbana, Ill. 1985, 3; interviews with Gutman and Montgomery in MARHO, ed., *Visions of History*, New York 1983. Alice Kessler-Harris, 'A New Agenda for American Labor History: A Gendered Analysis and the Question of Class', in J. Carroll Moody and Kessler-Harris, eds, *Perspectives on American Labor History: The Problems of Synthesis*, Dekalb, Ill. 1989, 221, similarly sets the crisis of US labor history within the decline of the labor movement. See also Meredith Tax, 'I Had Been Hungry All the Years', in Ellen Carol Du Bois and Vicki L. Ruiz, eds, *Unequal Sisters: A Multicultural Reader in US Women's History*, New York 1990, 169–71; and Eric Arnesen, 'Crusades against Crisis: A View from the United States on the "Rank–and–File" Critique and Other Catalogues of Labor History's Alleged Ills', *International Review of Social History* 35 (1900): 125.
7. For discussion of the prominence of trade unions in the new labor history, see Howard Kimeldorf, 'Bringing Unions Back In (Or Why We Need a New, Old Labor History)' and esp. the responses to Kimeldorf by Michael Kazin, Alice Kessler-Harris, David Montgomery, Bruce Nelson, and Daniel Nelson, all in *Labor History* 32 (Winter 1991): 104–27, with the quote from 99n14.
8. Brody, 'On Creating a New Synthesis of American Labor History', in Moody and Kessler-Harris, eds, *American Labor History*, 205.
9. Brody, 'The Breakdown of the Social Contract', *Dissent* (Winter 1992): 39. In the first instance Brody is quoting, and disagreeing with, management analyst Ben Fischer.
10. Paul Krause, 'The Life and Times of "Beeswax" Taylor: Origins and Paradoxes of the Gilded-Age Labor Movement', *Labor History* 33 (Winter 1992): esp. 54; I. A. Newby, *Plain Folk in the New South: Social Change and Culture Persistence, 1880–1915*, Baton Rouge, La. 1989; Christopher Lasch, *The True and Only Heaven: Progress and Its Critics*, New York 1991, and Steven Rosswurm, 'The Catholic Church and the Left-Led Unions' in Rosswurm, ed., *The CIO's Left-Led Unions*, New Brunswick, N.J. 1992, 119–38, offer a variety of examples.
11. For example, Christopher L. Tomlins, *The State and the Unions: Labor Relations, Law and the Organized Labor Movement in America, 1880–1960*, Cambridge 1985, and Steve Fraser, *Labor Will Rule: Sidney Hillman and the Rise of American Labor*, New York 1991.
12. For a sampling of this rich work, see Rosswurm, ed., *Left-Led Unions*.
13. Among the best recent examples are Vicki Ruiz, *Cannery Women, Cannery Lives: Mexican Women, Unionization and the California Food Processing Industry, 1930–1950*, Albuquerque, N.M. 1987; Ronald L. Filippelli, *American Labor and Postwar Italy, 1947–1953*, Stanford, Calif. 1989; James R. Barrett, 'Americanization from the Bottom Up: Immigration and the Remaking of the Working Class in the United States, 1880–1930', *Journal of American History* 79 (December 1992): 996–1020; Gwendolyn Mink, *Old Labor and New Immigrants in American*

Political Development: Union, Party and State, 1875–1920, Ithaca, N.Y. 1986; Lizabeth Cohen, *Making a New Deal: Industrial Workers in Chicago, 1919–1939*, Cambridge 1990.

14. Michael Goldfield, *The Decline of Organized Labor in the United States*, Chicago 1987; Mike Davis, *Prisoners of the American Dream*, London 1986, 256–300; Bruce Nelson, 'Response to Kimeldorf', *Labor History* 32 (Winter 1991): 119–20; Gregory DeFreitas, 'Unionization among Racial and Ethnic Minorities', *Industrial and Labor Relations Review* 46 (January 1993): 299.

15. The panel 'Remaking the Southern Working Class' at the October 1992 North American Labor History Conference at Wayne State University in Detroit was convened by John Campbell and featured superb papers by Leslie Schwalm, Joseph Reidy and Thavolia Glymph as well as trenchant comments by Daniel Letwin and Elsa Barkley Brown. W. E. B. Du Bois, *Black Reconstruction in America, 1860–1880*, New York 1962 (1935), 727; cf. David Montgomery, 'The Conventional Wisdom', *Labor History* 13 (Winter 1972): 134.

16. See Berlin's introduction to Herbert Gutman, *Power and Culture: Essays on the American Working Class* and the interviews with Montgomery and Gutman in MARHO, *Visions of History* and 'Roediger Interviews Rawick', 9. As David Brody observes, however, Gutman sometimes took positions on the place of slavery and race in working class history that were not fully consistent and altogether clearly drawn. See Brody, 'Synthesis', in Moody and Kessler-Harris, eds, *American Labor History*, 216n9, and Mimi Rosenberg, 'An Unpublished Interview with Herbert Gutman on United States Labor History', *Socialism and Democracy*, no. 10 (Spring-Summer 1990): 58.

17. Saxton, *Indispensable Enemy: Labor and the Anti-Chinese Movement in California*, Berkeley, Calif. 1971; Baron, 'The Demand for Black Labor: Historical Notes on the Political Economy of Racism', in James Green, ed., *Workers' Struggles, Past and Present*, Philadelphia 1983; Paul Worthman, 'Black Labor and Labor Unions in Birmingham, Alabama, 1897–1904' in Milton Cantor, ed., *Black Labor in America*, Westport, Conn. 1969; Green, 'The Brotherhood of Timber Workers, 1910–1913', *Past and Present*, 60 (August 1973): 161–200; Gutman, 'The Negro and the United Mine Workers of America: The Career and Letters of Richard L. Davis and Something of Their Meaning, 1890–1900', in Julius Jacobson, ed., *The Negro and the American Labor Movement*, Garden City, N.Y. 1968, 49–127.

18. Barry H. Goldberg, 'Beyond Free Labor: Labor, Socialism and the Idea of Wage Slavery, 1890–1920' (Ph.D. dissertation, Columbia University, 1979); Mary Ellen Freifeld, 'The Emergence of the American Working Classes: The Roots of Division, 1865–1885' (Ph.D. dissertation, New York University, 1980); Eric Foner, *Free Soil, Free Labor, Free Men: The Ideology of the Republican Party before the Civil War*, New York 1970; Foner, *Reconstruction: America's Unfinished Revolution, 1863–1877*, New York 1988; Montgomery, *Beyond Equality: Labor and the Radical Republicans, 1862–1872*, New York 1967; Sean Wilentz, 'The Rise of the American Working Class, 1776–1877: A Survey' in Moody and Kessler–Harris, eds, *American Labor History*, 83–151.

19. See, for example, Hill, 'Mythmaking as Labor History: Herbert Gutman and the United Mine Workers of America', *International Journal of Politics, Culture and Society* 2 (Winter 1988): 132–98. My own fuller reflections on race and the new labor history are found in '"Labor in White Skin": Race and Working Class History' in Mike Davis and Michael Sprinker, eds, *Reshaping the US Left* London 1988, 287–308, and reprinted in this volume.

20. See Philip S. Foner, *Organized Labor and the Black Worker, 1819–1973*, New York 1974; Bettina Aptheker, ed., *The Unfolding Drama: Studies in United States History by Herbert Aptheker*, New York 1979; Melvyn Dubofsky, 'Give Us That Old Time Labor History: Philip S. Foner and the American Worker', *Labor History* 26 (1985): 118–37.

21. See Brody, 'Synthesis', in Moody and Kessler–Harris, eds, *American Labor History*, 216n9 and my 'Precapitalism in One Confederacy: Genovese and the Politics of History', Chapter 3 in this volume. Note, however, that Genovese's practice in comparing labor under slavery and under the wage system has been more supple than his theory. See esp. *Roll, Jordan, Roll: The World the Slaves Made*, New York 1976, esp. 285–324.

22. Rosenberg, 'Unpublished Interview', 58.

23. Morrison, '"Unspeakable Things Unspoken": The Afro–American Presence in American Literature', *Michigan Quarterly Review* 28 (Winter 1989), esp. 2–3 and 38.

24. A quite incomplete list of major recent works would feature Christine Stansell, *City*

of Women: Sex and Class in New York, 1789–1860, New York 1986; Susan Porter Benson, *Counter Cultures: Salewomen, Managers and Customers in American Department Stores, 1890–1910*, Urbana, Ill. 1986; Barbara Melosh, *The Physician's Hand: Work Culture and Conflict in American Nursing*, Philadelphia 1982; Mary Blewett, *Men, Women and Work: Class, Gender and Protest in the New England Shoe Industry, 1780–1910*, Urbana, Ill. 1988; Alice Kessler-Harris, *A Woman's Wage: Historical Meanings and Social Consequences*, Lexington, Ky. 1990; Ava Baron, ed., *Work Engendered: Toward a New History of Men, Women and Work*, Ithaca, N.Y. 1991; Jacqueline Dowd Hall, 'Disorderly Women: Gender and Labor Militancy in the Appalachian South' in Du Bois and Ruiz, eds, *Unequal Sisters*, 298–321; Kathy Peiss, *Cheap Amusements: Working Women and Leisure in Turn-of-the-Century New York*, Philadelphia 1986. See also Lois Helmbold and Ann Schofield, 'Women's Labor History, 1790–1945', *Reviews in American Labor History* 17 (December 1989), and notes 25 and 26 below.

25. Glenn, 'The Dialectics of Wage Work: Japanese-American Women and Domestic Service, 1905–1940' in DuBois and Ruiz, eds, *Unequal Sisters*, 345–72; Joanne J. Meyerowitz, *Women Adrift: Independent Wage Earners in Chicago, 1880–1930*, Chicago 1988; Dana Frank, 'Race, Class and the Politics of Consumption: Race Relations and the Seattle Labor Movement, 1915–1929' (unpublished paper delivered at Organization of American Historians meeting, 1991); essays by Hewitt and Janiewski in Baron, ed., *Work Engendered*; Janiewski, *Sisterhood Denied: Race, Gender, and Class in a New South Community*, Philadelphia 1985; Ruiz, *Cannery Lives*; Patricia A. Cooper, *Once a Cigarmaker: Men, Women, and Work Culture in American Cigar Factories, 1900–1919*, Urbana, Ill. 1987. I particularly thank Tèra Hunter for sharing with me a manuscript version of her powerful *Contesting the New South: The Politics and Culture of Wage Household Labor in Atlanta, 1861–1920*.

26. Joy Parr, *The Gender of Breadwinners: Women, Men and Change in Two Industrial Towns, 1888–1950*, Toronto 1990; Faue, *Community of Suffering and Struggle: Women, Men, and the Labor Movement in Minneapolis, 1915–1945*, Chapel Hill, N.C. 1991; Boydston, *Home and Work: Housework, Wages, and the Ideology of Labor in the Early Republic*, New York 1990.

27. Again, the list is quite incomplete, but see Rick Halpern, 'Race, Ethnicity and the Union in the Chicago Stockyards, 1917–1922', *International Review of Social History* 37 (1992): 25–58; Iver Bernstein, *The New York City Draft Riots: Their Significance for American Society and Politics in the Age of the Civil War*, New York 1990; Griffith, *The Crisis of American Labor: Operation Dixie and the Defeat of the CIO*, Philadelphia 1988; Eric Arnesen, *Waterfront Workers of New Orleans, Race, Class and Politics*, New York 1990; Arnesen, 'Rethinking the Historical Relationship between Black Workers and the Labor Movement', forthcoming in *Radical History Review* (1993); Wayne Durrill, *War of Another Kind: A Southern Community in the Great Rebellion*, New York 1990; Nancy Quam Wickham, 'Who Controls the Hiring Hall? The Struggle for Job Control in the ILWU during World War II'; and Bruce Nelson, 'Class and Race in the Crescent City: The ILWU from San Francisco to New Orleans', both in Rosswurm, ed., *Left-Led Unions*, 19–68; the essays in Robert Zieger, ed., *Organized Labor in the Twentieth Century South*, Knoxville, Tenn. 1991; Leon Fink and Brian Greenberg, *Upheaval in the Quiet Zone: A History of Hospital Workers' Union Local 1199*, Urbana, Ill. 1989; and, above all, Peter Rachleff, *Black Labor in the South: Richmond, Virginia, 1865–1890*, Philadelphia 1984.

28. Takaki, *Paui Hana: Plantation Life and Labor in Hawaii, 1835–1920*, Honolulu, Ha. 1983; Lewis, *In Their Own Interest: Race, Class and Power in Twentieth-Century Norfolk, Virginia*, Berkeley, Calif. 1991; Trotter, *Black Milwaukee: The Making of an Industrial Proletariat, 1914–45*, Urbana, Ill. 1984, and *Coal, Class and Color: Blacks in Southern West Virginia, 1915–32*, Urbana, Ill. 1990; Ruiz, *Cannery Lives*; Kelley, '"We Are Not What We Seem": Towards a Black Working-Class Infrapolitics in the Twentieth-Century South', forthcoming in *Journal of American History*; Hunter, *Contesting the New South*. Both Kelley and Hunter are particularly adept at drawing on the literature on slave resistance to inform studies of resistance by later Black wage workers. See also Kelley, *Hammer and Hoe: Alabama Communists during the Great Depression*, Chapel Hill, N.C. 1990, 101. Mario T. Garcia's fine 'Border Proletarians: Mexican-Americans and the International Union of Mine, Mill and Smelter Workers, 1939–1946', in Robert Asher and Charles Stephenson, eds, *Labor Divided: Race and Ethnicity in United States Labor Struggles*, Albany, N.Y. 1990, 83–104; and, on slavery, Norrece T. Jones, Jr, *Born a Child of Freedom Yet a Slave: Mechanisms of Control and Strategies of Resistance in Antebellum South Carolina*, Hanover, N.H. 1990.

29. Morrison, 'Afro-American Presence' and *Playing in the Dark: Whiteness and the Literary Imagination*, Cambridge, Mass. 1992; bell hooks, 'Representations of Whiteness', in *Black Looks: Race and Representation*, London 1992, 165–78, with material from Fusco.

30. Du Bois, *Black Reconstruction*, 700–701; Saxton, *The Rise and Fall of the White Republic: Class Politics and Mass Culture in Nineteenth-Century America*, London 1990; See also Eric Lott, '"The Seeming Counterfeit": Racial Politics and Early Blackface Minstrelsy', *American Quarterly* 43 (June 1991): 223–54; Lott, *Blackface Minstrelsy and the American Working Class*, forthcoming; Michael Rogin, 'Blackface, White Noise: The Jewish Jazz Singer Finds His Voice', *Critical Inquiry* 18 (Spring 1992); Vron Ware, *Beyond the Pale: White Women, Racism and History*, New York 1992; Ruth Frankenberg, *White Women, Race Matters: The Social Construction of Whiteness*, Minneapolis, Minn. 1993.

31. Hunter, in her forthcoming *Contesting the New South*, urges the examination of 'gender, race, and class in their simulaneity, in the way that human beings actually experience these social relations.'

32. See, for example, the reviews of *Wages of Whiteness* by Iver Bernstein in *Journal of American History* 79 (December 1992): 1120–21; by Joe William Trotter in *Journal of Social History* 25 (1992): 674–6; and by Lawrence B. Glickman in *Nation*, 17 February 1992, 207–9.

33. Steven Watts, 'The Idiocy of American Studies: Poststructuralism, Language and Politics in the Age of Self-Fulfillment', *American Quarterly* 43 (December 1991): 653; Stein, 'Race and Class Consciousness Revisited', *Reviews in American History* 19 (December 1991): esp. 556–9.

PART II

Studies in Whiteness and the Replotting of US History

'All [Negroes] were friends of ours [and] those of our own age were in fact comrades. We were comrades and yet not comrades; color and condition interposed a subtle line which both parties were conscious of and which rendered complete fusion impossible.'

Mark Twain, on his youth in Missouri

'Sexual politics, like class ... struggle, will thus necessarily be caught up in the very metaphysical categories it hopes finally to abolish; and any such movement will demand a difficult, perhaps ultimately impossible, double optic, at once fighting on a terrain already mapped out by its antagonists and seeking even now to prefigure within that mundane strategy styles and being and identity for which we have as yet no proper name.'

Terry Eagleton
Nationalism, Irony and Commitment (1988)

7

'The So-Called Mob': Race, Class, Skill and Community in the St Louis General Strike

In July 1877 the US economy suffered from continuing depression and trade union fortunes from continuing decline. Nonetheless, during that month a remarkable nationwide railroad strike sparked an even more re- markable chain of events in the large industrial city of St Louis.[1] The railroad walkout stopped traffic in the rail center of East St Louis by Sunday, 22 July. The following day saw demonstrations of solidarity in- itiated by leaders of the socialist Workingmen's Party of the United States of America (WPUSA) coincide with sporadic strikes to restore wage cuts by several St Louis trades outside the railroad industry. Such strikes spread on Tuesday, especially among coopers, iron molders, wire workers and rivermen. At a Tuesday night mass meeting of about 10,000, the WPUSA, an organization of scarcely a thousand members in St Louis, proposed that the strikes become general, with an end to child labor and the institution of the eight-hour working day as their political demands. On Wednesday, Thursday and Friday, a stormy series of tramping processions, initially WPUSA-directed but featuring many spontaneous offshoots by integrated crowds, enforced the general strike order. A general strike under different, but also WPUSA-influenced, leadership developed as well in the heavily industrial enclave of Caron- delet, which had recently been annexed to the city.

Not only was the general strike the first in an industrial city in the United States, but the Executive Committee which led it attempted to set up a workers' assembly of WPUSA leaders and delegates from organized trades, one of the world's first workers' councils. The Executive Commit- tee pressed demands for shorter hours and abolition of child labor and added (or let speakers using its platforms add) calls for banking and cur- rency reforms, provision of food to those on strike, nonintervention by federal troops, public works and nationalization of railroads. While demanding much, the Executive Committee also displayed a desire to negotiate and to achieve some results. Indeed, the first WPUSA speech suggesting expanding the railroad strike stressed, 'This strike will extend to all kinds of business, and in the end capitalists and the government must grant at least a portion of the rights demanded.'[2]

With the economic activity of the city of 350,000 at a standstill – even bars and brothels closing – the Executive Committee conferred with industrialists and with the mayor and took to itself some of the functions of government. Provision of guards for factories, of permission for mail and passenger trains to move and of emergency plans for continued medical services fell to the strike leaders, who even asked St Louis Mayor Henry Overstolz to recognize their efforts to keep order by deputizing strikers. In East St Louis and apparently in the Carondelet section of St Louis, such recognition of the strikers' police powers did occur.

But even as the St Louis mayor thrice met with delegations from the Executive Committee, he coordinated the organization of an armed anti-strike Committee of Public Safety which he and many of the city's elite had convened. The English- and German-language press solidly arrayed itself against the strike. Federal troops and guns massed in St Louis, and additional arms and men came from the state government for suppression of the strike. On Thursday, 26 July, Missouri's governor, John Phelps, came to the city to join his efforts with those of Overstolz and the Committee of Public Safety. A handful of workplaces reopened.

The Executive Committee, so bold in its early proclamations, became increasingly timid in its tactics by midweek, cancelling all authorizations for mass meetings and parades after Wednesday. But this circumspection failed to convince the mayor and the Committee of Public Safety that the Executive Committee was a voice of restraint. On Friday, when its forces were sufficiently large and well-armed, the Committee of Public Safety, invested with powers as a *posse comitatus* and under orders to shoot to kill resisters, raided Executive Committee headquarters and ended the strike with wholesale arrests that eventually totalled 150 or more. The strike leaders offered no resistance. The crowds, after two days of almost no communication from the Executive Committee, mounted only token opposition. Continuing strike action in Carondelet and East St Louis came to a quick end with the intervention of federal troops.

The labor upheaval in St Louis has received attention as an early general strike and as a proto-'soviet'.[3] It is the subject of two excellent books giving narrative accounts and a large body of other historical literature.[4] But if the novelty and the drama, and even the irony and anomalies, of the 1877 general strike have been successfully captured by historians, the analysis of why the strike unfolded as it did and of how it fit into the larger pattern of post-Reconstruction labor and urban history has hardly begun. The formation of a huge private army to confront the strikers requires explanation, as does the scenario of a socialist leadership using a situation of shared power to bargain with the mayor and ultimately defusing a mass movement. Both these developments take on special significance in the context of a growing consensus among historians that, at least in small and medium-sized cities, working-class leaders often felt themselves to be important parts of communities, held exalted ideas of republican citizenship, and were able to achieve a measure of local power during the Gilded Age.[5]

Both the behavior of the St Louis Executive Committee and of the Committee of Public Safety best make sense in the light of a social analysis of who was leading the strike, who was participating in the processions spreading it, and who acted to oppose it. But accounts from the press, participants, and Gilded Age historians of the general strike amount almost to a cautionary tale against the use of such evidence to determine the social composition of groups in conflict. So contradictory are the accounts and so unrestrained the rhetoric that few conclusions can be drawn about who fought whom. The Committee of Public Safety, for example, usually drew descriptions as representing 'order', the 'people', 'citizens', the 'city', and 'our best young men' rather than any class or interest. However, other accounts found merchants and clerks to be the social base of the Committee.[6]

The strikers and demonstrators attracted more varied and passionate assessments. Describing this group as '*canaille*', 'the mob', or 'rabble', the St Louis press was of several minds concerning the composition of its leadership and its ranks. Early in the week, the *Dispatch* distinguished between 'real railroad strikers' and 'tramps and loafers' anxious to 'pillage and plunder'. By Tuesday the paper found the strike movement dominated by 'hordes of idle loafers and tramps'. Its editorials nonetheless included continued attempts to reason with 'the workingmen'. According to the *Missouri Republican*, the radical labor movement drew support from a 'few unprincipled demagogues, more rattlebrained visionaries, and a lot of honest but deceived workingmen'.[7] The *Globe-Democrat* christened the strike leadership the 'Executive Committee of United Tramps', while the *Republican* saw them as representative of 'no one but themselves and a crowd of bummers'. But both the papers also spoke of 'turbulent workingmen' as the backbone of the movement, even alluding to the 'better class of workingmen' bulking large in crowds. The *Globe-Democrat* found unnamed persons secure 'in the enjoyment of comfortable income' helping to lead the strike in which the 'toiling masses ... allowed themselves to get mixed up with the spoiling masses.' The German-language press similarly vacillated between seeing 'arbeiter' and 'bummler' as chief strike participants, with the liberal German Catholic daily *Amerika* blaming 'homeless and stateless journeymen'.[8]

Missouri Republican reporter J. A. Dacus's 1877 study of the strikes nationwide, the best such contemporary account, fell prey to the same inconsistencies. Dacus denied that there was any 'such thing as a united and enthusiastic labor strike in St Louis'. He described those in the streets as a 'disreputable rabble, in the ranks of which very few members of the operative and industrial classes were to be found.' Those dominant he added, were 'pariahs, the men who never perform useful labor'. But at other junctures Dacus allowed for participation by the 'large mass of ... unemployed poor, dispirited, hopeless, ready to seize upon any occasion to improve their really deplorable condition' and characterized crowds as composed of 'mechanics and molders'. Support came from 'tradesmen and artisans, with here and there a man of thought and culture, who believed with earnestness of martyr-confessors that labor ... did not receive its just rewards.'[9]

Other impressionistic accounts are just as inconsistent. Committee of Public Safety leader Albert Warren Kelsey, in memoirs written over three decades after the general strike, recalled a 'howling band of Anarchists', although there is no other evidence of any anarchist role in the strike. Early St Louis historian J. T. Scharf found 'the mass of the disaffected ... were tramps and irresponsible persons, idlers, and curiosity seekers'. But the somewhat later history by Russell Nolen, based on *Missouri Republican* articles, portrays a labor strike rooted mainly among railroaders. The Signal Service reports to Washington, D.C. during the upheaval most often simply refer to the crowds as being made up of 'strikers'.[10]

Along with a common tendency in contemporary accounts to blame outsiders, tramps, or 'unwanted strangers',[11] went a marked emphasis on African American participation in strike processions. The *Missouri Republican* analyzed such crowds as mostly Black, writing of 'squads of squalid negroes' and of 'whooping ... dangerous-looking' aggregations of 'brutal negroes'. The *Globe-Democrat* found a more equal division among Black and white demonstrators, while complaining of 'maniacal yelling' by the former. Dacus repeatedly referred to crowds composed 'largely of negroes' in some cases joined by a few 'sorry specimens of the Caucasian race'. Out-of-town newspapers allude to important, but minority, Black participation in strike processions.[12]

Of course the range of descriptions reflected in part the real variety of the crowds and the changes in their composition from day to day. However, the contradictions in the evidence, the offhandedness of the observations, and the tenor of vehemence suggest that most of the documents describing the strike bespeak at least as much a desire to end it as to analyze its roots. In such a situation statistical evidence regarding those arrested and those identified as the leaders of the strike and of the Committee of Public Safety assumes special importance.

This article attempts a social analysis of the strike based on evidence from documentary sources, from city directories and from the 1880 manuscript census. It seeks to describe the occupational, racial and ethnic composition of strike and Committee of Public Safety leaders and of rank-and-filers arrested or identified as participants in strike crowds. It also considers the age and rootedness in the community of members of these groups. It argues that the last of these factors played a vital role in uniting the strike and Committee of Public Safety leaders in a common perception that the rank-and-file demonstrators constituted a grave threat to social order despite the absence of violence. Such fear, accentuated by an intense civic boosterism rooted in a contest among St Louis, Chicago and other developing cities for trade and industry,[13] contributed to the willingness and ability of the Committee of Public Safety to act decisively against the general strike and to the failure of the Executive Committee to act much at all after spectacularly setting the strike into motion.

Albert Warren Kelsey's memoirs, however inaccurate in narrative details and bias against the strike, constitute a useful point of departure as the only primary account to attempt a relatively full record of the Committee of Public Safety and its composition. Although nearly as anxious as the St Louis press to identify the Committee with the whole city, Kelsey observed that all groups did not participate equally. 'I saw among the prominent citizens present', Kelsey wrote in describing the first Committee meeting he attended, 'the Catholic Bishop Ryan ... , the principal Bank Presidents, the Police Commissioners, Editors of Journals, etc., etc., just a representative assemblage of the various classes, including the merchant princes and moneyed men of the city.' Rank-and-file citizens' militiamen, he recalled, 'were respectable members of the body politic, who had responded to a call from their employers to ... enroll themselves as being willing to assist ... in the preservation of law and order – mostly clerks and bookkeepers.'[14]

If we discount the reference to a 'representative assemblage of the various classes', Kelsey's summary comports well with the evidence on the 107 ward leaders of the Committee of Public Safety and the 176 members listed in three surviving 'police militia' rosters, one from the week of the general strike and the others from fourteen and twenty-three months later (see Tables 1 and 3). The miniscule proportion of skilled workers and laborers, which together comprise only 1.30 percent of Committee leadership and 5.52 percent of the membership, disqualifies the citizens' militia from representativeness and makes its class nature contrast with other, more broadly based, late-nineteenth-century militia units that historians have studied.[15] But outside of the wage-working class, the Committee did draw on a spectrum of social groups. Its leadership included merchants (23.38 percent), financiers (5.19 percent), manufacturers and builders (23.38 percent), professional men (23.38 percent), government officials (5.19 percent in addition to a pair of former governors), small business-men (10.39 percent, particularly grocers and saloonkeepers), and railway managers (6.49 percent). Among members, clerks and bookkeepers pre-dominated, with those two groups plus salesmen and collectors account-ing for 51.18 percent. Eleven lawyers joined nine other professionals in comprising 15.75 percent of the membership. Manufacturers (9.45 per-cent) and merchants (7.87 percent) filled the ranks in about equal num-bers, with railway officials adding 3.94 percent. Small proprietors (2.36 percent) were underrepresented in the membership, perhaps because the exigencies of drill one or more nights per week conflicted with late-clos-ing schedules.[16]

Kelsey's stress on the rootedness of the Committee in St Louis's 'body politic' was also accurate. Of the leadership, a higher percentage (94.62 percent) of those cases not compromised by too common names or insuf-ficient data can be identified through the 1877 city directory than can be for either strike leaders (79.17 percent) or strike rank-and-filers (60.00 percent and 25.00 percent in two samples). The geographical persistence of Committee leaders in St Louis from 1875 to 1877 (83.25 percent) and from 1877 to 1879 (76.92 percent) far outdistanced that for other groups, as did the proportion of Committee leaders identifiable in the 1880 manuscript census. Committee leaders, at an average of 46.89 years, were also older than members of any of the other samples.[17]

The Committee of Public Safety succeeded in uniting members of the non-wage working class of the community across ethnic lines, as Table 2 illustrates). Although almost half (47.83 percent) of the recoverable cases among its leadership were born in the United States, significant numbers of German natives (32.61 percent) and Irish immigrants (10.87 percent) were present. The former group was overrepresented in proportion to its place in the general population of the city by a factor of 2.08 and the latter by a factor of 1.33[18]

German participation is particularly striking because relatively few Germans were among the city's executives, supervisors, managers, mer-chants, professionals or proprietors – the groups from which the leader-ship of the Committee of Public Safety overwhelmingly came. In part the extent of German leadership mirrored a similar overrepresentation of Germans among the strike's leaders and among its rank-and-file. The strike was very much, though far from exclusively, a German problem, and the elite sections of the German community responded to it force-fully.[19] In addition, the leading members of the German population had had ample opportunity to ponder how they would choose to define their commitments to 'free labor' and republicanism, some of them since the 1848 European revolutions. Through the American Civil War and the labor insurgency that followed, through Radical Reconstruction and a turn to Liberal Republicanism, German political and opinion leaders in St Louis had developed a sophisticated ideology drawing on republican ideals but admitting, after the Civil War, no significant social divisions in the US.[20] The *Westliche Post*, for example, briefly supported the eight-hour working day at the end of the Civil War before aligning itself against labor candidates. Its part-owner, Carl Schurz, the most prominent German American politician in America and the Secretary of the Interior during the 1877 strikes, played a critical role from his St Louis base in the de-emphasis on civil rights in Republican Party politics during Reconstruction and was author of the epigram 'There are many social questions in America but there is no social question.' The German press was as vociferous in its opposition to the general strike as its English-language counterpart. Perhaps its most influential editor, Karl Daenzer of the *Anzeiger des Westens*, was a convener of the Committee of Public Safety.[21]

The partly German St Louis Hegelians, one of the leading schools of philosophical thought in the US in the late nineteenth century, developed the German American elite's outlook into a potent public philosophy which stressed the centrality of private property in civilization, the critical role of the working capitalist in transcending the contradiction between workers and owners, the inviolability of the power and unity of the American state, and the mission of education in keeping 'property safe from confiscation by a majority composed of communists'. Counting in the ranks of their leading thinkers Missouri's lieutenant-governor during the general strike and St Louis's top educational officials, the St Louis Hegelians both gave voice to and molded a German American conservatism that steered far away from reaction, a philosophy that identified the American tradition as anti-aristocratic, meritocratic and bourgeois. In Henry Brokmeyer, the lieutenant-governor, they also furnished a major leader of the suppression of the general strike.[22]

In addition to sustaining an ethnic unity, the Committee of Public Safety, led by an former Civil War general from each side, brought together ex-rebels and ex-Yankees in the St Louis elite. The city, antebellum home to the nation's first Chamber of Commerce, had experienced a major sectional rift among its upper classes, culminating during Reconstruction in the formation of a separate Union Merchants' Exchange for pro-Northern businessmen. A single Merchants' Exchange was reestablished only shortly before the 1877 strike, but no sectional animosities appear to have surfaced inside the Committee of Public Safety. Ten identifiable Southern-born Americans (21.7 percent of the sample) joined eight Northern-born Americans (17.39 percent) and four from Missouri

(8.70 percent) among Committee leaders.[23]

The unity and zeal displayed by those composing the Committee of Public Safety deserve consideration. Especially striking was the participation of merchants and small proprietors. Historians have recently noticed, and possible overemphasized, the fact that Gilded Age businessmen, especially in smaller cities, often sided with labor in wage disputes. One study has applied this perception of a split between vendors and manufacturers specifically to the 1877 general strike in St Louis. Several contemporary accounts refer to business support for the 1877 railroad strikes nationally, with one even suggesting business leadership of crowd violence and the transfer of looted goods to the inventories of those involved.[24] But despite some small business participation in the leadership of the strike and attempts by the Executive Committee of the strikers to broaden such support (as discussed below), the data on the Committee of Public Safety indicate that merchants and their white-collar employees acted decisively against the general strike in St Louis. Consistent participation by both industrial and commercial capitalists, illustrated by the statistical evidence and press accounts of who funded the volunteer troops, suggests that analyses positing a merchant sector relatively sympathetic to labor's demands may apply poorly in a large mercantile-manufacturing center like St Louis. Indeed a 'merchants' militia', at first separate from the Committee of Public Safety, itself armed as many as a thousand men.[25]

If there was a split between the mercantile sectors of the economy and those of the manufacturers and railroad executives, it lay in the realm of tactics. Railway officials, especially Thomas A. Scott, president of the Pennsylvania Railroad and the nation's most politically powerful entrepreneur, vigorously argued for action by the federal army against the railroad strike.[26] From St Louis, James Harrison Wilson, a former Union military officer and federal receiver of the failed St Louis and Southwestern Railroad, joined former Governor Thomas Fletcher, a pro-railroad political leader, and Charles Belcher, head of a large sugar refinery, in calls, often directed to Schurz, for increased federal intervention and declarations of martial law.[27] Although such pressure resulted in the administration of Rutherford B. Hayes preparing, but never issuing, a proclamation to 'put these rioters in the position of levying war against the US',[28] it found little echo among St Louis businessmen, who regarded the strike as a state and local matter. The Committee of Public Safety confined its substantive requests of Washington to the 'loan' of 12,000 arms for use by local citizens.[29]

Even in the realm of tactics, the differences between Wilson and his associates on one hand and the Mayor and Committee of Public Safety on the other can easily receive too much emphasis. First, there was little legal justification for a broad call for federal troops. Lacking, particularly in St

Louis, was any firm evidence of insurrection; thus, only the strikes on the mail-carrying railroads, the rail lines in federal receivership and an odd industry like Belcher's (whose warehouses were government-bonded) could support the argument for intervention.[30]

More important, the scenario of massive federal intervention was not a live policy option from the standpoint of manpower. The 25,000-man national army, already spread thin in Indian wars in the Dakotas (a year after Custer's defeat), the Southwest and the Northwest and in Mexican border troubles, could not attack strikers at all points. The 42 officers and 410 regular troops who were assigned to St Louis – and who played an important part in escorting in guns, storming the railroad strike strongholds in East St Louis and Carondelet and exerting 'moral' power against the general strike – represented nearly one American soldier in fifty. Their assignment left their commander fretting about the undermanned defense of Kansas City against strikers there. Secretary of the Interior Schurz meanwhile complained of the lack of troops for prosecution of Indian wars.[31] The National Guard had by 1877 reached what one of its leading historians has called its 'nadir' nationally. Its few units, ill-trained and poorly equipped, showed a propensity, both inside the St Louis area and elsewhere, to refuse service and to fraternize with strikers. In Missouri the disintegration of the militia was serious. The late Reconstruction efforts to reform, and especially to fund, the militia had come to little. The handful of extant units played a negligible role in policing the general strike.[32]

Finally, the disputed 1876 presidential election, which had brought Hayes, a loser in the popular vote and the barest winner in the electoral vote, into office, narrowed options. Hayes's election resulted from a bargain to gain Southern Democratic support regarding contested electoral votes by removing federal troops protecting Black civil rights in that region. Neither he nor Democratic governors then had much reason to advocate a vigorous role for the federal army during the strike. The Democratic governors who did call for troops won derision in the socialist and, to an extent, in the Republican, press. Missouri's Governor John Phelps, a Democrat, did not request troops.[33] The Hayes administration more or less scrupulously directed the regular army to act only in defense of federal property or on orders from state officials.[34] All reports from federal officers in the St Louis area accept the authority of the Committee of Public Safety and uphold its authority, largely on pragmatic grounds, to lead the suppression of the strike. So, for that matter, might have Wilson, who punctuated his appeals to Schurz for federal action by serving as a leader of the Committee.[35]

However, the wide participation in and acceptance of the Committee of Public Safety by the city's elite should not obscure what an unorthodox formation it was. That the leaders of a major metropolis could call for the mustering of a 10,000-man army, armed by loans of munitions from other levels of government and by private subscriptions, is in retrospect amazing. At the time it was likewise regarded as a last-ditch experiment. According to Kelsey's memoirs, even the legal device of forming a *posse comitatus* to legitimate Committee of Public Safety actions was not at first considered. 'As all authority from the state or city officials … had already been exerted without effect', he wrote, 'we were compelled to assume extra-legal powers, in the hope that any action taken would later be approved by the legislature.'[36]

It is not possible to account for so bold a move by a municipal elite known for its conservatism on the grounds of opposition to strike violence.[37] The Committee of Public Safety formed on Tuesday, 25 July, the day before the first full day of the general strike and before any acts of vandalism or physical intimidation had occurred. As the week progressed an inflamed press could point only to a single police casualty, a fire allegedly of suspicious origin, minor looting of bread and soap, a pair of alleged assaults on strikebreakers, and the reportedly menacing stance of the tramping strikers. In its more sober moments, the local press allowed that good order generally prevailed. WPUSA speeches transcribed in the St Louis papers and proclamations of the Executive Committee followed the national WPUSA policy of consistently warning strikers against initiating violence. In the wake of the general strike, Mayor Overstolz could boast of its suppression without 'the destruction of a dollar's worth of property'.[38]

In part, racism and published rumors accentuated fears of disorder out of proportion to its occurrence. The press regarded any participation by African Americans in a labor disturbance as unexpected and threatening, with even the Republican *Globe-Democrat* advising summary execution of Blacks involved in disorderly strike processions. Strikers, according to the newspapers, possessed several thousand arms.[39] That 'Internationalists' led the upheaval provoked the most sensational reportage. 'They are the sworn foes of every establishment in society', wrote the *Missouri Republican*, which continued, '… they demand the abolition of public worship, the seizure and transformation of churches into halls and hospitals, the abrogation of the relation of marriage, and the substitution of promiscuous freedom between the sexes, … the repeal of all property laws and a redistribution of wealth equally among all members of society.'[40]

But rumor, racism, anti-Communism and rhetorical excess overlay a more fundamental opposition to the strike as a strike. Hard by the *Republican*'s reports on the terrors of the 'Internationals' was another article in the same edition insisting that 'none of the wild ravings of the communists in St Louis have surpassed the inflammatory addresses /of/ the railroad strike in East St Louis.'[41] The *Dispatch* complained [of] 'mechanics and workingmen' who 'increase the prevailing disorder, ... damage business, and endanger the peace of the city, and incite rioting, by getting up strikes for higher wages.' Another account described strike processions, however lacking in violence, as 'rioting', a position which resonates well with Mayor Overstolz's back-to-work proclamation of 26 July, a document forbidding 'interference, by intimidation or otherwise, with the employees of any mill, factory, business or business establishment or railway.'[42]

Such broad opposition to the general strike among the leading citizens – and their willingness to undertake the ambitious, unorthodox step of forming the Committee of Public Safety – rested on the elite class status and rootedness of the participants and took shape around the protection of property and the defense of the city and its image. The nearly total stoppage of retail and wholesale trade gave merchants and small proprietors a material stake in seeing that the strike was settled even if the terms of settlement did not much involve their interests. Governor Phelps' 26 July order to end the strike appealed strongly to such business concerns over ending the suspension of trade.[43] Moreover, the city was not rigidly segregated by class with the result that homes of the well-to-do were sometimes near centers of strike activity.[44] This was particularly true of the Lucas Market environs, the site of the largest nightly strike meetings and an area of longstanding concern to wealthy residents nearby. The name of the Committee of Public Safety was sometimes rendered as the 'Citizens' Organization for the Protection of Property'.[45]

The members of the Committee of Public Safety also acted out of a concern for St Louis, as they defined it. On the one hand there was a concrete dimension to this concern. For many years, the city had operated amidst a fiscal crisis. The business community had long feared municipal bankruptcy, a fact which had given impetus to a reform/home rule campaign which reached fruition in 1875 and 1876 and to the reelection of Overstolz in 1877 as a fiscal reformer. According to the prevailing interpretation of Missouri law, the perpetrators of damage to 'person or property' in an 'unlawful assemblage' were liable for damages but (and this feature of the law suggests how anxious developing areas were to provide a climate favorable for capital investment) the city in which the disturbance occurred was also responsible for repayment of damages up to 75 percent of the total amount. From its inception, Committee of Public Safety efforts found justification in terms of forestalling the city's financial collapse.[46]

Also at stake was St Louis's reputation – a commodity that, in the context of boosterist rivalry with Chicago and other developing cities, was as precious as its bank account. From the start, the city's press perceived the nationwide strikes of 1877 as an opportunity to show the superiority of St Louis. The St Louis *Daily Market Reporter* found early in the conflict that in its home city, in contrast to others, 'the wild mob spirit is unknown'. The *Globe-Democrat* understood the troubles in Baltimore and Pittsburgh, those 'exceptionally disorderly cities', but thought St Louis to be 're-moved from the danger of such outbreaks by the diffusion of prosperity and the consequent interests of all classes of citizens in the preservation of peace.'[47] When sharp labor conflict did develop, the press could only stress the presence of 'a sufficient number of brave and law-abiding citizens to take care of their families and themselves'.[48] The Committee of Public Safety became a symbol of municipal order and a repository of civic virtue in newspaper accounts. These were roles to which the Committee was not loath to assume. But carrying them out, and salvaging the city's honor, depended on an end to *any* disorder or disruption of business. When such a successful suppression of the general strike had been achieved, the *Missouri Republican* headlined 'SAINT LOUIS REDEEMS HER CREDIT AS A CITY', possibly with puns intended. A huge and festive military parade reaffirmed St Louis's reputation for good order. An odd kind of civic pride even developed around the idea that St Louis had generated, and defused, America's only 'genuine Commune'.[49]

The leaders of St Louis's general strike, many of them in jail, did not participate in the celebrations in which the Committee of Public Safety paraded its victory. But as surely as the social facts typifying the Committee of Public Safety shaped its behavior, so too did those characterizing the identifiable strike leaders contribute to their extraordinary actions in boldly initiating and then largely abandoning a general strike. In its root-edness and its social composition, the strike leadership differed as much from those identifiable as rank-and-file tramping strikers as it did from Committee of Public Safety leaders. A year after the general strike, Peter Lofgreen, one of its leaders, argued that socialists faced a dual task: 'They not only have the ruling classes to overcome but also the so-called mob to control.'[50] In accounting for the seemingly contradictory behavior of strike leaders, the social and demographic differences between leaders and rank-and-filers that underlay a statement like Lofgreen's deserve emphasis, as do racism and tactical considerations.

The occupations of the strike leaders, summarized in Table 4, contrast sharply with the press accounts stressing the presence of vagrants and manipulative wealthy persons at the head of the upheaval. More than two in five (40.43 percent) of the 47 identifiable leaders were skilled workers. Professionals, white-collar workers, and small proprietors accounted for 27.66 percent of the leadership, equaling the proportion of unskilled workers. While far more working class than the Committee of Public Safety, this sample also sharply differed from the two available samples of rank-and-file tramping strikers occupationally. The first and less reliable of the latter samples, that representing the group arrested outside strike headquarters, included two strike leaders, both skilled workers, and 71 rank-and-filers. For the entire sample, as summarized in Table 7, unskilled workers outnumbered the skilled by 55.48 percent to 34.93 percent. If we disregard the two leaders and the four cases in which no occupation is given, the proportions are 60.45 percent versus 35.07 percent. Most of these men seized in the raid on strike headquarters were, however, released for lack of evidence. The second and more reliable rank-and-file sample, drawn from evidence of later arrests and prosecutions and an occasional press mention of a tramping striker during the strike, tips, as Table 8 illustrates, still more heavily toward the unskilled (61.76 percent) over the skilled (32.35 percent). In both rank-and-file samples, non-wage-working-class groups constitute a negligible proportion. Since recent work finds wide disparities in standards of living between the American skilled and unskilled, the leadership and the rank-and-file likely differed significantly in material circumstances.[51]

Of the nine top leaders of the strike's Executive Committee, arrested together and charged with riot, none was unskilled. Only two were even skilled workers, a shoemaker and a printer, with the latter having recently run his own newspaper. Joining these two were a student/party organizer (formerly a baker), two clerks (one formerly a lawyer), a doctor (formerly a lawyer and soon to be a sign painter), a drug and bleach maker and peddler, a newsdealer (soon to be a bookkeeper) and a self-employed bootfitter.[52] That several of the parenthetical references are to downward mobility fits the larger leadership sample as well. Five of the recoverable cases (10.64 percent) slid from having a trade to laboring status between 1875 and 1877. Three more (6.38 percent) moved downward from proprietorship or professional work to wage work or to joblessness. Another four (23.79 percent of those remaining in St Louis) had experienced downward mobility by 1879.[53]

Such data reflect statistically the precariousness of the social position of members of the general strike leadership. More human examples lie in the careers of Henry Allen and Peter Lofgreen. Allen, the Welsh immigrant who led the American section of the WPUSA, was a self-taught physician who practiced among the poor. Unable to earn enough from medicine, he was moonlighting as a sign painter at the time of the general strike. By 1878 he identified himself solely with the painting trade. Lofgreen, a Dane who also led the American section, would write in 1878, 'Thousands of young persons, to my knowledge, lawyers and professional men, now live a very precarious existence, glad to sleep on a lounge in some office, and not knowing whether they will have a meal the next day.' The words were in part autobiographical, as Lofgreen had secured only a clerkship after passing the bar. Losing a white-collar job at a newspaper hostile to the general strike, Lofgreen was by 1878 a tailor. Since six of the unskilled strike leaders (46.15 percent) had held higher status occupations just before 1877, the proportion of leaders who had reason to conceive of themselves as unskilled workers in the long term might be put as low as 14.89 percent of the sample.[54]

Conversely, if the numbers of recently lapsed proprietors and professionals are added to those in the strike leadership still involved in such pursuits in 1877, these groups together form over a quarter (25.53 percent) and, with the addition of white-collar workers over a third (34.04 percent) of the leadership.[55] Although businessmen were more important in the suppression of the strike than in its leadership, there was a large enough pool of lapsed and practicing business and professional men at the head of the strike to make understandable the Executive Committee's overtures to merchants for support. As late as Friday, 27 July, when the strike headquarters was seized, these overtures continued with the strike leadership asking for mercantile support and resolving:

> We deem it to the true interests of all businessmen, particularly the retail dealers, to use their best endeavors to further the passage of an eight-hour law and living wages. The working classes in times of prosperity constitute the great circulating medium of the country. Good times for the mechanic means active industries ... and plenty of business to the storekeepers.[56]

The large numbers of skilled workers and of such workers recently descended into unskilled jobs, which together comprise 51.06 percent of the recoverable cases among the general strike leadership, join other evidence in suggesting the possibility that trade unions played a more important role in setting the stage for the general strike than any historical accounts have yet argued. No less than twenty-one separate crafts had locals in St Louis in 1877 with another score of locals having disappeared the previous year. Only three of the thirty skilled workers identified as strike leaders or as rank-and-filers in the more reliable rank-and-file sample came from trades with no evidence of extant or very recent trade union activity. Moreover, the broader radical milieu in St Louis, involving the WPUSA, unions, secret societies, Greenback groups, cooperatives and Turner societies organized many skilled workers, in many cases alongside small proprietors. Such organization makes more explicable the boldness of the WPUSA in envisioning the possibility of a general strike and its early tactical successes in coordinating it. That the unskilled were generally not active unionists, nor, from the available evidence, likely to be in other radical organizations, further distanced the strike leaders from the rank-and-file in terms of experience and contacts as well as occupation.[57]

Strike leaders also differed dramatically from rank-and-file tramping strikers in terms of rootedness in the community. Over three-fourths of the leaders (79.17 percent) are identifiable from the 1877 city directory as against 60.00 percent from the more reliable rank-and-file sample and 25.00 percent of the less reliable rank-and-file sample (in every case disregarding cases compromised by too common names or insufficient data). While the 60 percent figure should warn against acceptance of the press's view of the tramping strikers as a rootless, transient mob, the strike leaders are nonetheless nearer the Committee of Public Safety than to even the more settled sample of the rank-and-file. The same holds true for rates of retrievability from the 1880 census. Moreover, the incidence of strike leaders' persistence in St Louis from 1875 through 1877 (64.95 percent) and from 1877 through 1879 (60.42 percent) more than double those of the rank-and-filers and again more closely approximate figures for Committee of Public Safety leaders (see Table 9). The mean age of the strike leaders, 39.2 years, trails that of the Committee of Public Safety by over seven years but exceeds the mean age of the more reliable rank-and-file sample by 2.32 years and of the less reliable one by 8.84 years.[58]

The 18.46 percent illiteracy rate among those seized outside strike headquarters is also significant in light of the extent to which the socialist movement, which provided much of the strike leadership, prized education, literacy and culture. The constitution of the German section of the International Workingmen's Association in St Louis, an immediate precursor of the WPUSA, insisted on the knowledge of English as a criterion for membership.[59] Four of the nine top Executive Committee leaders became newspaper editors in the two years following the general strike, as did two important secondary leaders. Another top leader had just stopped producing his own paper. Two top leaders went on to write popular utopian socialist books, one to a leading position as a freethought writer and another to translate part of *The Autobiographies of the Haymarket Martyrs* before owning a chain of California newspapers.[60] That so many of the strike leaders came from the German community in St Louis, an immigrant community in which literacy and education were important badges of status, made distinctions as to the ability to read and write still more vital.[61] So did a strong strain of eight-hour philosophy, which stressed the cultural degradation of workers under the long hours system and at times verged on holding that only an educated working class could make serious reforms – but that only with reform could the greater portion of the working class become educated.[62] Strike leaders considered themselves representative of the aspirations, but not the condition, of the working class.

The leaders also saw themselves as enough a part of the community to entertain hopes that Mayor Overstolz would deputize them to police the general strike. They appealed to the mayor on Tuesday, 24 July, asking that he oppose federal intervention, and on Wednesday, with offers of a peacekeeping force and requests that strikers be fed. Even after Overstolz had unequivocally armed the Committee of Public Safety instead, after the Friday raid on strike headquarters, and after wholesale arrests, two strike leaders still at large went to the office of Overstolz to negotiate. There they were taken into custody.[63]

Perhaps more laden with symbolism than these consistent appeals to municipal authority was the scene on 24 July, in which Executive Committee leaders asked Logan U. Reavis, the author of the most unabashed St Louis booster literature and the leader of a campaign to move the capital of the United States to St Louis, onto their speaking platform. Having bought the formerly trade union–owned *Daily Press* on his arrival in St Louis eleven years before, for a short time in that failing paper and then in tracts and speeches, Reavis preached a populist boosterism that stressed the 'industrial mission' of the citizenry as one of St Louis's prime resources. Reavis refused offers to speak at the strike meeting, pleading his lack of information and arguing for development as the key to the city's well-being. But had he assented, the brand of boosterism which was his trademark would likely have found a sympathetic ear among the strike leaders who sought to recruit him to speak.[64]

The strike leadership's constant appeals to republicanism, its repeated cautions against the initiation of violence, and its persistent efforts to bargain, even in the face of the seizure of its headquarters, all argue against the press's view that the Executive Committee negotiated insincerely while planning violence. Only the slimmest threads of evidence point to the contemplation of even small trade union self-defense squads and these might well have been seen as attempting to keep order.[65] Nor can the strategy of asking the mayor for deputization and arms be regarded as a ploy to get guns and prestige useful in fighting opponents of the strike. In Carondelet, where a separate striker-based and WPUSA-led Executive Committee was probably sanctioned as a peacekeeping body by St Louis municipal authorities, that group peacefully disbanded with the suppression of the strike in other parts of the city.[66]

The Carondelet example is also one of several that suggest that the strategy of continued appeals to the mayor, though ultimately unsuccessful, was not as ill-conceived as it appears in retrospect. East St Louis's mayor, for example, also deputized strikers. St Louis's Overstolz displayed unfailing cordiality to Executive Committee delegations through Thursday of the general strike. Belcher's Sugar Refinery asked both the federal government and the strikers' Executive Committee to guard its premises. A local meat packer appealed successfully to the Executive Committee to haul ice to preserve his wares and pronounced 'three cheers for the strikers' upon announcement of the decision. Stockyards recognized the authority of the Executive Committee by securing approval for the movement of corn and hay.[67]

However, far more difficult to explain than the strategy of appealing to municipal authorities were the decisions taken after Wednesday, 25 July, to end strike parades and mass meetings and to concentrate solely on negotiations. In effect, the Executive Committee, lacking a press of its own, divorced itself from contact with the strike's rank-and-file. It might be argued that the Executive Committee had to follow such a course to make its overtures to Overstolz convincing. But by midweek Overstolz was already drilling Committee of Public Safety troops and was preparing a back-to-work order. There was mounting evidence that mere appeals would not work. More important, the leverage in making such appeals lay in control over the alleged mob, control which the Executive Committee increasingly abdicated. Since unsanctioned meetings continued, featuring militant rhetoric for which the Executive Committee still drew censure in the press, the withdrawal of sponsorship for processions and demonstrations did not make sense even as a law-and-order measure.[68] The lone other tactical explanation of the leadership's actions and inaction, that hearing of the carnage and defeats of labor in Chicago and Pittsburgh, the Executive Committee foresaw defeat and sought to head off bloodshed and subsequent prosecutions, is also unsatisfactory.[69] A leadership with such a view would have called for abandonment of the general strike, not just of strike parades.

The ending of mass strike support activities is best viewed as the product of fear rather than hardheaded strike (let alone, revolutionary) strategy. Any general strike in a city like St Louis, where mean factory or workshop employment was but 8.92 workers, had to involve marches from workplace to workplace.[70] On Wednesday morning the Executive Committee had initiated just such a tramping strike. But the strike leadership envisioned processions in which 'none but workingmen over the age of eighteen should take part'.[71] The strike parades turned out quite differently, involving significant numbers of women and children.[72] Crucially, if the statistics presented above are indicative, unskilled workers may have far outnumbered the skilled in strike parades. The reverse characterized the strike leadership. On Wednesday evening, Executive Committee member Thomas Curtis sounded not a little like the city's press in finding it necessary to address his speech to 'workingmen ... and not to "scalawags and loafers" who attached themselves to the movement'.[73] In its subsequent limitation of attendance at Executive Committee deliberations to WPUSA delegates and representatives of organized trade unions, a wary leadership sought in effect to convene a soviet of the skilled and small proprietors, the groups already active in labor and radical organizations. The Executive Committee's new motto validated the worst fears being spread in the city's newspapers with the words 'Death to thieves, incendiaries and murderers'.[74] Those words must also have expressed the terrors of a leadership watching a strike grow on very different lines from those with which it was comfortable.

The Executive Committee was close enough to the situation to know that virtually no violence had occurred, but the largely preindustrial and often flamboyant strike symbols would have reminded them that the upheaval was a broad one not wholly subject to forces they controlled or understood. Although republican fifes and drums were much in evidence, urchins paraded to the accompaniment of a banner reading 'WE DON'T WANT BREAD. WE WANT CAKE AND PIE, OR BLOOD'.[75] The banner parodied the main symbol of the strike, a loaf of break on a stick. The focus on bread rather than specific trade union demands also found expression in the most popular song of the strikers, which began 'Bread for our little ones, wine for our sick ones'.[76] Along the Missouri Pacific Railroad tracks there appeared 'a rude kind of cross' with a dead rat hanging from it and a sign appropriating the Executive Committee's slogan, misspelling it 'DEATH TO THEEVES'. Neither the spelling nor the implication that rats (strikebreakers) faced fatal reprisals would have pleased the Executive Committee.[77] Moreover, there is evidence that some skilled, unionized workers, perhaps recoiling at such symbols and at Black participation, failed to support the general strike by Thursday, 27 July.[78]

Given that the leadership of the strike and the rank-and-file appear to have been well-integrated ethnically (as, for that matter were the leadership of the Committee of Public Safety and, to some extent, the residential patterns of the city),[79] ethnic prejudices could ill serve as vehicles for describing tensions between leaders and tramping strikers. Racism could and did. Indeed the role of racism is probably the most subtle and vital issue in an analysis of the dynamics of the general strike. After the Civil War, the labor movement in St Louis had developed a pattern of alternating active bursts of anti-Black rhetoric with neglect of civil rights and union organizing among African Americans. J. J. McBride typified the combination of racism and concern for the interests of white labor in the immediate postwar years. McBride, and other Irish pro-labor leaders in St Louis, fought for the eight-hour day and conservative racial policies; he was to be a major general strike spokesman in 1877. St Louis socialists did not challenge labor racism prior to the strike. Like the WPUSA nationally, they ignored the issues of Black civil rights.[80]

Nonetheless, perhaps moved by Black self-activity and the necessity to enlist the aid of African American rivermen in shutting down trade, the WPUSA became more flexible at the beginning of the general strike. At an early strike meeting an eloquent address by a Black speaker asked whether whites were ready to support the demands made by Black workers: he received a resounding 'We will!' in reply.[81] One of the five early

Executive Committee members was Black, as was one member of the first delegation to visit Overstolz. In all three Black strike leaders cooperating with the Executive Committee are mentioned. Integrated crowds were the rule in St Louis.[82] Just after the strike, a WPUSA leader advocated unity of the races behind labor demands and shortly thereafter St Louis had one of the few Black sections of the Socialist Labor Party in the United States.[83]

But alongside these developments was continued racism. Anti-Chinese and anti-Black rhetoric marked speeches from Executive Committee platforms, especially after reports that Black troops had arrived in St Louis to police the strike.[84] The fullest reminiscences of a strike leader, given from jail by Albert Currlin, blamed disorder and the movement's failure on a 'gang of niggers'. Currlin indicated that the Executive Committee's retreat from sanctioning public activities stemmed from anxieties concerning Black participation. His fellow leader Henry Allen also gave a post mortem of the strike suggestive of the connection between racism and retreat.[85]

What makes such racist recrimination fascinating is that evidence regarding the rank-and-file tramping strikers does not suggest a very high incidence of Black participation in the strike processions. Only 6 of the 77 rank-and-filers mentioned (7.79 percent) are identifiable as African Americans. That proportion slightly exceeds the Black share of the St Louis population but hardly indicates that the tramping strikers were dominated by minority workers. Of course it is possible that the newspapers sometimes departed from their usual practice at the time of identifying the race of Blacks charged with crimes, but so charged was the press with awareness of race during the strike and so full are the references to race where they do appear that this seems unlikely to have occurred widely. An alternative explanation, that police apprehended Black strikers less zealously or effectively is unlikely. For 1877, Black St Louisans were arrested in proportions greater than their share in the population by a factor of 1.91.[86] It thus appears that both the press and some strike leaders looked at an integrated tramping strike in which African Americans were an important but decided minority and saw a Black mob.

This ability to find in the 'mob' that group which best fit with the prejudices of the beholder was hardly peculiar to white strike leaders. The press made similar judgements, and the British vice-consul in St Louis went the American racists one better, identifying the participants in the processions as 'ignorant negroes and Irishmen of the lowest class, ready for any job that has the promise of wiskey [sic] in it.'[87] But in the mouths of socialist leaders who had cast themselves as heads of a general strike putatively representing the aspirations of all workers, indeed of a whole city, racist epithets had a particularly harsh ring. They recall and even illustrate a particularly full and brilliant passage by W. E. B. Du Bois on the many-sided ways in which racism undercut not only trade union unity but also the political and moral promise of the labor movement. The same passage also speaks to the events of 1877 in St Louis as it addresses the way in which racism could serve as a metaphor for, and a goad toward, an animus against all unskilled labor:

> Despite the fact that the nineteenth century saw an upsurge in the power of the laboring classes and a fight toward economic equality and political democracy, this movement ... lagged far behind the accumulation of wealth, because in popular opinion labor was fundamentally degrading and the just burden of inferior peoples. ... It was bad enough to have the consequences of [racist] thought ... fall upon colored people the world over; but in the end it was even worse when one considers what this attitude did to the European worker. His aim and ideal was distorted. ... He began to want not comfort for all men but power over other men. ... He did not love humanity and he hated 'niggers'.[88]

In the wake of the general strike the leadership's judgment that it played a valued part in the community received some vindication. Although rank-and-filers, especially Black rank-and-file strikers, often went to the workhouse on convictions for breaching the peace, all nine top leaders went free on a *nolle prosequi* verdict after a brief trial in which the prosecution was denied a vital delay.[89] A cheering crowd greeted their release. Hundreds of WPUSA supporters marched without interference in a funeral parade for one of their members just after the strike.[90] Committee of Public Safety members registered their opposition to late payment of wages by railroads, acknowledging that some strike grievances may have been legitimate. Democratic political leader Matthew J. Brennan's controversial cooperation with Carondelet strikers did not prevent his appointment as assistant fire chief weeks after the strike. The socialists began work in a variety of alliances with other parties and community organizations over such issues as German-language instruction in schools and municipal charter reform. WPUSA meetings quickly resumed and a socialist ticket took five of the fifteen School Board seats contested in October 1877. A month late a grand jury investigation of the strike failed to generate indictments against strike leaders, citing technical impediments.[91] Indeed, after August 1877 the main legal actions concerning the strike were proceedings brought by strike leaders who protested that their rights as US citizens, and in one case as a British national, had been violated. By May 1878, 200 organized St Louis socialists were allowed to drill regularly in public with arms.[92]

The following year Governor Phelps approved creation of a Missouri Bureau of Labor Statistics and appointed Socialist Labor Party sympathizers as its leading staffers. Shortly thereafter, such strike leaders as James Cope and Albert Currlin found their ways into the reform wing of the Republican Party. The latter, dubbed 'Albert the Agitator' during the general strike, was a Republican-appointed city water inspector and then a writer for an arch-opponent of the strikers, the *Westliche Post*, in the early 1880s, before Haymarket sent him back into revolutionary politics.

However, such openness to labor and radical input on the part of the local power structure did not undercut the development of mechanisms for suppressing future strikes. The St Louis police force was increased in size on the argument that it had been undermanned during the strike. By February 1878 nearly 500 police reservists drilled regularly in nine companies. Militia reform occurred in a burst. St Louis soon acquired a massive National Guard armory. In 1882 the city abolished Lucas Market, the center of strike demonstrations, 'at the instance of property holders'.[94]

The strong sense of belonging and of local republican citizenship held by skilled workers in late nineteenth century St Louis – sentiments at times fostered by the receptivity of local authorities to a radical presence but at other critical junctures, like the general strike, mocked by uncompromising repression – played a complex role in St Louis labor history of the period. Such ideas, along with the reality of a social position between that of the anti-strike elite and unskilled workers, imbued skilled workers and their allies with the confidence to pose labor demands. Such ideas acted, as Leon Fink, Herbert Gutman and Nick Salvatore have shown they did in other locales, to encourage democratic reform and to keep alive in the labor movement a sense of the possibility of self-improvement through collective improvement.[95]

But there was a cost. Ideas of local rootedness and republican citizenship widened the gap between unskilled and skilled workers, especially when differences of demography and education between the two groups were pronounced. Such ideas limited the tactical flexibility of labor organizations by committing them to a local boosterism shared with the upper and middle classes, a boosterism variously defined but generally anxious not to see the underclasses sully local reputation. The very ideas which encouraged labor reform activities also set boundaries on that activity, including limits which made it difficult to counter antistrike actions by the municipal authorities. They accentuated racism among skilled workers as a means of expressing those workers' inclusion in the community by dwelling on the otherness of Black workers (even, in a case like St Louis, when the Black workers were not imported strikebreakers). Fink's study of the skilled and unskilled in Milwaukee in 1886, Salvatore's work on the 1877 strike in Terre Haute, and accounts by Gutman of the reception of minority strikebreakers in small city strikes suggest such that costs were exacted in areas far beyond St Louis.[96]

TABLE 1

Occupations of Committee of Public Safety Leaders

Field	Number of Cases	Percent of Identified Cases
Professional	18	23.38
Banking and insurance	4	5.19
Manufacturing and construction	18	23.38
Merchants	18	23.38
Railway officials	5	6.49
Government officials	4	5.19
Grocers and saloonkeepers	8	10.39
Skilled workers	1	1.30
Other	1	1.30
Total	77	100.00

Based on 107 leaders listed in J. Thomas Scharf, *History of St Louis, City and County*, Philadelphia 1883, 2:1844–5, and originally in the *Missouri Republican*, 25 July 1877. Of these, 77 (71.96 percent) are identifiable from *Gould's St Louis City Directory for 1877*, St. Louis 1877. Fourteen of the unidentifiable cases simply do not appear in the directory (13.08%). Sixteen cases (14.96%) have names that are too common or are insufficiently identified as to first names to permit identification. All the percentages in the third column are of the 77 identifiable cases.

TABLE 2

Data from the 1880 Manuscript Census on St Louis Committee of Public Safety Leaders

Birthplace	Number of Cases	Percent of Identified Cases
German states	15	31.61
US, Total	22	47.83
US, South	10	21.74
US, North	8	17.39
US, Missouri	4	8.70
Ireland	5	10.87
England and Scotland	2	4.35
Other European	2	4.35
Total	46	100.00

Sex: Males, 100 percent   Mean age: 46.89 years   Race: 100 percent white

This table analyzes the same list of leaders as in Table 1. Of the 91 leaders whose cases are not complicated by having very common names or insufficient first names, 46 (50.55%) have been recovered from the US Census Soundex index to the Missouri manuscript census of 1880 (including both St Louis ennumerations). All the percentages in the third column are of the 46 identified cases. In all the tables using 1880 census data for St Louis some uncertainty is introduced by the questionable reliability of the enumerations. See Jeanette C. Lauer and Robert H. Lauer, 'St Louis and the 1880 Census: The Shock of Collective Failure', *Missouri Historical Review* 74 (January 1982): 151–63.

TABLE 3

Occupations of Committee of Public Safety and Police Militia Members

Field	Number of Cases	Percent of Identified Cases
White-collar employees	65	51.18
Merchants	10	7.87
Professionals	20 (11 lawyers)	15.75
Manufacturers and supervisors	12	9.45
Railway officials	5	3.94
Skilled workers	6	4.73
Unskilled workers	1	.79
Small proprietors	3	2.36
Other	5	3.94
Total	127	100.00

Based on 176 cases drawn from *Roll and Directory of the Branch Guards, September 20, 1878*, containing 67 entries; *Volunteers for the Citizen's Militia at St Louis and Southeastern Railroad Office, July 25, 1877*, containing 44 cases and *First Regiment, P.R., Lafayette Guard, Company A, Military Roll, June 11, 1879*, containing 65 entries. The first two sources are at the Missouri Historical Society at St Louis, and the last is at the Missouri Historical Society at Columbia. The 127 occupations identified through city directories comprise 72.16% of the sample. Of the remainder, 32 names (18.18%) fail to appear in the directory for the appropriate year, while 15 (8.52%) are unidentifiable because the names are too common or lack first names, or signatures are indistinguishable. All percentages in the third column are of the 127 identified cases.

TABLE 4

Occupations of Strike Leaders

Field	Number of Cases	Percent of Identified Cases
Skilled workers	19	40.43
Unskilled workers	13	27.66
Small proprietors	6	12.77
White-collar employess	4	8.51
Professionals	3	6.38
Others	2	4.26
Total	47	100.00

Based on press accounts in the St Louis *Times, Journal, Globe-Democrat* and *Dispatch, Missouri Republican, Western Watchman, Amerika, Irish World, Labor Standard* and *Westliche Post* (23 July– 15 August 1877). Leaders are defined as those identified as Executive Committee members, as leaders of the dominant pro-strike wing of the Carondelet citizens' committee, as those speaking in favor of the strike at sanctioned strike meetings or as union delegates to general strike meetings. Simple instances of trade union leadership, such as the cases of the many coopers delegated as negotiators with employers during the strike, have not been included. Were they included, the sample would be still more dominated by skilled workers. Identifications are from the 1877 city directory in 38 cases and from mentions of occupations in the press or in the researches of David Burbank in 9 cases. Of the remaining cases, 1 has left no evidence permitting identification and 2 have names that are too common or variously spelled to be identified.

TABLE 5

**Information on Strike Leaders' Birthplaces
Recoverable from the 1880 Manuscript Census**

Birthplace	Number of Cases	Percent of Identified Cases
German states	6	31.58
Ireland	4	21.05
England and Wales	2	10.53
US	4 (1 South/3 North)	21.05
Other Europe	1	5.26
Sweden	2	10.53
Total	19	100.00

The list of strike leaders is as in Table 4. The information in Table 2 applies to the census research here also. Percentages in the third column are of the 19 identified cases, which represent 39.58% of the 48 cases in Table 4 not complicated by insufficient data or names that are too common to be identified. Both Currlin and Lofgreen, two major strike leaders, apparently identified themselves to census takers as Swedish born. Other evidence indicates that in fact Lofgreen was Danish and Currlin was German.

TABLE 6

**Nonoccupational Data on Rank-and-File Strikers
Arrested in the Raid Upon the Executive Committee Headquarters**

Nationality	Number of Cases	Percent of Identified Cases
German	46	63.01
US	14	19.18
Irish	5	6.85
Polish	2	2.74
English	3	4.11
French	1	1.37
Cuban	1	1.37
None listed	1	1.37
Total	73	100.00

The source for this information is a list in the St Louis *Times* (27 July 1877). The newspaper apparently used information from police records which are no longer extant. The roster of the arrested gives age, nationality, marital status, job and literacy. Nationality probably refers not to birthplace but to place of origins of recent ancestors. It is unclear whether literacy meant only literacy in English. This apparently very fluid sample has not been followed with further directory and census analysis because even with the information on occupation provided, an aid in finding common and variously spelled names in directories, only 17 (23.29%) of the group can be identified in the 1877 directory. Five cases (6.85%) are vitiated by too common names or insufficient data. Most of those arrested in the raid were quickly released without trial.

TABLE 7

**Occupational Data on Rank-and-File Strikers
Arrested in the Raid Upon the Executive Committee Headquarters**

Field	Number of Cases	Percent of Identified Cases
Unskilled workers	40.5	55.48
Skilled workers	25.5	34.93
Other	3	4.11
None given	4	5.48
Total	73	100.00

The source is the St Louis *Times* (27 July 1877), as discussed in Table 6. One case listed as both a skilled worker and a laborer has been counted as a half in each category.

TABLE 8

**Occupational Data on Rank-and-File Strikers
Arrested and Those Identified as 'Mob' Participants**

Field	Number of Cases	Percent of Identified Cases
Skilled workers	11	32.35
Unskilled workers	21	61.76
Other	2	5.88
Total	34	100.00

For the sources, see Table 4. These sources generated 77 names of rank-and-file strikers allegedly participating in processions or demonstrations aimed at extending the strike. Most are mentioned with regard to their arrest or trial on minor charges arising from the attempt to prevent strikebreaking. Of the 77, 33 (42.86 percent) can be identified through the 1877 city directory and one other from the press. In 22 cases (28.57 percent) the name is variously spelled or too common to identify conclusively. In 21 cases (27.27 percent) there is simply no entry in the directory. The list that generated Tables 6 and 7 is *not* included here.

TABLE 9

Rates of Persistence in St Louis

Group	Rate of Persistence
Committee of Public Safety leaders (as per Table 1)	For 1875–77: 76/91=83.52 For 1877–79: 70/91=76.92
Strike leaders (as per Table 4)	For 1875–77: 31/48=64.59 For 1877–79: 29/48=60.42
Rank-and-File strikers (as per Table 8)	For 1875–77: 18/55=32.72 For 1877–79: 14/55=25.45

Based on the percentage of those identifiable as persisting in the listings in St Louis city directories for the years indicated. In each case the base from which the percentage is calculated is the total number of cases in a group minus those vitiated by having too common names, varied spelling, or lack of first names.

TABLE 10

Information on Rank-and-File Strikers' Birthplaces
Recoverable from the 1877 Manuscript Census

Birthplace	Number of Cases	Percent of Identified Cases
US–Total	6	35.29
US–Black	2	11.76
US–white	4 (1 South/3 North)	23.53
England	2	11.76
German states	5	29.41
Ireland	3	17.65
France	1	5.88
Total	17	100.00

See Tables 2 and 4 for sources and methods. Of the 55 cases not complicated by too common names or varied spellings, as given in Table 8, data on 17 (30.91 percent) can be recovered through the Soundex index to the 1880 Missouri manuscript census.

Notes

1. All further studies of the 1877 general strike in St Louis benefit from two solid factual accounts by David Thayer Burbank. They are the microcard edition of *City of Little Bread*, St Louis 1957, and *Reign of the Rabble*, New York 1966. The summary of the strike which begins this article draws on Burbank's work and on David Roediger, 'America's First General Strike: The St Louis "Commune" of 1877', *Midwest Quarterly* 21 (Winter 1989–90): 196-206. I thank the American Council of Learned Societies, the Exxon Educational Foundation, the American Philosophical Society and the American Association for State and Local History for financial contributions to the writing and research of this article. Philip Foner, David Burbank, Alex Yard, John Jentz, Anne Kenney, Tread Merrill, Susan Bowler, Jean Allman and the officers of St Louis Typographical Union Local 8 and Carpenters' Union 1596 also deserve thanks, as do the staffs of Northwestern University Library, Newberry Library, the Western Historical Collections at the Universities of Missouri at St Louis and Columbia, the Missouri Historical Society at St Louis and the State Historical Society of Wisconsin at Madison.

2. *Missouri Republican*, 23 July 1877.

3. Burbank, *Reign of the Rabble*, 55–6; Philip S. Foner, *The Great Labor Uprising of 1877*, New York 1977, 158; Albert Weisbord, *The Conquest of Power*, New York 1937, 1:413; Terry Moon and Ron Brokmeyer, *On the Hundredth Anniversary of the St Louis General Strike*, Detroit 1976; Walter B. Stevens, *St Louis: The Fourth City*, St Louis 1909, 1092–3.

4. See note 1 and Foner, *Great Labor Uprising*, 157–87; Robert V. Bruce, *1877: Year of Violence*, Indianapolis, Ind. 1959, esp. 255–60, 274–6 and 281–2; Russell M. Nolen, 'The Labor Movement in St Louis from 1860–1890', *Missouri Historical Review* 34 (1940): 161–73; Elliot J. Kanter, 'Class, Ethnicity and Socialist Politics: St Louis, 1876–1881', *UCLA Historical Journal* 3 (1982): 43–5; Alex Yard, 'Workers, Radicals and Capitalists: The St Louis Strikes of 1877' (unpublished seminar paper, Washington University, 1976).

5. For example, Herbert Gutman, 'Class Status and Community Power in Nineteenth-Century American Industrial Cities', in Gutman, *Work, Culture and Society in Industrializing America*, New York 1976, passim; Gutman, 'The Workers' Search for Power', in H. Wayne Morgan, ed., *The Gilded Age: A Reappraisal*, Syracuse, N.Y. 1968, 138–68; Nick Salvatore, *Eugene V. Debs: Citizen and Socialist*, Urbana, Ill. 1982; Leon Fink, *Workingmen's Democracy:*

The Knights of Labor and American Politics, Urbana, Ill. 1983.

6. *Missouri Republican*, 28 July 1877; St Louis *Dispatch*, 25 July 1877; 'Pope to E. D. Townsend', 27 July 1877, in Rutherford B. Hayes Manuscripts, Hayes Library, Fremont, Ohio [hereafter Hayes Papers]. See also 'Mayor Henry Overstolz to Municipal Assembly', 10 August 1877, in 'St Louis City Council Manuscript Proceedings', Archival Library, St Louis City Hall.

7. St Louis *Dispatch*, 23 and 25 July 1877; *Missouri Republican*, 15 August 1877.

8. St Louis *Globe-Democrat*, 24–27 July 1877; *Missouri Republican*, 25–28, July 1877; Burbank, *Reign of the Rabble*, 58; Foner, *Great Labor Uprising*, 174; *Amerika*, 26–28 July 1877. Cf. *Missouri Republican*, 11 November 1876, on the 'very respectable' workingmen at WPUSA affairs.

9. J. A. Dacus, *Annals of the Great Strikes in the United States*, St Louis 1877, 366–7, and 282–3 and 352–86 passim.

10. Albert Warren Kelsey, *Autobiographical Notes and Memoranda*, Baltimore 1911, 94; J. T. Scharf, *History of St Louis, City and County*, Philadelphia 1883, 2:1843. The Signal Service reports of William Finn from St Louis for the duration of the strike are in the Hayes Papers.

11. St Louis *Dispatch*, 27 July 1877.

12. *Missouri Republican*, 27 July 1877; St Louis *Globe-Democrat*, 26–27 July 1877; Dacus, *Annals*, 388–9; *Scranton Republican*, 26 July 1877. See also J. T. Headley, *Pen and Pencil Sketches of the Great Riots*, New York 1882, 455; Edward W. Martin, *The History of the Great Riots*, St Louis and Dayton 1877, 411.

13. Wyatt W. Belcher, *The Economic Rivalry between St Louis and Chicago, 1850–1880*, New York 1947.

14. Kelsey, *Notes and Memoranda*, 96 and 93.

15. Robert Reinders, 'Militia and Public Order in Nineteenth-Century America', *Journal of American Studies* 11 (1977): 96–7.

16. Statistics from Tables 1 and 3.

17. Data from Tables 1, 2, 3, and 10; Tables 4, 6 and 8 used for comparative purposes.

18. Computations and data from Table 2 and James Neal Primm, *Lion of the Valley: St Louis, Missouri*, Boulder, Colo. 1981, 331–2.

19. Frederick A. Hodes, 'The Urbanization of St Louis: A Study in Urban Residential Patterns in the Nineteenth Century' (PhD dissertation, St Louis University, 1973), 96–104; Audrey L. Olson, 'St Louis Germans, 1850–1920: The Nature of an Immigrant Community and Its Relation to the Assimilation Process' (PhD dissertation, University of Kansas, 1970), 56; and Tables 5 and 9. The same point applies to the Irish. See Hodes, 'Urbanization', 106.

20. Walter Kamphoefner, 'St Louis Germans and the Republican Party, 1848–1860', *Mid-America* 57 (April 1975); Steve Rowan and James Neal Primm, eds, *Germans for a Free Missouri: Translations from the St Louis Radical Press, 1857–1862*, Columbia, Mo. 1983, passim; Thomas Henry Clare, 'The Sociological Theories of William Torrey Harris' (PhD dissertation, Washington University, 1934), esp. 34, 75–6 and 85; Henry C. Brokmeyer, *A Mechanic's Diary*, Washington, D.C. 1910, 30ff; Maynard G. Redfield, 'Some Social and Intellectual Influences on the Development of Public Education in Missouri' (PhD dissertation, Washington University, 1956), esp. 121–3.

21. David R. Roediger, 'Racism, Reconstruction and the Labor Press: The Rise and Fall of the *St Louis Daily Press*, 1864–1866', *Science and Society* 42 (Summer 1978): 168; *Westliche Post*, 10–24 July 1866; William Parrish, *Missouri under Radical Rule, 1865–1870*, Columbia, Mo. 1965, 229–326; Schurz, quoted in J. R. Franz, 'History of the US, Part 4', *International Socialist Review* 3 (July 1902): 39. The quote is mocked in *Labor Standard*, 26 August 1877. On the German press and the general strike, see *Amerika*, 25–27 July 1877, and *Westliche Post*, 26–28 July 1877; Kelsey, *Notes and Memoranda*, 92–3; St Louis *Globe-Democrat*, 27 July 1877.

22. See note 20 above. The quote is from Clare, 'Harris', 75. Frances B. Harmon, *The Social Philosophy of the St Louis Hegelians*, New York 1943, 28–68, remains the most comprehensive study of the group's impact. On Brokmeyer, see Burbank, *Reign of the Rabble*, 104–5, and, for his role in the suppression of the strike, esp. St Louis *Globe-Democrat*, 24 July 1877.

23. Dena Lange and Merlin Ames, *St Louis: Child of the River, Parent of the West*, St Louis 1939: 204; Burbank, *Reign of the Rabble*, 51; Parrish, *Radical Rule*, 179; Table 2.

24. See Gutman as cited in note 5 above and his 'Social and Economic Structure and

Depression: American Labor in 1873 and 1874' (PhD dissertation, University of Wisconsin, 1959); David R. Roediger and Philip S. Foner, *Our Own Time: A History of American Labor and the Working Day*, London 1989, esp. Chapter 9. On local business and the 1877 strikes, see Foner, *Great Labor Uprising*, 55 and 201; *National Labor Tribune*, 28 July 1877. For a provocative attempt to apply Gutman's ideas to the St Louis general strike, see Yard, 'Workers', passim.

25. See Tables 1 and 2; St Louis *Globe-Democrat*, 28 July 1877; St Louis *Dispatch*, 27 July 1877; Scharf, *St Louis*, 2:1846.

26. On Scott, see C. Vann Woodward, *Reunion and Reaction: The Compromise of 1877 and the End of Reconstruction*, Boston 1951; Bruce, *1877*, 40–53, 86–7 and 209–21.

27. The relevant correspondence from Fletcher, Belcher and Wilson is in 'Military Division of the Missouri, Letters Sent and Received' in the National Archives, Washington, D.C. and in the Hayes Papers. See also Parrish, *Radical Rule*, 199, and Wilson, 'The Size and Organization of Armies', *International Review* 5 (July 1878): 514–29.

28. T. Harry Williams, ed. *Hayes: Diary of a President, 1875–1881*, New York 1964, 89.

29. 'Henry Overstolz et al. (including J. H. Wilson) to Secretary of War', 24 July 1877, in 'Missouri Letters', National Archives.

30. Gerald G. Eggert, *Railroad Labor Disputes: The Beginnings of Federal Strike Policy*, Ann Arbor, Mich. 1967, 3–49; Richard B. Morris, 'Andrew Jackson, Strikebreaker', *American Historical Review* 60 (1949): 54–68; Marlin S. Reichley, 'Federal Military Intervention in Civil Disturbances' (PhD dissertation, Georgetown University, 1939); Roediger, 'Racism, Reconstruction and the Labor Press', 158, treats Civil War anti-strike action by federal troops in St Louis.

31. Both Bennett M. Rich, *The Presidents and Civil Disorder*, Washington D.C. 1941, 84, and Harry Barnard, *Rutherford B. Hayes and His America*, New York 1954, 446ff, credit Hayes's circumspection with limiting the scale of federal intervention. Eggert, *Railroad Labor Disputes*, 29, points to manpower constraints among other factors. On shortages of troops, see 'Jno Pope to Adjutant General, USA', 24 July 1877, in 'Missouri Letters', National Archives and 'Cabinet Meeting', 27 July 1877, original notes in Hayes's handwriting, Hayes Papers. See also *Report of the Secretary of War, 1877*, in *Executive Documents of the House of Representatives*, Washington, D.C. 1878, 96.

32. Reinders, 'Militia', 91; William Riker, *Soldiers of the States: The Role of the National Guard in American Democracy*, Washington, D.C. 1957, 43–6; *Irish World*, 4 August 1877; Foner, *Great Labor Uprising*, 83 and 212; Eggert, *Railroad Labor Disputes*, 25; Kelsey, *Notes and Memoranda*, 95; *Missouri Republican*, 31 July 1877; Burbank, *Reign of the Rabble*, 154; John G. Westover, 'The Evolution of the Missouri Militia, 1804–1919' (PhD dissertation, University of Missouri, 1948), 180–88; William Hyde and H. L. Conard, eds, *Encyclopedia of the History of St Louis*, New York 1899, 3:1515.

33. Vann Woodward, *Reunion and Reaction*, 17ff; *Sandusky Weekly Register*, 5 June 1878; St Louis *Globe-Democrat*, 27 July 1877; (St Louis) *Christian Advocate*, 1 August 1877; *Labor Standard*, 28 July 1877.

34. The constraints on Hayes stemming from his disputed election had interesting parallels in St Louis, where Overstolz first took office, the city's fifth mayor in less than a year, as a result of a disputed election. His rival had served nine months before Overstolz was inaugurated. John Finn, the sheriff who led formation of the *posse comitatus* opposing the strike, also served after contestation of the legality of his title to the office. See J. T. Scharf, *History of St Louis, City and County*, Philadelphia 1883, 1:708–11; Charles H. Cromwell, ed., *St Louis Mayors: Brief Biographies*, St Louis 1965, 24; *Irish World*, 14 July 1877.

35. See above, notes 29 and 31; the Finn telegrams as cited in note 10 and the Cabinet minutes in the Hayes Papers.

36. Kelsey, *Notes and Memoranda*, 102.

37. Belcher, *Economic Rivalry*, esp. 115–16.

38. St Louis *Globe-Democrat*, 25–27 July 1877; St Louis *Times*, 25 July 1877; *Missouri Republican*, 28 July 1877; 'General Myer to the President', 25 July 1877, in Hayes Papers; Overstolz as quoted in *Missouri Republican*, 1 August 1877; Allan Pinkerton, *Strikers, Communists, Tramps and Detectives*, New York 1878, 407; Morris Hilquit, *History of Socialism in the United States*, New York 1903, 223.

39. St Louis *Globe-Democrat*, 26 and 27 July 1877; *St Louis Dispatch*, 26 and 27 July 1877.

40. *Missouri Republican*, 27 July 1877.

41. Ibid.

42. St Louis *Dispatch*, 24 July 1877; *Missouri Republican*, 28 July and 1 August 1877; St Louis *Globe-Democrat*, 27 July 1877.

43. St Louis *Globe-Democrat*, 27 July 1877; Floyd C. Shoemaker and Grace G. Avery, eds, *The Messages and Proclamations of the Governors of the State of Missouri*, Columbia, Mo. 1924, 6:180–81.

44. Hodes, 'Urbanization', 105–10, does, however, find some tendency to concentrate residentially among the wealthy.

45. Philip Taylor, *A Brief History of Public Markets and Private Markets Referred to as Public Markets in the City of St Louis*, St Louis 1961, 19–20; *Missouri Republican*, 27 July 1877; Martin, *Great Riots*, 408. Note also the *Missouri Republican*, 1 August 1877, citing large numbers of upper class spectators during the strike.

46. St Louis *Dispatch*, 17 July 1877; *Missouri Republican*, 25 July 1877.

47. *St Louis Daily Market Reporter*, 27 July 1877; *St Louis Globe-Democrat*, 28 July 1877; St Louis *Times*, 28 July 1877.

48. St Louis *Dispatch*, 25 July 1877; St Louis *Globe-Democrat*, 28 July 1877; St Louis *Times*, 28 July 1877.

49. Burbank, *Reign of the Rabble*, 177–8 and 161.

50. Peter Lofgreen [as Laurence Gronlund], *The Coming Revolution: Its Principles*, St Louis 1878, 38.

51. Tables 4, 6, 7 and 8; Peter Shergold, *Working-Class Life: The 'American Standard' in Comparative Perspective, 1899–1913*, Pittsburgh 1982.

52. *Gould's St Louis City Directory for 1877*, St Louis 1877: *Gould's St Louis City Directory for 1878*, St Louis 1878; St Louis *Globe-Democrat*, 11 August 1877; Foner, *Great Labor Uprising*, 161; Mayor Henry Overstolz Scrapbooks at Missouri Historical Society at St Louis, 3:10–11; Philip S. Foner, ed., *The Autobiographies of the Haymarket Martyrs*, New York 1969, 73.

53. The sources here are as listed in Table 4 and the St Louis city directories from 1875 through 1879.

54. Overstolz Scrapbooks, 3:10–11; Lofgreen, *Coming Revolution*, 27; Foner, *Great Labor Uprising*, 161; *Gould's City Directory for 1878*; see also Table 4.

55. Computed from Table 4.

56. St Louis *Globe-Democrat*, 28 July 1877; Lofgreen, *Coming Revolution*, 13, expands on the common interests of workers and merchants.

57. See notes 10, 21 and 23 and my 'What Was the Labor Movement?: Organization and the St Louis General Strike of 1877', forthcoming in *Mid-America*.

58. Compares all the tables.

59. Table 6 and 'Constitution' of Section One (St Louis) of the International Working-men's Association in the microfilm edition of the International Workingmen's Association Papers available from State Historical Society of Wisconsin at Madison, Reel 2.

60. *Gould's City Directory for 1878*; Foner, ed., *Autobiographies of the Haymarket Martyrs*, 73; *Irish World*, 1 September 1877; Burbank, *Reign of the Rabble*, 189–201.

61. George H. Kellner, 'The German Element on the Urban Frontier: St Louis, 1830–1860' (PhD dissertation, University of Missouri at Columbia, 1973), esp. 172.

62. *Labor Standard*, 25 November and 9 December 1876, and 8 March 1877; Yard, 'St Louis', 27–8. See also the slightly later article, also emanating from St Louis, by Peter J. McGuire on 'Socialism and Eight Hours' in *Chicago Socialist*, 5 July 1879. For the eight-hour movement and uplift generally, see Roediger and Foner, *Our Own Time*.

63. St Louis *Globe-Democrat*, 28 September 1877; *St Louis Times*, 4 August 1877; Burbank, *Reign of the Rabble*, 82–3; *St Louis Dispatch*, 24 July 1877.

64. St Louis *Times*, 4 August 1877; Primm, *Lion of the Valley*, 288–90; Reavis, *St Louis: The Future Great City*, St Louis 1870, esp. 86–110; Roediger, 'Racism, Reconstruction and the Labor Press', 156–77.

65. Burbank, *Reign of the Rabble*, 114 and 131–2; *Missouri Republican*, 28 July 1877.

66. Burbank, *Reign of the Rabble*, 82, 138 and 145.

67. Bruce, *1877*, 257; *Missouri Republican*, 1 August 1877; St Louis *Globe-Democrat*, 26 and 27 July 1877; Foner, *Great Labor Uprising*, 179–80.

68. *Missouri Republican*, 27 July 1877; St Louis *Daily Journal*, 27 July 1877.

69. Bruce, *1877*, 131–61 and 236–53; Pinkerton, *Strikers, Communists, Tramps, Detectives*, 404.

70. Computed from tables in *St Louis Times*, 19 November 1877; St Louis *Globe-Democrat*, 26 July 1877. See also Richard Schneirov, 'Chicago's Great Upheaval of 1877', *Chicago History*, 9 (1980): 4.

71. St Louis *Times*, 4 August 1877.

72. *Missouri Republican*, 26–27 July 1877; St Louis *Globe-Democrat*, 24 July 1877; St Louis *Dispatch*, 27 July 1877.

73. *Missouri Republican*, 26 July 1877.

74. Burbank, *Reign of the Rabble*, 133; *St Louis Globe-Democrat*, 26 July 1877.

75. *Missouri Republican*, 26 July 1877.

76. St Louis *Globe-Democrat*, 26 July 1877.

77. Ibid.

78. Ibid.; Burbank, *City of Little Bread*, 120; Burbank, *Reign of the Rabble*, 99; St Louis Carpenters Union No. 1596 (formerly *Moebel-Arbeiter* Union Number 12) Papers, esp. the minutes from 28 July to 4 August 1877. These papers were examined in the local's office but are now part of the Western Historical Collections, University of Missouri at St Louis.

79. Hodes, 'Urbanization', 47–62; Tables 2, 5 and 9.

80. Roediger, 'Racism, Reconstruction and the Labor Press', passim; Parrish, *Radical Rule*, 224; Foner, *Great Labor Uprising*, 181–3; Foner, ed., *The Formation of the Workingmen's Party of the United States*, New York 1976, 18. On St Louis racism during this period, the best work is Lawrence O. Christensen, 'Black St Louis: A Study in Race Relations, 1865–1916' (PhD dissertation, University of Missouri at Columbia, 1972), esp. 194ff.

81. St Louis *Dispatch*, 23 July 1877; Ralph and Mildred Fletcher, 'Some Data on Occupations among Negroes in St Louis from 1866 to 1897', *Journal of Negro History* 20 (1935): 338–41; Foner, *Great Labor Uprising*, 181.

82. See note 12; *New York Sun*, 27 July 1877: Burbank, *Reign of the Rabble*, 33. One recent account terms the general strike a model of 'interracial solidarity'; see Don Fitz and Ray Eberle, Racism in St Louis, 1877 to 1914', *Workers' Democracy* 2 (1982): 11–13.

83. St Louis *Times*, 4 September 1877; Kanter, 'Class, Ethnicity and Socialist Politics', 56.

84. St Louis *Globe-Democrat*, 26 July 1877; Burbank, *Reign of the Rabble*, 50: *Missouri Republican*, 26 July 1877. Putative evidence of rank-and-file racism is found in one of the several strike stories, intended to be humorous and generally told in Irish or German dialect, to appear in the St Louis press during or after the strike. See St Louis *Globe-Democrat*, 28 July 1877.

85. St Louis *Times*, 4 August 1877; Overstolz Scrapbooks, 3:10–11, has Allen comparing the crowds to 'wild heathens'.

86. Arrest sources are as given in Table 4. On African American arrests in proportion to the Black population, see Primm, *Lion of the Valley*, 331–2, and Board of Police Commissioners of the City of St Louis, *Seventeenth Annual Report*, St Louis 1878, 53–6.

87. See note 12 and 'Report by Vice-Consul Bagshawe on the Late Industrial Conflicts at St Louis' in *Reports Respecting the Late Industrial Conflicts in the United States, Presented to Both Houses of Parliament by Order of Her Majesty*, London 1877, 46.

88. Du Bois's concentrated discussion of the full impact of racism on the labor movement, a discussion which deserves close consideration from those who would abandon the concept of false consciousness, is in his *The World and Africa: An Inquiry into the Part Which Africa Has Played in World History*, New York 1965, 18–21.

89. Cf. *Missouri Republican*, 11 August 1877, with St Louis *Globe-Democrat*, 10 and 14 August 1877.

90. Burbank, *Reign of the Rabble*, 182; St Louis *Globe-Democrat*, 11 August 1877.

91. *Missouri Republican*, 2 August 1877; Kanter, 'Class, Ethnicity and Socialist Politics', 43, and passim; Burbank, *Reign of the Rabble*, 114 and 186–9; *Missouri Republican*, 6 November 177; St Louis *Times*, 27 August 1877; St Louis *Globe-Democrat*, 25 September 1877; Charles

W. Swingley, *History of the St Louis Fire Department*, St Louis 1914, 182.

92. 'One of the Strikers Sues' in Overstolz Scrapbooks, vol. 3 (*circa* 5 April 1878); St Louis *Globe-Democrat*, 28–9 September 1877; St Louis *Times*, 2 October 1877; St Louis *Evening Post*, 30 April and 4 May 1878.

93. Burbank, *Reign of the Rabble*, 191–2 and 198–9.

94. Board of Police Commissioners, *Seventeenth Annual Report*, esp. 40–42; Annetta J. Morris, 'The Police Department of St Louis: Its Development, History, Methods and Service from 1808 to 1919' (MS at Missouri Historical Society at St Louis, 1919), 13ff; *Official Programme and Souvenir of the Great Historical Encampment at New Armory*, St Louis n.d.; Westover, 'Evolution of Missouri Militia', 194ff; Taylor, *Public Markets*, 20.

95. See note 5.

96. Note especially Salvatore's discussion of the 1877 strike in Terre Haute in his 'The Small Town Strike: Terre Haute, Indiana' (paper delivered to the American Historical Association, Washington, D.C., 28 December 1976), and *Debs*, esp. 31–8; Fink, *Workingmen's Democracy*, 188–95; Gutman, 'Reconstruction in Ohio: Negroes in the Hocking Valley Coal Mines in 1873 and 1874', *Labor History* 3 (Fall 1962): 243–64, and 'The Braidwood Lockout of 1874', *Journal of the Illinois State Historical Society* 53 (1960): 5–28.

8

Gook: The Short History of an Americanism

'The Haitians, in whose service United States Marines are presumably restoring peace and order in Haiti, are nicknamed "Gooks" and have been treated with every variety of contempt, insult and bestiality.' So wrote Herbert J. Seligman in *The Nation* in 1920. The contempt and bestiality will scarcely surprise those who have much studied American imperialism, but hearing the term *gook* applied to Black people may. In the last forty years, *gook* has chiefly slurred Asian people, especially, but far from exclusively, those actively opposing American presence in Korea and Indochina. But the broader pan-racist past of *gook* provides almost a short history of modern US imperial aggression and particularly of the connections between racial oppression and war.

The origins of *gook* are mysterious, but the dictionary-makers agree that it is an Americanism. The *Oxford English Dictionary* counts the word 'orig[inally] and chiefly US' and identifies it as 'a term of contempt; a foreigner; a coloured inhabitant of (south-)east Asia.' It offers a 1935 first usage, applied mainly to Filipinos, and notes use by US troops in Korea and Vietnam, without considering that such usages in fact applied to *natives* in lands where Americans were *foreigners*. The *OED* adds 'origins unknown' as its verdict regarding scholarly knowledge of the coining of the term.

If *gook* did originate in the Phillipines, it probably did so far earlier than 1935. Irving Lewis Allen, in *The Language of Ethnic Conflict*, refers to *goo-goo* as 'originally a Filipino in the Spanish-American War, 1899–1902', and some scholars of American English suggest that *gook* itself found usage during the same conflict. If so, *gook* developed among troops who were probably connecting contempt for natives with contempt for 'promiscuous' women and for poor people generally. An 1893 citation from

Slang and Its Analogues finds *gooks* to be 'tarts' and particularly camp-following prostitutes or 'barrack hacks', catering to the army. A 1914 source similarly defines *gook* as 'a tramp, low'.

Another explanation – and it is surely preferable to think of the various possible sources of ethnic slurs as overlapping rather than as alternatives – is that *gook* developed from *goo-goo*, which, as Stuart Flexner suggests, may have been a mocking imitation of Filipino speech. If so, the origins would square with the roughly contemporaneous 'spik', the derivation of which, H. L. Mencken held, came from Spanish-speakers' alleged attempts to say that they did not 'spik' [speak] English. One account from the 1930s specifically identifies gooks on language grounds as Spanish-speakers. Finally, the use of *gook* in the Philippines had a specifically racial dimension, with the term applied particularly to those natives who had no mixture of European 'blood' – a particularly despised (or pitied) category that imperialists freely predicted would die out as 'progress' occurred.

By the 1920s, gooks were French- and creole-speaking Black Haitians and Spanish-speaking Nicaraguans. Marines, as we have seen, made the Haitians into gooks. They also, after the 1926 invasion of Nicaragua, were responsible for so naming 'natives' there. Into the 1930s in Costa Rica, *goo-goo* described the citizenry, at least to Americans. Such a term, in the Philippines or Latin America, could hardly have failed to conjure up an image of an infantilized subject population.

During World War II, the identity of the gook expanded again. The West Coast's brilliant amateur student of language, Peter Tamony, took notes on radio commentator Deane Dickason's 1943 comments on *gook* – the Marines' 'word for natives everywhere' but especially for Arabs. The latter of Dickason's conclusions is likely closer to the mark than the former. 'Natives' of France, or of Britain, or of Holland, were not gooks, but people of color were. In particular, the mainly Arab population of North Africa acquired the status of gook. Indeed the usage spread to French colonialists so that, even a decade after the war, panicked settlers reacted to Algeria's national liberation struggle by indiscriminately slaughtering villagers in 'gook-hunts'.

In the Pacific, World War II witnessed the usage of *gook* to apply to peoples far beyond the Philippines. Neither was coming from a nation supporting the US nor from an American territory, proof against being called a gook. At the war's end, extensive riots between servicemen and natives erupted in Hawaii. *Life* commented in November 1945 that the rioting servicemen saw their enemies as 'gooks – that stupid, dirty lower strata of Honolulu citizen'. The San Francisco *News* explained to a California audience that same month that *gook* was 'a Hawaii servicemen's name roughly the equivalent to the mainland "zoot-suiter"' – the latter term describing the stylishly dressed Latinos and Blacks who were often the victims of mob violence stateside.

When the Korean War followed fast on the heels of World War II, *gook* quickly named Korean friend and foe in that conflict. Anti-Communism and racism mixed promiscuously. A 1950 San Francisco *News* headline blared 'HILLS ARE LOUSY WITH GOOKS' before the subhead 'Red Mortars Keep Yanks Pinned Down'. One source cited South Korean soldiers fighting alongside Americans as calling North Koreans *gooks*. But it is unlikely that many Koreans saw the term as anti-Communist rather than racist.

Although one San Francisco *Examiner* report from 1950 maintained that *gook* was 'soldier's slang for almost any non-American', there is so far no evidence that non-American whites in the United Nations force in Korea were so called. On the other hand, so prevalent was the reference to Koreans as gooks that in September 1950 General Douglas MacArthur directed that the use of the term be discontinued because it gave 'aid and comfort to the enemy' by opening the US commitment to democratic ideals to question. Although one October 1953 newspaper account optimistically held that *gook* 'has disappeared from the GI vocabulary', the word's use certainly continued quite prominently after MacArthur's pronouncement. *Life*'s December 1951 'A Marine Tells What Korea Is Really Like', for example, is littered with casual references to gooks.

That Vietnam followed Korea with no other sustained US interventions between solidified the modern meaning of *gook* as an Asian. Clearly the American command during the Vietnam fighting did not effectively press MacArthur's campaign against use of the word. One of the most revealing of the countless such references to gooks came in a 1969 report by war correspondent Robert Kaiser entitled 'The GI's and the Gooks'. Kaiser wrote, in a sentence suggestive of how anti-Vietnamese racism drew on formulations as old as the Indian Wars, 'The only good gook, it is said again and again on US bases throughout Vietnam, is a dead gook.'

The stark dehumanization of enemies in such a line reminds us that racism is not only a way to motivate fighters in wars of aggression but also that militarism has helped to foster racism. The frenetic gook-baiting that so many antiwar ex-GI's later reported as a feature of basic training during Vietnam was easily enough turned on but, despite the remarkable, hardwon antiracism developed by some soldiers, it was not always easily turned off on US soil. For example, Steve Jacobs, a Missouri-based psychiatric nurse counselling veterans of Vietnam, challenges clients when they use *gook* to describe their 'enemies' not just because the word is repugnant but because it signals a continuing denial to acknowledge the war's horrors and a holding on to pain.

The 1991 US imperial adventure in the Gulf came complete with references to 'Indian country' as a military synonym for 'enemy territory'.

My students tell me that the more gung-ho stateside supporters of the war referred to Arabs as *sand niggers*. The combination of racism, imperialism and war produces hideous things, including words. Those who would champion 'ethnic civility' must oppose such barbarisms, and not just at the level of language.

NOTE: This article was made possible by the late Peter Tamony's research notes on *gook* in the University of Missouri-Columbia's Western Historical Manuscripts Collection and was written during the first days of the Gulf War.

9

The Racial Crisis
of American Liberalism

Andrew Hacker's *Two Nations: Black and White, Separate, Hostile, Unequal* indicts race relations in the contemporary US as a system of what its publicity packet calls '*de facto* apartheid'.[1] But its most chilling contribution to showing just how bad things are is an unwitting one. Unlike earlier liberal studies of racism, *Two Nations* can only indict. Hacker sketches an apartheid system and adds 'I wouldn't know where to begin', so far as strategies for changing it are concerned. The pessimism of *Two Nations* stands out especially when compared with the tradition of the liberal epics on race relations with which it identifies itself. Gunnar Myrdal's 1944 *An American Dilemma*, which Hacker counts as 'America's most notable book on race' (p. xi), matched *Two Nations* in its stark portrayal of Black life and of the consistent betrayals of the 'American Creed' of equality by whites. But Myrdal stressed the tension between an overarching American commitment to justice and the brutalities of white supremacy. He saw room for progress and offered policy prescriptions with that end in view.

Two Nations takes its title and subtitle from a combination of Disraeli's celebrated remark about the social distance between the rich and poor in Victorian England and the conclusion of the 1968 report of the US National Advisory Commission on Civil Disorders: 'Our nation is moving toward two societies, one black, one white, separate and unequal.' But the 1968 report also offered plans to combat inequality. *Newsweek's* laudatory review of *Two Nations* illustrates how different Hacker's approach is. The review features his photograph with the apt caption 'A bleak diagnosis and no prescription'.[2]

Though it is striking and sobering that Hacker could write (and reviewers could unproblematically praise) a study that posits a more or less unchallenged and unchallengeable apartheid system in the US, his despair is hardly unique among American liberals. The old grounds for hope for racial justice have fled. Although African American support for organized labor remains high and trade union leadership is more integrated than in the past, the traditional 'Black and White, Unite and Fight' strategies of struggle suffer from the burdensome history of labor racism and the fact that the unions themselves have been decimated and shorn of both vision and social power. *Two Nations* makes virtually no mention of trade unions, either as vehicles for transforming society or even as factors shaping African American job prospects. The dream that integrated education would automatically produce racial harmony similarly stands discredited, both because of alleged failures of integration and, more broadly, because the perceived collapse of the educational system itself. Expanded job opportunities seemed a panacea in 1968 and seem an impossibility in the no-growth nineties.

However, Hacker's study differs from those of the many liberals who share his gloom regarding race. He does not follow most liberals in arguing that we need to minimize emphasis on racial inequality and to turn instead to the practical task of building raceless coalitions to address economic growth and educational reform, which too many liberals see as prior and practical issues as opposed to the impossibilities of antiracist political action. For example, Hacker writes eloquently of Republican electoral successes resting on the fit between the self-conscious whiteness of voters and the Republicans Party's willingness 'to have itself regarded as a white party' (p. 102). He proposes no counterstrategy. Thomas and Mary Edsall's influential analysis of race and contemporary politics, *Chain Reaction*, meanwhile approvingly quotes a description of a representative group of white Democrats-turned-Reagan-supporters as people for whom African Americans 'constitute the explanation for nearly everything that has gone wrong', and for whom 'virtually all progressive symbols and themes have been redefined in racial and pejorative terms'. They propose that the Democrats downplay appeals to 'special interests' (for example, racial justice).[3] In both cases, the diagnoses are bleak, but while Hacker offers no prescriptions, the Edsalls prescribe a deft sidestepping of the issue of race. Given these choices, I would confess a preference for Hacker's refusal, as one reviewer has put it, to pencil in 'upbeat final chapters' over the notion that the pale populism of a Bill Clinton will start a process that builds a class coalition that in turn will ameliorate racial oppression.[4] However, the choices need not be so limited. We ought to be able to learn from Hacker's unreconstructed racial liberalism without accepting its apoliticism and to criticize his assumptions without supposing that the 'left wing of the possible' is located in the family rooms of Reagan Democrats.

'While joining in the chorus of "Yeas" which the book has so deservedly evoked', the great novelist Ralph Ellison wrote in his review of Myrdal's *American Dilemma*, it is also necessary to 'utter a lusty and simultaneous "Nay".'[5] *Two Nations* provokes the same divided response. On the one hand it provides a useful mélange of information, and especially of statistical information, that debunks reigning myths concerning African Americans and crime, welfare, voting and jobs. At a time when many liberals and a fair share of the left have shied away from support for affirmative action, Hacker offers a vigorous, commonsensical defense of partly race-based strategies to overcome partly race-based injustices. His central insight, that the story of race relations in the US should focus on how 'white America ... has made being Black so disconsolate an estate' (p. 218) signals an unwillingness to blame the victim and places him in the best of the antiracist liberal tradition. But the same line also signals why that tradition is in ruins and why we should say 'Nay' to the overall message of Hacker's study even as we applaud individual sections within it. Failing to see anything but 'disconsolation' in the African American experience, and failing to see that on some levels whites know better than that, Hacker can offer no substantive grounds for hope that racial oppression can be fought. The inability of not only Hacker, but also American liberalism generally to keep hope alive influences the very structure of *Two Nations*. Pitching his argument defensively to a white audience, Hacker organizes his work around a series of 'debunkings' of popular myths about African Americans. In comparison with Myrdal or the National Advisory Commission, his work is quite limited. *Two Nations* is a short book and one based on the drawing together of other researchers' data, not the generation of new research. Where Hacker does provide startling new interpretations, too often a laborious check of the ill-designed citations reveals that the assertion is unsupported. For example, he argues, without citation and despite voluminous documentation to the contrary by the Boston-based Center for the Study of Sport and Society's studies of racism and athletics, that members of professional teams are 'all ... obviously hired on merit' (p. 121). Similarly, the interesting assertion that 'very few white Americans have ever set foot inside a Black family's home' (p. 21) turns out to rest on no cited evidence. And how would one document the bizarre contention that African-Americans 'sense that much that is "Black" is missing in artists like ... Toni Morrison [and] Paul Robeson?' (p. 40).

Even so, there is much to applaud in Hacker's gathering of statistical material to dismantle myths. He shows, for example, that the typical welfare mother is as likely to be white as Black, that in half of all cases her family receives aid for less than two years and that 43.2 percent of the time she has only one child and 30.6 percent of the time, just two. Moreover, he adds, 'most single mothers are not on welfare, but in fact hold full-time jobs' (pp. 86–7). Hacker likewise carefully demolishes the myth that affirmative action has exercised a strong negative influence on white male job and education opportunities. He deflates the notion that a privileged generation of African American 'affirmative action babies' has moved up with uncommon speed economically. Black male attorneys between the ages of 35 and 45, for example, make only $790 for each $1000 made by their white counterparts. Hacker excels especially at presenting provocative statistics, in either tables or prose, with little commentary. He demonstrates, for example, that recent rape victims identify their assailants as white in two-thirds to more than three-quarters of cases, depending on the sources used. He adds that in 'close to half' of rape arrests, the subject is Black (pp. 182–3).

But structuring a book around the statistical puncturing of racist mythology has its clear dangers as well. These myths set the book's agenda and sometimes leave Hacker arguing narrowly and rather pleadingly that African American life is not so pathological or degraded as has been thought. The lamentable detail Hacker lavishes on discussion of African American scores on standardized achievement tests is a perfect example of this problem. Penetrating points on the cultural biases and limited usefulness of the tests drown in numbers and graphs. Nor does Hacker avoid being trapped at times in variants of the myths he attacks. As Micaela di Leonardo's withering critique of *Two Nations* has shown, this is particularly the case where gender is concerned. Hacker argues, here following rather than challenging popular fashion, that Black women are catching up to white society as Black men are not, and that by one measure Black women have caught up in income. But the comparisons are always with white women and the fact that African American women still earn just 62 percent of what African American men earn gets lost in the shuffle.[6]

That Hacker stands out among popularly publicized academic writers on race reflects his own modest but real contributions, the generally abysmal state of the art, and the extent to which stronger critiques of popular racelore among whites have been marginalized. Sociological and anthropological accounts of the "Black underclass" have done so much to legitimate such racelore that even the best of recent studies often fight over poorly and dishonestly mapped terrain. As the political scientist Adolph Reed has acutely observed,

> Since the late 1970s … there have been on average, no fewer than three books and scores of popular, middlebrow and faux-scholarly articles published annually on 'the underclass' and its sordid and defective ways, all repeating the same vicious idiocies and all claiming to break courageously with a silence imposed by sentimental liberals' and defensive Blacks' censorship.

The works of Reed and essays by Julianne Malveaux, Mack Jones and Charles P. Henry in James Jennings's fine collection *Race, Politics, and Economic Development*, for example, challenge the underclass/racelore arguments much more thoroughly than Hacker does, but, alas, to far fewer readers.[7]

Most important, the reactive nature of *Two Nations* does not allow Hacker to question whether being Black really is 'so disconsolate an estate'. Hacker not only reacts to white racism but assumes that African American life is *merely* a panoply of reactions to, if not agonizings over, oppression by whites. Here too Ellison's commentary on Myrdal wears all too well as criticism of Hacker. 'But can a people ... ', Ellison asks, 'live and develop over three hundred years simply by *reacting*?' He continues: 'Men have made a way of life in caves and upon cliffs, why cannot Negroes have made a life upon the horns of the white man's dilemma?'[8] That way of life is missing in *Two Nations*, with Hacker's imagination failing especially when it looks at (or fails to look at) what African American youth (particularly young single mothers) and working class people have created, not just out of their oppression but also out of their activity and reflection. Hiphop music and poetry, for example, is discussed in three lines and only as evidence of misogyny. There is no sense in Hacker's work that masses of African Americans are still answering and even increasingly answering the question of who 'wills to be' African American with the same assurance as Ellison: 'I do.'[9] Nor is there any sense of the extent to which, or the levels on which, many so-called white Americans question whether they want to be white. Hacker at once holds that most whites sincerely consider themselves to be the victims of 'reverse discrimination' *and* that 'no white American ... would change places with even the most successful Black American' (p. 131). If both these assertions contain elements of truth – the second is clearly overstated – racial consciousness among whites is fascinatingly complex and deserving of sustained attention. In any case, the development by whites of the racelore Hacker discredits must be explained if we are to assess whether debunking has a realistic chance of changing attitudes.

Two Nations is most reticent in its discussion of whiteness, especially in contrast to its volubility on the question of what it is like to be Black. It offers useful, fugitive hints that consciousness of being white is an insubstantial substitute for living a real life, calling whiteness an 'artifact' (p. 217). It shows excellent taste in briefly quoting parts of James Baldwin's penetrating account of the way in which whiteness took shape as 'the white man's unadmitted – and apparently, to him, unspeakable – private fears and longings were projected onto the Negro.' But these observations fill but perhaps two pages in good-sized book. The pathology under debate for Hacker is that alleged to exist in African-America, not that which formed the very idea of a 'white America'.

Because of his assumption that race equals Blackness, Hacker does not see the tremendous (often superficial, but also at times deep) attraction to nonwhite cultures and the increasing suspicion of the emptiness of whiteness among white American youth. Hacker cannot imagine the redemptive possibilities Baldwin did when he hoped that the 'white man' might yet 'become a part of that suffering and dancing country that he now watches wistfully.'[10]

In concluding his 1944 essay on Myrdal, Ellison observed: 'What is needed ... is not an exchange of pathologies but a change in the basis of society. This is a job which both Negroes and whites must perform together. In Negro culture there is much of value for America as a whole. What is needed are Negroes to take it and create of it "the uncreated consciousness of their race". In doing so they'll do far more, they'll create a more human America.'[11]

Culturally, if not politically, the US has moved considerably in the direction mapped by Ellison in the half-century since he wrote those lines. The process is neither pretty nor even. A fair share of those white kids you see with Malcolm X t-shirts still have Confederate flag belt buckles. But what Baldwin called the 'lie' of whiteness is on the run and precisely because of the creations – in fiction, music, film, dance, social criticism, speech, fashion and everyday life – of people of color. This process is not easily reduced to statistics, least of all to election results, but it decidedly is a ground for the hope currently absent among American liberals.

Notes

1. Andrew Hacker, *Two Nations: Black and White, Separate, Hostile, Unequal*, New York 1992. All subsequent page references to *Two Nations* are in parentheses in the text. This review essay originally appeared in *New Left Review*, no. 196 (November-December 1992).

2. *Report of the National Advisory Commission on Civil Disorders*, New York 1968; David Gates, 'Apartheid, American Style', *Newsweek*, 23 March 1992, 61. See also Gunnar Myrdal, *An American Dilemma: The Negro Problem and Modern Democracy*, New York 1944.

3. Thomas and Mary Edsall, *Chain Reaction: The Impact of Race, Rights and Taxes on American Politics*, New York 1991, 182 and passim. *The American Prospect: A Journal for the Liberal Imagination* has been a leading force in policy argument for a strategy like that of the Edsalls.

4. Gates, 'Apartheid', 61.

5. Ellison, *Shadow and Act*, 303.

6. Micaela di Leonardo, 'Boyz on the Hood', *Nation*, 17/24 August 1992, 182.

7. Adolph Reed, Jr, 'The Race/Class Conundrum', *Nation*, 23 November 1992, 636; Reed, 'The "Underclass" as Myth and Symbol', *Radical America* (January 1992); Jennings, ed., *Race, Politics and Economic Development: Community Perspectives*, London 1992.

8. Ellison, *Shadow and Act*, 315-16. Emphasis original.

9. Ellison, *Shadow and Act*, 132.

10. James Baldwin, *The Fire Next Time*, New York 1964, 110.

11. Ellison, *Shadow and Act*, 317.

10

Gaining a Hearing for
Black–White Unity: Covington Hall
and the Complexities of Race,
Gender and Class

On a 1913 organizing campaign in DeRidder, Louisiana, Ed Lehman faced the familiar problem of a white worker who refused to join the union because 'it took in niggers'. In a masterful example of soapbox oratory, Lehman drew the racist worker into an exchange which entertained the assembled crowd. 'There is not a nigger in the union', Lehman said in the quiet voice which street speakers often used early in their performances to ward off hoarseness and to encourage listeners to move forward and pay close attention. 'The hell there ain't', came the reply. 'Not one', Lehman insisted. 'Well, what in the hell is Gaines, if he ain't a nigger?' asked the racist, seeking to clinch the argument by referring to a Black member of the Industrial Workers of World (IWW), one whose release on a bombing charge growing out of the Merryville lumber strike. 'Yes', Lehman granted, 'he is black as the ace of spades, but he isn't a nigger.' Surely the racist's voice was raised by this point: 'What the devil is he then?' It was just the question Lehman wanted and he shot back, 'He is a man, a union man, an IWW – a MAN! ... and he has proven it by his action, [which is] more than you have done in all your boss-sucking life.' Lehman finished his transformation of the discussion from racial division to class and gender unity by observing, 'There are white *men*, Negro *men* and Mexican *men* in this union, but no niggers, greasers or white trash.'[1]

We know about this splendid exchange because of the writings of Covington Hall, the poet, humorist and fellow worker with Lehman in the organization of the IWW-affiliated Brotherhood of Timber Workers (BTW) in Louisiana and Texas. Hall recorded Lehman's exploits in an especially vivid section of 'Labor Struggles in the Deep South', his superb unpublished work of history and reminiscence. He credited Lehman with a breakthrough in organizing. 'The assertion that all real men were for the union', he wrote, 'spread all over the lumber country.' That the 'rank and file' adopted Lehman's language and logic 'had a tremendous effect in countering the bosses' efforts to stir up race prejudice' in a Louisiana industry in which, according to the 1910 census, 49.2 percent of timber workers and 64 percent of saw- and planing-mill laborers were African Americans.[2]

If Lehman pioneered in the formulation of the argument that 'no niggers but only men' were found in radical unions, Hall was its popularizer. Editing *The Lumberjack* (later *Voice of the People*) in 1913 and 1914 as the integrated BTW reached its height of 20,000 members, he immediately took up Lehman's language. As early as 6 March 1913 he offered the following 'definitions' in *The Lumberjack*: 'Negro: A MAN, a UNION MAN, an I.W.W. Nigger: A dirty scab, a company sucker.'[3] Over the next year Hall's papers drove the same point home consistently with even cartoons enjoining, 'Let all white MEN and Negro MEN get on the same side of this rotten log.'[4]

Indeed, although this article concentrates on the years of 1913 and 1914 in Louisiana and East Texas, Hall may have carried Lehman's words across decades and state lines. The Southern Tenant Farmers Union (STFU) repopularized the phrasing of Lehman in answering racists during interracial organizing in Arkansas and Missouri in the 1930s, echoing him almost verbatim, minus the mention of the IWW, of course. The reminiscences of H. L. Mitchell, a leader and historian of the STFU, suggest that the formulation had the same galvanizing impact on Black–white unity in Arkansas and Missouri as Hall claimed for it in Louisiana and Texas. It is of course possible that Lehman's example survived in popular memory or that an STFUer hit upon the same logic and wording as Lehman independently. However, it is worth noting that Hall was teaching at Arkansas' leftwing Commonwealth College in the 1930s and that both Hall and John D. Rust, his former associate at Louisiana's New Llano cooperative experiment, were gurus to younger STFU activists. Hall 'could really make things clear', Mitchell recalled in a 1988 interview in which he mused that Hall's 'fascinating' and didactic stories were much like the ones he himself had taken to telling young people in older age. Whether one such story told by Hall to STFUers (or by Hall to Rust to STFUers) concerned Ed Lehman's breakthrough at DeRidder must remain a matter of speculation.[5] In any case, both the great early-twentieth-century Southern experiments in Black–white labor unity, those of the IWW/BTW and the STFU, justified their egalitarianism in the same way. Lehman's words, popularized by Hall, therefore echo over the decades and through the writings of historians searching for a usable Southern past.[6]

Hall's seemingly modern (or perhaps postmodern) appreciation of the

power of language typified early IWW writing. The union's press regularly featured poems, puns, neologisms and pointed redefinitions of important terms. From reprints of Jack London's rollicking essay in
definition, 'What Is a Scab?' to small, bottom-of-the-column fillers pro-
posing a new meaning for 'boss' or 'wage slave', the IWW papers connected the task of remaking the world with that of redefining it and made
workers talk and hear differently. When T-Bone Slim, surely the IWW's
and perhaps the nation's most linguistically playful writer, held, 'Wher-
ever you find injustice, the proper form of politeness is attack', or when
Joe Hill dubbed the Salvation Army the Starvation Army, they aimed to
shake established certainties even at the level of language. For T-Bone
Slim, this activity mattered even if the words involved had no immediate
'political' import. 'Juice', he wrote, 'is stranger than friction.'[7] Leading
students of American speech, from H. L. Mencken to Peter Tamony to
Archie Green, have therefore concentrated on the IWW.[8] 'Wobblies' took
their words seriously in part because they had time to do so. Often highly
educated, autodidactically and by each other, they talked for long
stretches in the bunkhouses of mining and lumber camps, on the job, in
boxcars carrying hoboes, and in circles surrounding the kettles and coffee
pots of soup kitchens and union halls. Such environments produced a
number of worker-intellectuals who connected the search for a new society with new ways of naming the old.[9]

Hall displayed a special concern with the use and redefinition of words
and with the ways white Southern workers spoke and heard. As the veteran anarchist Esther Dolgoff put it in her reminiscences, Hall 'spoke the
Southern workers' language, their idioms, their accent, their colloquial-
isms.' His substantial efforts as an organizer and as perhaps the most pro-
lific labor poet of his time, not to mention his work as an insurance
salesman, doubtless honed this attention to language.[10] His emphasis on
developing a 'republic of the imagination' led to the embellishment of
what he heard. Nonetheless, at least in comparison with T-Bone Slim,
Hall was not wildly playful in his use of language. He tended not so much
to invent new words as to pick up, popularize and recast in purposeful
ways existing Southern expressions. His papers featured not only steady
use of Lehman's new language of race and labor, but also redefinitions of
'rebels', 'slaves', 'Mothers of Dixie' and even 'clansmen'.[11]

Hall's politically charged recasting of language raises a serious question as to whether his (and Lehman's) new and improved Southern discourse represented an indigenous response to white Southern experiences
or merely an opportunistic playing with words by radicals who did not in
fact share the values of white workers in the region. A letter from the
IWW organizer and historian Fred W. Thompson provides an apt point
of entry into this question. Thompson, a friend of Hall's from the time

both taught at Minnesota's Work People's College during the Great Depression, objected to the inadequate treatment of Hall's Southern identity in one of my early essays on Hall's poetry. The essay viewed Hall's Southernness as the product of attempts to preserve a sense of personal heritage, but Thompson saw it shaped at least as much by virtue of its being a tool in mobilizing Southern workers:

> He was a Southerner and had no intention of ... apologizing for it; his sense of self-respect, and respect for his people and roots, made him boast his Southernness, just as 'black is beautiful' did for others later. He integrated this view with the populist perception that Wall Street was milking the South and West and with the obvious union practicality of uniting black and white against the employer. His ... audience consisted of fellow Southerners, whose prejudices he could best combat by advising them not to fall for the game of ... Northern capitalists.[12]

The virtue of Thompson's assessment is that it allows that Hall *both* acted out of a genuine commitment to white Southern values and traditions *and* sought in every possible way to turn those values and traditions to his own purposes. Indeed had Hall's new language been conceived in cynicism, it is most doubtful that it could have achieved the real, if limited, popular resonance it enjoyed.[13]

Only by seeing Hall as writing both within and against the Southern grain can we come to grips with the paradox which runs through his, and Lehman's, innovations in Southern language. On the one hand, Hall's mission was to demystify Dixie by showing it as a class society. But on the other hand, every attempt to do so invoked categories redolent of race, gender and regional identities: 'nigger scabs', 'rebel women', 'white men', 'company suckers', 'real men', 'white trash' and so on. Thus even the most popular attempt at a materialist language describing the Southern social structure could not get along without race and gender as pivotal social categories.

Proposals to do so were present, at least where race was concerned, but they found few takers. Phineas Eastman, another Wobbly leader of the Southern lumber organizing drive, urged workers in 1912 'to please stop calling the colored man "Nigger" – the tone some use is an insult, much less the word. Call him Negro if you must refer to his race, but "fellow worker" is the only form of salutation a rebel should use.' However, the Lehman/Hall approach, which sought to redefine existing Southern words like 'nigger' in terms of manliness, rather than to replace such words, persisted during the Lumber Wars to an extent that Eastman's more purely class-based discourse could not.[14]

Some modern readers will prefer Eastman's logic as better grounded in morality and/or surer about the centrality of class. Others will contrast the failure of Eastman's language to catch on with the brief success of Hall's in literally 'gaining a hearing' from white Southern male workers. The latter readers may praise Hall for a pragmatic populism that did not attempt to insist on a pure, essentialist class consciousness but instead built upon the existing consciousness of flesh-and-blood workers. Some may even see him as almost a premature poststructuralist radical, fashioning reversals in meaning via skillful reading and turning of symbols.[15] While I greatly admire Hall – he belongs with A. Philip Randolph, Lucy Randolph Mason, Isaac Myers, Nat Turner, Vincent St John and Albert Parsons at the front rank of Southern-born labor leaders – the purpose of this article's close examination and contextualization of his language of race, class and gender is neither to praise nor to condemn. Instead it is to use his proximity to the Southern white, male working class worldview during the period between Reconstruction and World War I to look anew at that worldview as well as at Hall by skipping promisicuously and often from Hall to the broader picture.

Southern values and traditions, along with the South's curious patchwork of occupational color bars and relatively integrated workplaces, opened space in which a 'son of Dixie' like Hall could attempt to fashion a radical new manly language of race designed to promote class unity. But the 'shell of the old society' in which Hall and other labor radicals attempted to build the new one, had its distinct chambers of gender and race, as well as of class. These imposed limits on the imagination of even a Covington Hall. If, as one historian has argued, the BTW leadership learned to struggle 'inside the racist vocabulary' of the region, it was not easy to get back out especially when issues of opening new job categories to Black workers arose. Escape by way of a heightened emphasis on gender carried its own problems. Ultimately there was no class consciousness, here or elsewhere in the industrializing US, which was not also race and gender consciousness as well. For that reason, this highly experimental essay is an attempt to treat race, class and gender in what Tera Hunter has aptly called their 'simultaneity', although many individual sections lapse into discussion only two of the three factors.[16]

Hall, White Workers and Gender:
The Personal, the Political and the Paternal

Evaluating Hall's central role in popularizing a new language of labor, race and gender among Southern workers is complicated by the fact that, although the region's most famous IWW member, he was not himself working class. At various junctures in his ill-documented life Hall was unemployed, an insurance agent, a lawyer, an editor, a publicist, an organizer, a poet and a professor. Hall sometimes received the improbable title of Reverend when introduced during the Lumber Wars, although his combination of militant free thought and what would now be called liberation theology makes it quite unlikely that he ever had a church. Neither his memoirs nor other sources show Hall as a wage worker for extended periods. Coming from a patrician background, he suffered immiseration and often lived in dire poverty, but he was not proletarianized.[17]

Hall tended to draw his attitudes from two worlds, neither of which he was fully part of. Though without wealth, he grew up within the traditions of the Southern elite, which could at times justify its hesitant racial liberalism on the grounds of a paternal fondness for, and duty towards, Blacks. He was more enduringly conversant with the world of the Southern white working class, which justified its own hesitant challenges to Jim Crow on extremely hard-headed, pragmatic grounds. Although the racial paternalism of the elite marked his poetry, Hall managed to put it aside when he wrote agitational labor journalism. On the other hand, the paternalist gender politics which the elite and white masses of the South shared (though with varying emphases) ran through both Hall's poetry and his prose, and, as this section emphasizes, undergirded Hall's attempts to create a language and a practice of biracial class unity.[18]

Hall's youth ensured a sharp concern for paternal values. Born in Woodville, Mississippi in 1871, Hall descended on both sides from prominent planter families. His father, a Presbyterian minister, soon separated from his mother, with the result that Hall grew up living with a half-uncle, Ami Woods, in the Bayou Terrebonne in the Louisiana Sugar Bowl region. After the death of the treasured Ami – Hall would sign many of his poems Covami – he watched as an adolescent when the Knights of Labor mounted a stirring integrated strike in the sugar industry. As the strike unravelled, some white Knights joined with a local militia unit which, at Thibodeaux, invaded churches and other buildings in which evicted Black strikers had massed. Perhaps thirty African Americans were massacred. Hall's memoirs credited estimates as high as 600 dead and noted that Thibodeaux was by no means the only scene of carnage. The memoir clearly connected this tragedy with the personal losses Hall experienced at about the same time, noting its proximity to the death of Ami Woods and its role in leading to the loss of the Woods family plantation, Rural Retreat, in a foreclosure and sheriff's auction in 1891. The latter link rested on the fact that Rodney Woods, an uncle of Hall's who operated the plantation, had given in to the sugar strikers' demand in order to preserve his cane crop. He thereby compounded the family's social and economic problems by securing a reputation as 'disloyal to his class'.[19]

Thus Hall lost the opportunity to apply the paternalist values with which he had been raised at just the time when he 'became a man'. Hall's best poem, 'Us the Hoboes and Dreamers', called on the Southern masses to rebel with 'the fierce and frenzied fury of a fatherhood denied'. He had ample reasons to invoke such an image. Of his own family, he wrote 'I have seen my father lying on his death bed like a beast, / In his poverty forsaken, he a Southern soldier-priest.' In his poetry Hall showed great concern with family lines. He was, by Oscar Ameringer's reckoning, the 'handsomest young man' in New Orleans and a formidable rival in court- ing young women. Yet Hall apparently neither married legally nor had children. The loss of Uncle Ami and of Rural Retreat, amidst the class and race war of 1887, denied Hall a 'father' and the opportunity to act in the paternal style of the Southern elite. His poetry and his activities as a leader of the Sons of the Confederacy (the first word of which surely explains his passion for the organization as much as the last), hankered for what might have been, personally and politically.[20]

This hankering bonded Hall to recently proletarianized male workers in and beyond the Piney Woods. Often reared in patriarchial farm or artisan households, such workers faced difficulty in securing the resources necessary to raise a family and often spent lengthy periods as migrant, single workers. When they did marry, they generally remained wagework- ers who could not appeal, as their fathers did, to male status as unbossed producers to ground their authority at home. Amidst this crisis in mascu- linity, the male role as a 'breadwinner' whose wages protected his family received greater emphasis within the working class. Unions, as Joy Parr's superb study of Canadian furniture workers suggests, both reflected and forwarded this change, which dramatically 'shift[ed] the balance among the roles by which [male] workers could define their worth as men to- wards providing and away from producing'. Hall's exhortation to 'BE A MAN!' therefore implied not just union militancy but a union militancy which, as a BTW leaflet put it, made Wobblies able to earn a 'family wage' and 'to keep their old mothers, their wives and their babies from hunger.' Indeed, working class manhood was a particularly supercharged topic in the South generally and in Louisiana particularly, as significant numbers of Black workers were migrants, as a fair share of white workers in particular still had (or had very recently lost) tenuous claim on nearby farms and a more traditional patriarchal existence, as white men dealt with the heritage of Civil War defeat, and as Black men (and a considerable percentage of whites) lost the citizenship rights that had given symbol and substance to male power. Hall's poetry and his labor journalism took full advantage of the drama attached to these gender issues, often using the threat that all trees might be felled to stand in for threats to masculinity in the industrializing South.[21]

Racial Paternalism versus Redneck Double Consciousness

Not surprisingly, Hall's poetry also featured a strongly nostalgic racial paternalism, focussing on his Black 'uncles', his 'mammy', and his own (lost) alleged responsibilities for taking care of plantation hands. His racial poems were almost always cloying and poor. If, as a great Black critic put it at the time, dialect poetry suffered from having 'only two stops – pathos and humor', Hall's attempts to write in Black dialect had only the former. The ill-treatment of language in a work like 'Old Ned Am Dyin' may have stemmed in part from the fact that Hall was a monotone and heard Black speech less than well. But what could excuse 'Good Ol' Pete' in which the minstrel-like Slufoot Sam meets Saint Peter and in which dialect consists of spelling 'from' as 'frum' and rendering 'likewise' as 'lakwuz'? Certainly the jittery postscript that 'all the "Slufoot Sams" ... are not black and yellow skinned. Quite a few are "White Supremacy Democrats"', mitigates little when the stereotypical and faithless rendering of Black speech is compared to Hall's practice of having Southern whites almost always speak in standard English.[22]

In Hall's most embarrassing racial verse condescending dialect was not the problem, but paternalist sentiments were. Revealingly titled, 'My Negro Mammy's Son', it includes

> I don't want to see him crushed, my dear old Mammy's son,
> The boy I played with long ago, whose 'chinas' [marbles] I often won,
> Who stood with me in many fights in old plantation days,
> Whose heart was true and loyal in a thousand different ways.
> I don't want to see him crushed, his black face scarred with grief.
> His sorrows made unending, or his pleasures few and brief.
> And for his sake an Aryan pleads with Aryans today
> To rise in Aryan manhood and drive the wolves away.

Hall could manage only the lamest defense of this poem when Joseph Ettor objected to it in the IWW journal *Solidarity* with the criticism that 'a sentimental projection of the negro is not revolutionary; it is condescension.'[23]

In his agitational journalism Hall gave full play to more or less conventional, paternal views on gender and portrayed many of his ideas in terms of inspirations derived from the 'rebel fathers' and 'granddads'.[24] However, in the practical world of revolutionary labor organization there was simply no place for the kind of racial paternalism that had its appeals among the elite. Hall's journalistic arguments for white workers cooperating with Black workers came to be as hardheaded and unsentimental as his racial poetry was saccharine. The organizing tasks he faced, and the constituency he courted, guaranteed as much.

Race relations at the bottom of postbellum Southern society generated little sentimentality but some variety. While the biracial labor unity in lumbering and longshore in Louisiana stuck out as exceptional within a generally bleak early-twentieth-century picture, such cooperation was part of a substantial tradition going back to Reconstruction. As Harold Baron has written, 'It was actually more common in the South than in the North for black workers to hold a position so strong in particular industries that unions had to take them into account.' Because of demography and perhaps because of the precocity of the North in developing a specifically 'white workerist' consciousness, Dixie hosted most American experiments in biracial unionism before 1919. The Knights of Labor, the organization of the New Orleans waterfront, coal-mining unionism in Alabama and the BTW were the most spectacular such experiments. More modest local cooperation and unity in individual trades added to a durable tradition which, in some areas, survived the lowest points in Southern race relations.[25] If we count, as some historians have, Populism as a 'labor' mobilization, Black–white working class unity attracted Southerners by the hundreds, rather than tens, of thousands.[26]

On the other hand, many of the scores of US 'hate strikes' against employing Black workers between 1865 and 1914 also occurred in the South and experiments in biracialism were often contradictory and fragile. For example, although the National Labor Union (NLU) and its Southern affiliates began Reconstruction-era efforts at joint work with the Colored National Labor Union (CNLU), Baltimore's white waterfront workers united across lines of craft to push Black ship caulkers, whom CNLU leader Isaac Myers had helped to organize, out of their jobs. NLU biracialism ran a very short course and, near its demise, the union entertained proposals to deport Blacks from the Southern 'white rights' agitator, Hinton Rowan Helper.[27] Similarly the sad decline of the Knights of Labor saw that union, which had attracted such loyal support from Black Southern members, resolve in favor of emigration of African Americans as a solution to white workers' problems.[28] Even the remarkable biracial cooperation on the New Orleans waterfront suffered through a terrible hiatus in the 1890s. That city's general strike in 1892 marked what Eric Arnesen has called 'the climax ... of Gilded Age solidarity'. Less than two years later, white union men used both the strike and the riot to try to drive Black crewmen and longshoremen from the docks.[29]

While economic cycles, racist initiatives by white supremacy Democrats and successes of employers in exacerbating racial divisions help to account for such crazy-quilt patterns of biracialism and hate, it is important to emphasize that white Southern workers were not just manipulated into racism. Their consciousness was a double one that constantly pulled them towards urgent insistence on their whiteness and toward a questioning of whether their class grievances did not outweigh their racial privileges. The use of the word *redneck* tells much about this double consciousness. By 1900, *red-neck* had come into use as 'a name applied by the better class of people to the poorer [white] inhabitants of the rural districts of the South'. The *Oxford English Dictionary's* 1989 characterization of the word as 'originally, and still often, derogatory' captures the tone with which elite whites used the word but misses the extent to which 'rednecks' created their own identities. Southern journalists Billy Bowles and Remer Tyson trace *redneck* to the style of headgear adopted by poor whites in the wake of the emancipation of the slaves. Noting that ex-slaves wore broad-brimmed straw hats when working outdoors, such rural whites opted for narrow-brimmed wool headgear in the fields to set themselves apart. The Southern sun ensured red necks for working whites who made such a choice.[30]

But if red necks and wool hats signalled important changes in white racial formation in the South, they also heralded critical developments in class feeling. The 'wool-hat boys' (whose headwear hearkened back to that identified with Jacksonian Democrats) vigorously participated in populist politics, underpinning, for example, the successes of Georgia's Tom Watson, who vigorously championed the unity of 'black sheep' and 'white sheep' against the 'fleecers' of the world before turning to pitting the white poor against Blacks. *Redneck* itself at times expressed a fragile impetus toward class feeling across racial lines. A 1935 article in *American Speech* defined the term as 'any honest working man' but, more specifically 'one who belongs to a labor union or sympathizes with union men in a strike'. The latter meaning specifically reflected the practice of union miners who tied red bandannas over their necks to develop a nonracial 'redneck' identity and who sang during strikes, 'Red Necks, keep them scabs away'. So strong was the association of labor radicalism with the term that radical, often Communist, National Miners Union agitators in Appalachia in the early years of the Great Depression were slurred as 'rednecks', with the term roughly connoting 'Bolshevism'. The consciousness of the redneck thus took shape both against images of the 'straw hat' Black and of the 'silk hat' rich.[31]

That there is such a stark difference in symbolism between the 'wool-hat' redneck and the red bandanna one does not mean that the individual white worker irrevocably chose to identify with one image or the other. The 'wool-hat boy', in that he chose hot and not very protective headgear to prove himself different from Blacks, might serve as a textbook case of self-defeating white working class racism. The nonracial red bandanna redneck symbolizes a quite different logic. However, as the about-face of Tom Watson and his followers on race illustrates, white consciousness of race and class was both fluid and contradictory. On the one hand, being white did offer benefits in politics, in education, on the job and even in the ability to get into a park or theater. The performance of 'nigger work' and the consequent association (real or symbolic) with African Americans opened whites to harder driving, increased danger and stepped-up economic exploitation.[32] Moreover, as Patrick Huber has shown, the use of such terms as *redneck* and *hillbilly* by elite Southerners placed the very 'whiteness' of poor whites at issue, with elite spokepersons often referring to these groups as genetically inferior and as of a different color. In Hall's Louisiana, the question of whether Italian Americans, slow learners of Jim Crow, were white was sharply contested in the 1890s, as were at times the positions of 'coonass' Cajuns and the fine, fluctuating line between white and black Creoles. In the last of these cases, as Virginia Domínguez's perceptive *White by Definition* demonstrates, acceptance of 'colored jobs' served to heighten the fear of being cast(e) as nonwhite. Most tellingly, the very term *redbones*, used to describe many of the poor in the piney woods Louisiana timber region, bespoke the ways in which racial classification was the product of social struggle. On the one hand, the word applied to 'small groups' of isolated folk whose ancestry was said to be traced to the early presence, and mixture, of Indians, white fugitives and escaped slaves in the region. On the other hand, it was also more broadly applied to many who considered themselves 'white' and who considered *redbones* to be a 'fighting word'.[33]

At the same time, the common experiences of poor Black and white workers and farmers with credit merchants and employers, with poverty and slights, and, after 1890, with political disfranchisement, could cheapen the wages of whiteness and send white workers to look for their red bandannas. The 'wool-hat boy' could mock the way that elite Democrats ruled by manipulating white supremacy, as the *People's Party Paper* did in 1892:

The argument against the independent political movement in the South may be boiled down into one word – NIGGER!
Fatal word!
Why, for thirty years before our war, did the North and South hate each other?
NIGGER.
What brought disunion and war?
NIGGER.
With what did Abraham Lincoln break the backbone of the Confederacy?
NIGGER.
What impeded reconstruction?
NIGGER.
How did the Republicans rule the South for years after Appomatox?
NIGGER.

What has kept the South in a cast iron straight jacket?
NIGGER.
What will be the slogan of our old politicians until Gabriel calls them home?
NIGGER.

Hall's task was to make sure that his constituency saw such a passage in terms of class justice and did not, like the wool-hat redneck, take its moral to be that the problems of poor whites could only be addressed when Blacks were removed from the world of politics, or of work.[34]

Surely those whites with an ongoing experience working alongside large numbers of African Americans were most likely to resist seeing their interests undermined by racial divisions. That mining, a highly integrated occupation, generated the red bandanna as a nonracial symbol is no accident. Nor is it odd that the white workers of textile mill villages, protected in their poverty by color bars and often, as W. J. Cash observed, unfamiliar with Blacks, took particularly quick and sharp offense when middle-class reformers seemed to treat 'mill people' as a separate, less-than-white caste.[35] But even in biracial workplaces there were constant temptations to attempt to capitalize on whiteness and to shed the stigma of 'nigger work', whether by erecting full color bars, by creating a structure of white and 'nigger' jobs or simply by participating in racial abuse.[36]

At the turn of the century and beyond, *boss* remained so much a distinctively American English term that Sir Arthur Conan Doyle once referred to its use in a letter from Jack the Ripper as evidence that England's most famous mass murderer had spent time in the US. Independent-minded, self-consciously manly and often newly proletarianized, Southern white male workers despised the idea of being 'bossed'. However, after Reconstruction 'boss' also became a term by which virtually all Southern white men were called by virtually all Blacks. Although initially Blacks used 'boss' somewhat assertively, to avoid saying 'master', the word became a badge of humiliation for freedpeople and of self-satisfaction for poor whites.[37] Lillian Smith's brilliant *Killers of the Dream* argues intriguingly that the opportunities for poor white men in the South to be race and gender 'bosses' sealed the bargain that kept them subservient to patrician whites. However, it is worth reemphasizing that among white workers, such bossing could appear as paternalist, protective and benign only where gender, and not race, was concerned.[38] Moreover, since the very bargain that made poor whites 'bosses' also left them anxious regarding 'enslavement' and emasculation, their consciousness remained a contradictory and (at least) double one. Covington Hall and others could capitalize on such fears as they encouraged white workers to confront their bosses. They could denounce the twinned evils of 'wage slavery' and emasculation with considerable effect. What they could not do was to deny the importance of race or to sentimentalize racial divisions and hope to unionize white Southern males.

Stomach Equality and Its Context

Covington Hall and the BTW reflected, and faced, the double consciousness of poor whites in Louisiana and East Texas. Hall enjoyed particular success in organizing among the white farmers and sons of farmers from Louisiana's Winn Parish, home to both Huey Long Senior and Junior and to strong Populist and Socialist movements. In a tantalizing unfinished section of his memoirs, the lineage-minded Hall contended that 'Huey Long [Junior]'s Men [were] the sons and successors of the veterans of the Louisiana Lumber Wars'. Long Sr had great success in mobilizing Democratic voters at the time of the BTW's organization. He did so through remarkably class-conscious appeals. 'There wants to be a revolution. [I've] seen this domination of capital, seen it for seventy years. What do these rich folks care for the poor man?' he thundered in a jeremiad often quoted by those emphasizing the radical populism of the Long family. Less often quoted is the policy goal that followed in his remarks: '[to] get the niggers off our necks'.[39] Although poor rural whites in the timber region were as likely to be called 'redbones' as 'rednecks' and although Italian BTW members were the only ones who appear to have used red bandannas as symbols of labor unity, Hall's constituents shared the double consciousness of the 'wool-hat boys' throughout the South.[40]

In such a situation, Hall wrote, the BTW acted pragmatically and never 'overcame race prejudice [but] did smother it and prevent ... opponents from using it'.[41] Although he often pointed to the need for radical labor to provide a vision, a 'dream' or a 'republic of the imagination', Hall and his union emphasized only the immediate self-interest of white workers in a careful, bread-and-butter-based strategy to enroll whites in the biracial BTW. That strategy literally turned on winning men's hearts through their stomachs and the stomachs of their family members.

The best example of the BTW's argument for biracialism came in a short play, signed by 'Skag', in an early issue of *The Lumberjack*. Subtitled 'Union Men – Bill Wouldn't Organize the Negro Until – ' this highly didactic drama spelled out how the savvy white worker Tom won the more backward Bill to biracialism through a series of materialist lessons. 'I got seven members [to join the BTW] and could have got more if I had taken the "niggers" that wanted to join', Bill begins. Tom at once implicitly challenges Bill's language, referring to Blacks supporting the union as 'Negroes' – with that term being capitalized, as was done in neither the mainstream nor the labor press at the time. Slowly – the dialogue runs to nearly 150 lines of tiny type – Tom coaxes Bill into acknowledging that the Negro is 'a worker', who therefore potentially has 'power'. When Tom asks, 'Where would you sooner have that power, with us or against us?' Bill learns a little more, though he still thinks 'harmony' is better served by segregated locals. Tom's attempt to take Bill over this hurdle by arguing that strike strategy and union democracy cannot survive such separation meets with a serious objection when Bill asks with regard to mixed meetings, 'Wouldn't that be social equality?' 'No', Tom replies, clinching the argument, 'that would be "stomach equality".' Bill's conversion is complete. He announces that 'all of us have to come together the same way as we work' before running off to enroll 'colored fellow workers' into the BTW. Bill even agrees that it might be necessary to defy Jim Crow laws on behalf of 'stomach equality', if such laws interfere with bi-racial union meetings. Never in the whole catechismic exchange does Tom directly dispute Bill's views on white supremacy. Instead he 'smothers' Bill's racism on practical grounds.[42]

Tom and Bill reprised much of the BTW's celebrated 1912 convention. IWW leaders Hall and Big Bill Haywood persuaded white delegates at that convention to break from the union's segregated past and to hold biracial meetings, albeit with Blacks on one side of the hall and whites on the other. Hall later recalled that he and Haywood had insisted, 'If any arrests are made, all or none of us will go to jail, white and colored together'. The authorities, who had threatened to use Jim Crow laws to prevent mixed union meetings, backed down and apparently accepted Hall's argument that the law required only separation within the meeting place. Bill's – that is, Haywood's – transformation of the BTW set the stage for Tom's transformation of Bill. In both cases the logic was hard-headed. 'You cannot possibly do business this way', Haywood emphasized. Other BTW leaders extended the argument, pointing out that alarmist talk of 'social equality' was consciously spread by capitalists who opposed the union and who sought to sow disunity and to fool white men into valuing the hollow 'privilege' of lynching 'damnniggers' to obscure class and gender issues among whites by hiding the fact that capital worked white 'women and children to death'.[43]

Such emphasis on practical appeals to white workers and the refusal to be drawn into seemingly diversionary battles for social and political equality did not so much break new ground as they typified the most egalitarian ways in which the hesitant labor movement, North and South, conceptualized the inconsistently made case for Black–white unity from the Civil War through World War I. Even the rare labor paper that did support full equality for African Americans, as did the *Boston Daily Evening Voice* during Reconstruction, necessarily cast its appeals in terms of the interests of its largely white readership, asking, 'How many kicks ... will be required to give [workingmen] the hint that colored labor ... is henceforth in competition with the white; and if the white will not lift the colored up, the colored will drag the white down?' National Labor Union leader William Sylvis, who opposed 'social equality' vehemently and on highly gendered grounds (writing of his disdain for whites whose daughters 'entertain young negro gentlemen') was more stark in his evocation of white workers' economic self-interest as the basis of biracial trade union unity: 'The time will come when the negro will take possession of the shops if we have not taken possession of the negro.'[44] The Knights of Labor, a rare trade union with a massive Black membership during part of this period, often organized racially segregated 'assemblies' in the South and paid a considerable price in white membership when it did not. When, during its 1886 convention in Richmond, some Knights raised questions as to the propriety of social segregation, the storm was fierce and the retreat clear. Grand Master Workman Terence V. Powderly wrote to the Richmond *Dispatch*, promising that the Knights had 'no wish to interfere with the social relations which exist between the races of the South', that there 'need be no further cause for alarm' and that 'the colored representatives of this convention will not intrude where they are not wanted.'[45]

The AFL's ambivalence on racial equality shows most clearly in its important 1901 policy statement on the issue. In it, Samuel Gompers reaffirmed the federation's paper commitment to organizing without regard to race or color but hastened to add that this did not mean 'that the social barriers which exist between the whites and blacks could or should be obliterated.' Segregation, Gompers held, was a problem that 'the Southland' deserved to be able to consider 'without the interference ... of meddlers from the outside.'[46] When the *Labor Advocate*, in the AFL's Birmingham stronghold of biracial unionism, did launch an 'Obliterate the Color Line' campaign, it could be certain of being understood by regular readers to mean within the union only. And even Birmingham came to have a segregated city central labor body and few integrated locals. While it was possible at times to extend the field of 'labor' matters in which biracialism was permissible to include a parade, AFL unions seldom challenged Jim Crow outside the workplace and often did not do so within it. The AFL consistently tolerated color bars within its affiliates. As late as 1898, its *American Federationist* touted mass colonization of African Americans as a strategy to improve the lot of white workers. Some of its member unions did enroll significant numbers of Black workers, especially in mining, longshore and, to a lesser extent, tobacco processing. However, even these unions were capable of capitulating to, and pressing for, racial exclusion.[47]

AFL officials typically organized Blacks apologetically. That 'white and black workers are compelled to work side by side' necessitated biracial organizing, according to Gompers, who thereby placed the onus of race-mixing on the employer. John Mitchell, president of the United Mine Workers (UMW), confessed a personal belief that Blacks were morally inferior and depressed living standards, though he added that the UMW constitution forbade discrimination. When Atlanta's Carpenters and Joiners District Council president supported organizing of Blacks to prevent competition from lowering wage rates, he began his economic argument with, 'Let us lay aside all our prejudice. (I have as much as any Southern-born white man.)'[48] Chris Scully, a Hall associate who advocated biracial cooperation from his position as head of a white longshoremen's union in New Orleans, provided a classic expression of this forced-into-accepting-Blacks stance in replying to a false 1907 charge by a state senator that the unions advocated 'social equality':

> ... I wasn't always a nigger-lover. ... You made me work with niggers, eat with niggers, sleep with niggers, drink out of the same water bucket with niggers, and finally got me to the place where if one of them comes to me and blubbers something about more pay, I say, 'Come on, nigger, let's go after the white bastards.'[49]

The railway brotherhoods at best adopted this shamefaced biracialism. The editor of *Railroad Trainmen's Journal* in 1899 justified taking in Black members with the plea, 'It is humiliating, no one will take kindly to it ... but unless the negro is raised, the white man will have to come down.' Most skilled railway brotherhood members continued to resist such 'humiliation' in the name of masculinity, class and race, engaging in strikes and in terror to displace Black workers. When Georgia's railroad firemen engaged in a 1909 hate strike, they argued that Blacks had no right to skilled jobs in a 'white man's country' and that an integrated labor force amounted to 'social equality'.[50] None of this kept Gompers from blaming Black workers for being 'cheap men' or from threatening that if Blacks kept 'tearing down what the white man has built. ... Caucasian civilization will serve notice that its uplifting process is not to be interfered with in any way.'[51]

The countenancing of compromise with Jim Crow, though destructive in the long run, did not require hypocrisy or bad faith. 'Social equality' was not a live political possibility in the South, but it was a most useful stick with which antiunion forces could, partly be invoking gender fears, beat down labor. For this reason and others, Black unionists themselves often disavowed any intention to use the labor movement to address racial inequalities outside the workplace. Moreover, they took pride at times in all-Black locals as institutions strengthening the African American community. Prior to the historic 1912 decision of the BTW to integrate, the central demand of African Americans in the union was for a *separate* Black executive board to ensure that the existing all-white board not control the dues of African Americans. Even after 1912 Blacks often opted for separate locals in the BTW, whether out of preference, pressure from sheriffs enforcing Jim Crow laws or both. To argue that unions should go out of their way to raise the issue of racial equality would still seem an adventurist, exotic position as late as 1929, when the Communist-led textile workers union at Gastonia did so during a bitter strike, provoking strong public doubts among its own organizers as to the wisdom of exposing tender shoots of union growth to the icy outrage provoked by questioning of segregation.[52] In 1946, the fearless leftwing white Southern journalist Stetson Kennedy wrote that neither race could be helped by a union that 'went so far and so fast in the field of race relations' as to jeopardize its own existence.[53] Put in those terms, slow progress to 'stomach equality' represented a wise course and a considerable achievement.

The work of the Socialist Party (SP) in the South and nationally reflected the same sense that given the necessity to appeal to white workers' self-interest and given the surpassing importance of class, there was little room for specifically antiracist initiatives on the part of a workers' movement. In a mild form, such as Eugene V. Debs's 1903 statement that the Socialists 'have nothing special to offer the negro', such a stance implied that Blacks suffered oppression, and should seek redress, only as workers. But Socialist pragmatism in the South often led further, to a positive endorsement of the color line.[54] In some industries Black workers were a force to be reckoned with, pushing white unionists toward biracial organizing. But the SP functioned as an electoral party in a South where Blacks could almost never vote. Short of undertaking a campaign for reenfranchisement, the SP was left appealing for white votes by making certain that its advocacy of the downtrodden was not mistaken for an appeal for racial justice. With Hall as an early leader, the Louisiana SP insisted on 'the separation of the black and white races' so loudly that the national party delayed approving its charter. The 'Negro Clause' supporting Jim Crow was eventually dropped in Louisiana, and the state and national parties lived harmoniously with the *de facto* segregation into separate locals of the few Black Socialists enrolled.[55] At the height of the Lumber War in 1913, only South Carolina's SP openly banned African American membership, but Florida, Georgia and Mississippi had completely segregated parties. Arkansas had recruited no Black members, and Maryland and Tennessee but a few. Only parts of Texas and the border states of Kentucky and Oklahoma had substantial, racially mixed Socialist organizations. In Texas, Hall's sister paper, *The Rebel*, publicized the Texas SP's demands for an end to the poll tax, but its editor, Tom Hickey, specifically disavowed 'social equality' and refused to recruit Blacks to the SP, on the grounds that they could not vote.[56]

Hall was by 1913 far too much a syndicalist to more than episodically support the electoral solutions offered by the SP. He, and the BTW, did have excellent relations with the SP leaders around the *Appeal to Reason* newspaper in St Louis, however. The *Appeal* featured lively and sympathetic reports on the BTW alongside commentary on race by its editor, Kate Richards O'Hare. O'Hare carried to extremes the argument of many racist Socialists that the new society could perfect segregation. She argued that a Socialist America would solve 'the race question' with a policy of 'Segregation' that isolated African Americans on reservations. Her 1912 pamphlet '"Nigger" Equality' proposed a temporary, strategic alliance with Black workers, but it left no doubt that the 'nigger [is] getting the best of it all around in the South' and that whites needed to defend their racial sensibilities as well as their class *and gender* interests:

> Where is the Jim Crow law for the factory, workshop, mines or cotton field? A negro can't ride in a white street car in Memphis, but I saw a hundred men digging in a sewer ditch. Half of them were blacks and half white Democrats; there was no Jim Crow law there. ... When the water boy came along with the water pail and one dipper, a 'nigger' took a drink and then a white man ... and not a politician shouted 'nigger equality'. In the laundries of that aristocratic southern city the daughters of white Democrats work side by side with big, black negro men; in the cotton mills, the white children compete with negro children. In the cotton fields the white daughters of white voters drag the cotton sacks down the cotton row next to 'nigger bucks'.[57]

Against such a backdrop, we can appreciate why historians have stressed the exemplary egalitarianism of the BTW. It therefore bears emphasizing that what is being discussed here is not the cynical, 'incorrect', or immoral racial strategy of an evil union, but the limitations and costs of a good strategy in a exemplary union. There was clearly substantial antiracist opinion inside the BTW. Hall signed his letters 'Yours for the liberty of man, woman and child, regardless of creed, race or color.'[58] Eastman, surely the most consistently egalitarian white BTW organizer, wrote suggestively of a desire among the white rank-and-file to 'be friendly with their colored fellow workers' but also of that desire constantly being frustrated because the white worker 'feels abashed and is afraid he will be made fun of'.[59] Such a delicate situation required hard judgements. At times, the BTW did 'race-mix' outside the union hall. Hall, for example, joined hundreds of other white workers in union-sponsored, integrated celebration of 'Negro Emancipation Day' in 1912.[60]

Eastman once attempted an end run around Jim Crow by going to eat at a 'nigger restaurant' until a deputy sheriff drove him off at gunpoint. In telling the story of a Black worker thrown from a moving train for walking through a 'white' car in search of a 'colored' one, Eastman circumspectly challenged the caprice and brutality of the color line.[61] Finally, it is worth remarking that the strongly syndicalist ideology of BTW leaders made them regard the workplace and the union as the most important institutions in their present society and as the seedbeds of the new one. Thus in terms of racial equality, nothing was more critical to them than breaching the color line in the 'economic' realm.[62]

Finally and critically the BTW/IWW innovated to strengthen the ground on which arguments for 'stomach equality' could be made through its clear understanding that employers could use racial divisions not only to depress wages, break strikes and hurt unions, but to foster competition that made life worse every day on the job. Within unions with few Black members and few members at integrated workplaces, the call for industrial equality of the races could be quite abstract, as in the National Labor Union's celebrated post–Civil War question to white unionists: 'Shall we make [Black workers] our friends, or shall capital be allowed to turn them as an engine against us?'[63] The IWW in Louisiana, building on experiences in timber camps and on those of New Orleans longshore workers who knew how crews of differing races could literally be pitted against each other in daily competition, were far more concrete regarding what was at stake. The cartoons in Figures 1 and 2 suggest the extent to which race became associated with issues of workers' control. The perception that it was possible for management to exploit the race issue not just on pay day or during strikes, but throughout entire working lives – that, as one Southern tobacco worker put it, supervisors used 'the poor whites to whip the nigger and the nigger to whip the poor whites' – became a key to BTW strategy on race.[64]

Such sophisticated appeals to the class interest of workers took the logic of 'stomach equality' to impressive new levels. Nonetheless the BTW remained a product of American and Southern conditions and continued to think and speak in terms of racial and gender hierarchies. Even at its 1912 convention, the union stopped short on the issue of 'social equalities', a set of questions BTW leaders rarely mentioned without noting that it was the 'capitalist' who threw the races together.[65] Hall's speech to the convention echoed Gompers with regard to the alleged subservience of Black workers, noting that the Civil War had freed the slaves 'but many negroes in the South don't know it yet.' He premised the case for labor revolt, characteristically, on the decline in the position of Southern workers from that held by their 'fathers and grandfathers', despite the fact that the fathers and grandfathers of those on one entire side of the hall

Figure 1. 'Mr Block', from Ernest Riebe, *Mr. Block*, Franklin Rosemont, ed., Chicago 1984 (1913).

Figure 2. 'Same Side of the Log'. From *The Lumberjack*, 27 March 1913.

had overwhelmingly been slaves. He further argued, just as the AFL and openly racist Southern reformers did, that the presence of only white children (and 'no Republican negro children') at work in Southern textile mills was objectionable as example of the special victimization of whites, ignoring the color bar against all Black workers in production jobs in textiles. Finally, he added a racial swipe at white Southern workers, whom he derided to an uneasy audience as the servile 'white Chinese of the world'.[66] His newspaper would similarly appeal to, and at times become ensnared in, the common sense of the South.

'Niggers' and 'White Trash': Race amid Class

Hall was far from alone in the Southern labor movement in using the word *nigger* while trying to organize biracially. The desire to signal that one accepted Black participation but did not necessarily question white supremacy outside the union contributed to such usage. When Tobacco Workers International Union President E. Lewis Evans wrote to a white Durham activist in 1933 that 'the Nigs' had to be brought into the union for strategic reasons, his language reinforced his pledge elsewhere in the letter that biracialism could not mean that his union would ever countenance 'social equality'.[67] Some use of racist language was perhaps habitual. One Texas CIO organizer, according to an associate, 'never could get over saying "nigger"' despite being the 'biggest and best champion of civil rights you ever saw.'[68] Activists who were sure that the movements of classes, not races, would transform the world may have regarded such habits as less than important. When early white Alabama Communists referred to Black party members as 'comrade nigger' it is difficult to know if they did so out of habit, out of a need to reaffirm a sense of whiteness even as they broke racial taboos, out of a misplaced certainty that the power of the first of their words took all sting from the second, or for all of these reasons at once.[69]

Since class (like race) did matter, Black organizers often learned to look past racial epithets without breaking from the union. Richard L. Davis, a Black official on the United Mine Workers' Executive Board, once attempted to defuse the anger of Black unionists after white unionists had undertaken a hate strike rather than work under supervision of a Black worker. Holding that Black miners should stick with the union while resisting racism, Davis explained that when a man 'call[s] me a nigger, I call him a fool, so we keep even on that score.'[70]

Hall and the BTW found a way to retain old racial language and categorizations without exposing their own members to the insult of racial abuse. Like other Southern advocates of biracial unionism, they faced charges of being 'nigger-lovers'. In Alabama in 1903, for example, Black and white organizers of coal miners suffered the humiliation of being made to kiss another man of another race in public in addition to beatings. In Hall's New Orleans, the opponents of longshore unions could brand them as 'amalgamators', referring to the unions' willingness to federate across lines of skill but also playing distinctly on white fears of race-mixing.[71] Hall's papers frequently attacked 'niggers', but at the same time they accorded to 'colored fellow workers' the title of 'Negro'. In so doing, Hall again was giving a progressive twist to that longstanding and far from egalitarian Southern practice on differentiating between respectable and tractable 'Negroes' and disreputable 'niggers'. Moreover, *The Lumberjack* and *Voice of the People* offered a certain degree of equality in epithets. They emphasized that just as there were 'niggers' there also were 'white trash', employing a term that white and African American Southerners themselves often used. That 'black trash' came to take the jobs of the 'pure white trash' non-unionists at non-union mills was, for example, seen as poetic justice.[72] Hall offered the opportunity for workers to retain the idea that race mattered but also to transcend the stigma attached to race.

In effect, what Hall and the BTW did was to try to reverse the employer's use of competition among racial and ethnic groups portrayed in Figures 1 and 2 by encouraging the races to compete in their manly, family-defending labor militancy. Hall called upon, and refined, longstanding arguments for class unity across racial lines when he invoked such logic. As early as 1866, the New Orleans *Tribune*, the first African American daily newspaper in the US, argued, 'Labor equalizes all men; the handicraft of the worker has no color and belongs to no race.' In 1913 *The Lumberjack* maintained, 'Trees don't care who fells them. They make as good lumber when felled by the hand of a negro [or] a Hindoo ... as when coming from the hands of a white, American citizen. ... The interests of all who work in the woods and mills are the same.'[73]

But if labor was raceless for Hall, individuals were not, and their actions proved the mettle of the groups to which they belonged. Hall frequently compared the willingness to struggle of Southern whites with that of other peoples and races. Usually the comparison reflected poorly on the whites, though his expectation was that they ought to have excelled. Hall counted the Chinese Revolution (along with the Mexican) as the international inspiration that helped to set the stage for the Lumber Wars and reported a stirring Chinese workers' 'mutiny' during the Marine Transport Workers (MTW) 1913 campaign against United Fruit Company. Nevertheless he continued to use the Chinese as a touchstone of degradation. His 1914 'CHINESE OUTSCABBED' headline led a story on Swedish and Norwegian seamen who beat out the Chinese as 'the final word on scabbery' and thereby disgraced 'the Caucasian race and more particularly the Scandenavian [sic]'.[74] Hall 'learned to love and respect ... Latin fellow workers' during the MTW agitation in which Spanish and Canary Islands workers showed a persistence which he thought refuted the popular image that they were 'too emotional' and lacked the 'bulldog tenacity of Britishers and Americans'. The militancy of the 'Latins', Hall later recalled, put to shame that of later fruit ship workers 'recruited from the sod-busting farms of ... Mississippi, Alabama and Arkansas.' Other 'Latins' impressed Hall, again specifically in comparison to 'whites', during the Lumber Wars themselves. After Black workers near Carson, Louisiana had been driven off from a BTW street meeting by gunmen and deputy sheriffs, Hall and Lehman attempted to speak, shouting 'Long Live the Brotherhood!' and hearing in reply 'Viva la Brudderhoud!'. The answer had come from Mexican immigrants, members of an ethnic group so solidly pro-BTW that one company roster listed a worker's Mexican-sounding name and added 'presumably union (All Mexs. are)'. That same day thirty Italian workers also took up the 'Viva la Brudderhoud!' cry. However, according to Hall, 'no "freeborn" white Americans' dared answer back to the 'Long Live the Brotherhood!' cry at the time. Later some whites asked for understanding from Hall, saying they could not help their hesitancy. 'Oh, yes, you could', he answered, 'but unfortunately, unlike the Mexicans, Italians and Negroes, the spirit of solidarity was not in you. ... Now you will have to keep on crawling, and eating dirt, as usual.'[75]

Hall's invidious racial and ethnic comparisons sometimes had a distinctly playful quality, as when he discussed 'degenerate college scabs' almost as an ethnic minority. They were probably often reflexive, as when he criticized authorities in DeRidder for wishing to 'overthrow ... liberties respected even by Bushmen and Hottentots'.[76] More often they were pleas carefully designed to shame whites into a pro-union response. And yet Hall was not merely joking, free associating or angling for advantage. On some level he did think that the races were being tested. Reflecting, after more than thirty-five years had passed, on the day no white 'free-borns' would heed the BTW's call, he soberly remembered feeling 'ashamed of the breed to which [he] belonged by birth, which boasts itself "the free and the brave", but hasn't the manhood to take a stand when a battle for "Life, Liberty and the pursuit of Happiness" is on'.[77]

Insight and Blindness: 'Nigger Scabs', Syndicalism and the Klan

Today's readers, happily unused to seeing 'chinks' and 'niggers' denounced in labor publications, might object that Hall had not gone nearly far enough in eliminating white supremacy from his new language of labor and wish that the BTW had taken Phineas Eastman's advice to avoid reference to the race of workers altogether. Their uneasy response to Hall's playing with words to draw 'good' and 'bad' racial categories would raise an important point. Sometimes the line between a facility with language and facile language proved extremely thin. However, the option of a 'raceless' language was an illusory one, not only because white workers would not hear it, but also because race did shape work, politics and society in the South and therefore needed to be talked and struggled over. Hall's language was inadequate to the task of imagining a truly New South, or even of describing the complexity of the South in which he organized, but perhaps less because he paid too much attention to race than because he paid too little. Having broken from the sureties of white supremacy, his words and logic remained so tied to white South-ern male assumptions that he could construct the ideal 'rebel' without taking the experiences of 'others' into account. The failure to do so was the source of the strength of Hall's appeals to white male workers, of his inability to give them genuinely new ways to dream of the future, and of his sharply limited understanding of Black workers.

Hall's discussion of 'The NIGGER SCAB', in a short 1913 article carrying that title, shows well the attractions and the limits of his language. The passage begins with the standard *Lumberjack* distinction between 'niggers' and 'negroes', but concludes by threatening, with a vehemence very like that of Gompers, that whites would launch a race war if Black strikebreak-ing did not end. 'If the *negroes* of the South lay down on the job and allow *niggers* to continue to disgrace their race,' Hall warned, 'no earthly power can prevent a disaster to their people'. In pointing up the peril of the failure of 'the *negro* workers of New Orleans [to] ostracise the *nigger scabs* of the United Fruit Company', Hall minimized the record of Black labor militancy in Louisiana and Texas in order to emphasize the (real) threat that whites would conclude that Blacks as a race were 'nigger scabs'. He acknowledged the record of Black support for the BTW (which consisted at times of half or more minority members) in other contexts, but when it came to discussing the 'nigger scab' he remembered only 'a brave handful of *negro* workers, who have fought the good fight with us against the Lumber Trust'.[78] To have reflected on the actual record, in lumber, in sugar or in longshore, would have rendered ridiculous any attempt to cast Blacks as a 'scab race' in Louisiana.

Even in this amnesiac discussion of 'nigger scabs', Hall probably man-aged to stay barely within the left wing of the possible where race–class discourse among white workers was concerned. He clearly did not buy into the argument that Blacks were genetically or, because of the heritage of slavery, culturally programmed to break strikes. His language, even when discussing '*negro* workers' and '*nigger* scabs', shows that something other than race caused strikebreaking, a point much reinforced by the

151

presence of countless indictments of 'white trash' strikebreakers in Hall's papers. Harold M. Baron, writing of the nation in the early twentieth century, and William M. Tuttle, writing of Chicago's stockyards during the same period, have both offered the politely worded view that for many white workers *scab* and *Negro* were synonymous. Hall at least undermined that destructive mythology which, as Baron has written, persisted despite the fact that 'whites were used as scabs more frequently and in larger numbers'.[79]

Hall was far from alone among Southerners in his critique of the literal equation between Blackness and strikebreaking. The best examples of the conflation of scabbing and race tend to come from the North, especially from mining areas there and from industrial cities like Chicago, East St Louis and Pittsburgh. In Dixie, where traditions of biracial unionism had more strength and where it was less easy to brand African Americans as outsiders, it was harder to be misled. Moreover, the substantial record of white workers and white militias in undermining the strikes and unions of Black Southern workers – a topic much deserving historians' attention – undermined any imagined congruence between Blacks and enemies of unionism.[80] So did the image of poor whites in the South, and especially in the Southern mountains, as too individualistic, quarrelsome and ill-disciplined to be organized into unions.[81]

North or South, the connections between race and strikebreaking running through the use of an expression like *nigger scab* were extremely complex. Hideous as the term was, the need to add a racial prefix to *scab* suggests that Blackness and betrayal were not quite made one in white workers' consciousness. Just as the 'hobo lingo' spoken by so many Wobblies required two words, 'faded boogy', to describe a Black stool pigeon, so too was there no simple, single word connoting a Black strike breaker.[82] However, the behavior of a loyal union member during a strike was often described as 'proving that he was white', while disloyalty to the union revealed a 'black heart'. These usages reflected longstanding Anglo American traditions pairing whiteness with morality and drew on the well-established precedent of calling anti-unionists 'blacklegs' or 'black sheep'. Such terms did not directly invoke, but neither did they wholly transcend, racial categories. As a Birmingham *Labor Advocate* correspondent remarked in 1894, 'all the blacklegs [are] not "niggers." From the color of their skins at least.'[83] Whites in unions at times agreed with the Atlanta ironmolder who wrote in 1907 that 'the negro with a white heart, be his skin ever so black, is an angel in comparison to the black-hearted, job stealing, "scabby" white skin creature shaped like a man.' The willingness to allow Black workers to prove themselves 'white' by proving themselves men had a keenly pragmatic edge in that it allowed white strikers to appeal to Black strikebreakers to change course. Had the whites fully accepted that the Black race was bound to scab, they would not have been able to mix so intimately the racial abuse of 'nigger scabs' with hopeful pleas that African Americans would yet show their white-hearted manliness by walking off the job. On this reading of white workers' attitudes, Hall's distinction between 'nigger scabs' and 'negro workers' seems an approximation of distinctions then being made by a number of relatively egalitarian white unionists, especially in the South. Hall, however, offered African American workers the chance to 'prove themselves *negro*' rather than to 'prove themselves white'.[84]

That the IWW fought, in Hall's words, to 'bring *all* the workers into ONE BIG UNION for the mutual protection and final freedom of all', of course set him apart from those white AFL unionists who too often both demanded that African American workers show 'white hearts' by honoring picket lines and claimed the right to bar them from jobs afterwards. The strikebreakers whom Hall threatened could join and fully participate in the unions he championed, as those Gompers threatened typically could not.[85] Moreover, the BTW explicitly refused to waste its sympathies on those white unionists who erected color bars in their trades and who then waxed indignantly when Blacks broke their strikes.[86]

Nonetheless, Hall's emphasis on the idea that each race could unproblematically be judged by the same standard, that of 'loyalty to their class', missed the extent to which Jim Crow made the calculations of Black workers regarding unionism different from those of whites. Migrating from longer distances to the timber camps than white lumber workers, they could rely less on the support of nearby kin on farms during strikes and lockouts. A long pattern of exclusion of Blacks from unions by a labor movement that, as W. E. B. Du Bois complained, 'mobs white scabs to force them into labor fellowship [but] mobs black scabs to starve and kill them', left a bitter heritage not easily erased by episodically egalitarian labor organization.[87] As Du Bois's words further suggest, Blacks could be singled out for especially brutal intimidation. Such intimidation came from labor when Blacks broke strikes and from the police forces of corporations and of the state when they engaged in class protests. Typically able neither to vote nor to serve on juries, Black workers had few defenders against lynch mobs or judges. Hall did acknowledge that the presence of limited voting rights was all that saved Black unionists in the Sugar Bowl region in the 1880s from even harsher repression than they in fact received. He also wrote of the success of white labor radicals in New Orleans in making use of splits in the Democratic Party there. However, to have pressed for the franchise for Black Louisiana citizens as a *labor* demand would have verged too dangerously close to 'social equality' and would have clashed with the syndicalist disdain for politics Hall and other BTW leaders were professing in 1913 and 1914.[88]

Syndicalist Southerners were also slow to acknowledge that color bars severely limited the industries in which Blacks could work, a fact that complicated any decision to risk employment through union activity and that limited the extent to which the egalitarian logic of 'stomach equality' in fact applied in the South. Hall's syndicalism envisioned wide powers for workers in each industry to rule themselves and justified biracialism on the grounds of the need to respond to employers' divide-and-conquer tactics in mixed workplaces. Given this view, it is hard to see what dynamic would lead to the union challenging color bars in industries like textiles, where employers were not pursuing an immediate divide-and-conquer strategy and where the rank and file apparently had little interest in championing Black employment.[89]

Hall's certainty that 'while the colors in question are two, the class in question is only one' also caused him to overlook at times racial inequalities within 'good' unions. His memoirs found no reason to object when Black dock workers in New Orleans were forced in 1907 to give in on the issue of equality in the hiring of foremen in order to maintain 'harmony' with white unionists. More seriously, the *Voice of the People* in August 1913 featured an article by H. M. Whitt, a frequent contributor, which rehearsed familiar arguments for pragmatic Black–white unity but then specifically warned that without a commitment by whites to the biracial BTW, the 'nigger lovers' in management would succeed in placing Blacks in skilled jobs filing saws. Whitt raised fears that employers would 'give the "nigger" preference until ... black supremacy reigns.' There was no mention of the threat of 'white trash' filers. Hall appended a lame editorial comment which explained that 'in Southern lumberjack parlance, a "nigger" is a black skinned scab. ... A negro is a man, an IWW.' He did not at all comment on the vital issue of how rebel unionists should regard hierarchies of skill based on race. Since, as Robert Norrell has shown, so noble a concept as 'workers' control' could be turned in the South into an argument reinforcing 'caste' in job classification, this was no trifling omission. Hall's belief that the expansion of industrial capitalism would undermine distinctions of skill may have contributed to his neglect of the issues of race and job classification, but in the BTW's industry the problem was a pressing one. In the East Texas forests the union organized, virtually complete color bars kept Blacks from many skilled timbering jobs. In Louisiana's forests local white residents pressed, with some success, for color bars and in Mississippi some forests were closed to all Black workers, skilled or unskilled.[90]

Hall's Southern nationalism deepened his inability to see the situation of Black workers in the South as different from that of white workers. Although he at times couched his nationalism in humorous terms, there can be little doubt that Hall did regard the South as the 'First Conquered

Province of the American Plutocratic Empire', as a 'foreign country' and as a colony which, like Ireland, needed national liberation. He saw the Civil War as an invasion of the South by the 'Coming Class' in 'Samsland', who branded the 'Dixieans' as 'Too Lazy and Unprogressive' and fought them to gain 'the best Undeveloped Market in sight'. Reconstruction, the regime of that 'Coming Class', was 'never overthrown. All that happened was that politicians called "Democrats" ousted from office politicians called "Republicans" and in the name of "white supremacy" instead of black "social equality" sold out their native land to as soulless a gang of industrial Carpet-Baggers as ever plundered a nation of its resources.'[91]

The core of such a view of the post-Redemption South as a colony of Northeastern capital finds much support in modern historical literature.[92] Some of Southern tradition, such as an emphasis on decentralism, on rebellion and on love of nature, held obvious attractions for the BTW. On occasion, Confederate veterans' organization did provide valuable assistance to biracial labor initiatives.[93] Southern nationalism was not, therefore, a patently ridiculous notion for a radical like Hall to embrace. However it was, at least as developed by Hall, a problematic ideology in its implications for race relations. It combined with a vulgar Marxism to make doubly unlikely any examination of the specific plight of the Black worker, who was seen as the victim of capital and of colonizers but not of racists.

The perverse upshot of Hall's Southern nationalism was that he advocated that Southern workers organize across race lines in organizations named and modelled, right down to the sheets, after the Ku Klux Klan. As early as 1905, Hall had chided the New Orleans *Picayune* for supporting the Klan 'that operated in the South during [R]econstruction' but then opposing the equally praiseworthy 1905 Russian Revolution, which Hall found embodying many of the same principles.[94] He replied to charges that the BTW advocated self-defense and sabotage with mock horror that such accusations could be raised against the heirs to the Klan's tradition. By 1913, Hall specifically called the secret labor organizations that he envisioned taking shape as responses to repression in the lumber industry, the Clans of Toil. He hoped that 'ignorant Southerners' would 'copycat' their 'forbears' by forming such secret societies. He promoted his papers with the slogan 'Join the Silent Clan', and advised that if company police harmed 'a single one of our heroic women fellow workers' it would become necessary to 'let the sheeted Clansmen rise from their graves and ride again'. When the Clan of Toil was actually formed in 1916, one of its most influential advisers was J. J. Eager, whom Hall proudly described as 'a Confederate veteran and a leader of the old Ku Klux Klan'.[95]

In both prose and verse, Hall romanticized the Klan. His 1915 poem, characteristically titled 'Our Father's Way', looked back longingly to days when 'The wood was thick, the moon was bright. / The Clansmen knew that might was right.'[96] Other poems invoked the 'fiery cross' and the 'Souls of the Clansmen'. His prose explained why he thought none of this was racist:

> The great [Reconstruction-era] Klan of the Southern people [was hated] not because it killed a few 'niggers'. Except as a tool, the negro had very little part in the great war ... between the Northern capitalists and their Southern allies and the Southern planters and farmers. ... 'Democratic' politicians [raised] the issue of 'nigger domination' and hid behind the false race issue. ... What interests me most today is ... the marvelous manner of organization of the Ku Klux Klan.[97]

Hall wrote such lines at just the time when another advocate of the 'people' of the South and of the 'great Klan', D. W. Griffith, was filming *Birth of a Nation*. Hall was no Griffith, and no Klansman. He hated the North–South reconciliation glorified in the climax of *Birth of a Nation*. He had no use for the twentieth-century Klan, which he derided as a 'moronocracy'.[98] In his many litanies of 'rebel' heroes, Hall invoked antislavery luminaries such as Wendell Phillips and William Lloyd Garrison rather than flesh-and-blood Confederates. He stressed that, in his dream, Black, Mexican and white clans would come together around a common fire to form the Clan of Toil. Nonetheless, in a nation ripe for the triumph of *Birth of a Nation*, and for a new Ku Klux Klan, with his own associates praising the racist tradition of 'whitecapping' and echoing the words of the proslavery Dred Scott decision by arguing that 'the scab has no rights an honest man is bound to respect', Hall asked much of the Black workers he invited to come around that fire.[100] Given the Klan's record of sustained political *and economic* terror against Blacks, and given the confusion between Blackness and strikebreaking as he wrote, Hall's choice of the Klan as a model to organize interracially was an act of extraordinary impracticality.[101]

For Hall to have managed to rewrite Southern history, seeing Blacks as central actors in it, would have required more insight than we perhaps have any right to expect. Lists of slave 'rebels' to grace his hymns to freedom were not found in the dominant histories of slavery, which saw antebellum Blacks as capable of 'crime' but not of sustained resistance to bondage. On the left, Hall's friend Oscar Ameringer had written a highly popular history of the US in 1909 and had reached the same conclusions as Hall regarding the Civil War: 'No working class interests were at stake in the war between the [N]orth and [S]outh' and slavery hardly mattered in it. Griffith could easily stud *Birth of a Nation* with enough expert historical opinion for the film to win the endorsement of President Woodrow Wilson, himself one of the quoted historians.[102] Hall occasionally suggested that he recognized that Black traditions of what he called 'voodoo' undergirded BTW sabotage campaigns and that secret labor organizations in the South grew from Black as well as white traditions. However, outside of the early writings of Black historians, no body of knowledge at his time could have helped him to follow up these insights and to appreciate that the strongest Southern roots of 'silent' organization and direct action protest went back to the community of slaves. Nor could he have known that the freed people he dismissed as pawns during Reconstruction fought, against the murderous opposition of the Klan, an impressive battle for the very demand of land reform to which remnants of the BTW turned after their defeat as an above-ground union.[103] Given his background and opinions he would not have heard the truth about slavery, Reconstruction or the Klan from his 'fathers', his 'Negro Mammy's Son', nor even perhaps his 'colored fellow workers'.

More troubling is that same background and outlook may have kept Hall from realizing the extent of Black militancy even when he witnessed it. He came close to posing very important questions as to why, in Louisiana, Blacks were willing to take risks for the BTW that 'freeborn' whites would not. But he did not pursue the matter. He remained sure that 'nigger scab' and 'white trash' anti-unionists acted under the same pressures, judging both by a common standard that minimized the extent to which Blacks were, for historical rather than racial reasons, making more class-conscious choices, despite constraints, than whites. When Black workers broke strikes, Hall argued that they were discrediting their race, but when they led protests, he counted them as simply workers. Thus in describing the overwhelmingly Black strike in the Sugar Bowl during his youth, Hall emphasized white participation and noted that the Black leader of the strike was 'a "griffe" (about one-quarter white)'. He held that the strike disproved contentions that 'we cannot have the races together ... without danger of riot or bloodshed'. Of course, on Hall's own account, the strike did end with wholesale bloodshed. But he cast the 1887 'massacre' as an attack on those whom the wealthy called 'black bastards and white anarchists' rather than as the racially motivated, as well as class-based, slaughter of Black strikers in which some white Knights of Labor took part on the side of the attackers and remained undisciplined by the union for having done so. The same inappropriate rush to racelessness characterized Hall's discussion of the terrible 1919 Elaine, Arkansas riot by whites against Blacks engaged in rural labor protests. 'It is like all the rest of the "race wars" I've seen in Dixie, at bottom a struggle between landlords and tenants', Hall argued, before noting that since 'several WHITE men' had been arrested on charges of supporting the protests, it was ridiculous to see race as a central theme in the riots.[104]

Hall was tantalizingly close to questioning whether white supremacy hurt the labor movement simply because it divided workers or whether it did damage also because it deprived whites in that movement of the models established by Black workers. At every turn in the high spots of Hall's experience, Blacks played a leading role. Such was the case in the Sugar Bowl and on the New Orleans docks, where, according to Ameringer, 'there was considerably less danger of the Negroes deserting the whites' than vice-versa. Hall frequently noted the same situation in the BTW. His poems and humor concerning the wisdom of 'savages', Black and white, in the 'uncivilized' South suggest that he might almost have been able to see that the 'pickaninny' stereotype required criticism both because of its racism and because that racism hid from whites an attractive African American critique of alienated work. But instead of pursuing such glimmers of sharp insight, Hall busied himself separating 'niggers' from 'negroes'.[105]

'Slaves or Men, Which?'

When Hall offered the definition of 'Nigger' as 'A dirty scab, a company sucker', he glided from race to class to gender. In defining 'Negro' as 'A MAN, a UNION MAN, an I.W.W.', he moved from race to class by inserting gender as a middle term. When he wrote that he would 'rather be on the battleline of human freedom with a black MAN any day than down in the filth licking boots with a white SUCKER', he showed vividly his faith that gender – indeed heterosexism – combined with class, could overcome race. Black workers, like whites, could avoid being 'boss suckers', 'cringing cowards', 'bootlickers' and 'eunuchs' if they would only stand as men. The moral, indeed existential, question facing all workers found clear expression in the title of a major *Lumberjack* article: 'SLAVES OR MEN, WHICH?'[106]

The former choice indicated emasculation, while the latter demonstrated a manly fitness to take a place on the 'battleline of labor', protecting women and children. As Hall put it, the anti-IWW worker helped to send 'his WIFE and MOTHER to the SWEATSHOP, his DAUGHTER to the REDLIGHT, his BABIES to a worse than living death.' Such a worker, Hall continued, 'is not a Man – he is below the BRUTES, for the BRUTES PROTECT their YOUNG and their MOTHERS to the LAST EXTREMITY.'[107] Against those who projected the 'black brute rapist' as the central threat to the gender system of the South, Hall replied that corporations, 'gunmen' and 'suckers' were the real menaces to family life.

In Southern lumber, where there were seven married male workers for every six single ones – the ratio was less than four to six in the Northern and Western lumber industries – family responsibilities were facts of life.

Indeed Southern timber workers were often called 'homeguards' in contrast to their footloose counterparts in other regions. Hall consistently spoke, for all his personal dash and bachelorhood, to the values of the homeguards.[108]

If historians have amply appreciated that Hall advanced a class viewpoint in attacking racism, they have not much commented on how thoroughly gendered were his class arguments. Scholarly discussions of the BTW and gender, brief as they are, have downplayed discussion of the union's traditional values while stressing the egalitarian policy toward women adopted by the BTW's 1912 convention. At that meeting, the same one at which affiliation with the IWW and the turn to biracialism took place, delegates voted overwhelmingly to admit dues-paying wives of members to full union membership, which included the right to vote in strike ballots. Mothers, sisters and daughters of males in the BTW could also join and vote on strikes, provided that they did housework in a member's home. Since, in addition, the union included a remarkable female representative, Fredonia Stevenson, on its executive board, and since it demanded 'for the women workers the same wages and conditions it demands for men workers – ALL they PRODUCE and a FREE WORLD', the BTW has rightly been portrayed as having exceedingly advanced policies on gender equality.[109] Hall himself praised 'warrior women' and saw their willingness to struggle as 'presag[ing] the fall of the existing order of society'. He even defended the 'Sufferingets', as he called suffragettes, against mob attacks, though his syndicalism made him skeptical as to the ultimate good of their (or males') voting.[110]

However, egalitarian *policies* of the BTW did not necessarily signal a break with traditional attitudes regarding gender. The specific rationale for allowing women to vote on strikes was that 'when a strike is on, the man can go hunting and fishing, and not have to hear hungry children whimpering for something to eat, while the woman has to stay at home and take it all.' Women were to make sure that their husbands did not 'show the white feather' and male union leaders boasted of women able to exercise feminine influence by telling fainthearted men, 'Get out of this house and join the union, or I'll leave it and try to find a man to live with.'[111] Like the Latina cigar makers in Tampa who offered to lend their skirts to insufficiently militant male workers, BTW women attempted to shame men into being good union members. However, unlike the Tampa women, those in the BTW intervened almost solely as wives and mothers rather than as wage-earners. Hall idealized this aspect of their activism, referring to women as the 'Mothers of Dixie' the 'MOTHERS OF THE RACE' or the 'wives of the men'. Such roles did not preclude their being 'warriors'. (Indeed Hall's memoirs credit the grand old lady of labor, Mother Jones, with instructing her 'boys' in Louisiana on where to get cheap, reliable guns.) But in the main, Hall identified women's roles on the 'battleline' with nurturing. As workers, he thought women needed protection, especially from sliding into prostitution. As mothers, women defended families by sustaining the union. They ideally raised money, spoke to church groups, ran soup kitchens and saw their suffering households through strikes. *The Lumberjack* posed the first two of these womanly activities as specific alternatives to 'foolish' women's suffrage agitation. One of the major BTW solidarity campaigns revolved around the right of a mother to see her son, who had been jailed for union activities.[111]

Seeing men as protecting women through workplace struggles while women protected the home left little room for the BTW to imagine white women coming to antiracist conclusions except in the tow of men. The argument that a biracial wage-work experience provided the dynamic leading to limited challenges to white supremacy left white women out, as they were largely unwaged, working in private homes or working in industries featuring color bars. Moreover, since the BTW's biracialism derived its justification from 'stomach equality' and generally abjured 'social equality', it tended to accept mixing of the races in the male world of work and to reject such mixing precisely in the female realm of the home. Occasionally, and impressively, women could come to join in the breaking of the color line. Herbert Gutman fondly cited one such instance, that of an early-twentieth-century Irish woman who spoke to the reformer Mary White Ovington. As Ovington wrote:

> An Irish friend was talking on trade union matters, and she said: 'Do you know, yesterday I dined wid a naygur. Little did I ivir think I wud do sich a thing, but it was this way. You know my man is sicretary of his union, and the min are on strike, and who should come to the door at twelve o'clock but a big black naygur. 'Is Brother O'Neill at home?' says he. 'Brother O'Neill', thinks I; 'well, if I'm brother to you I'd better have stayed in Ireland.' But I axed him in, and in a minute my man comes and he shakes the naygur by the and, and says he, 'You must stay and ate wid us.' So I puts the dinner on the table and I sat down and ate wid a naygur. ... To tell you the truth', she said, 'he seemed just like anybody else.'

Even in this lovely passage, however, the expectation was that biracialism was first of all for men at work and that a woman got it secondhand, if at all. The logic of manly work and protected homes found more typical expression in an 1894 letter from 'Mississippi' to the *Machinists' Monthly Journals*. 'Mississippi', a white machinist, could scarcely imagine bringing a Black 'brother' home:

I can imagine myself saying, 'Wife, this is Mr Washington, a brother machinist', and I can imagine what would be her surprise, but I can't imagine what would be the results. I can realize how much lower myself and the machinist at large would be rated in the eyes of one who had always looked upon the machinists as an intelligent and worthy class of men. ...[112]

Hall's views on gender were likewise traditional where Blacks in the union were concerned. Although African American timber workers in the piney woods typically came as single workers they began families while living in company housing. However, the wives of Black timber workers are virtually absent in BTW propaganda. They receive scant mention individually or as a group and do not figure in BTW proceedings. In contrast to the highly racialized language used in referring to male lumber workers, union publications referred to Southern women and mothers in generic ways that implied their whiteness. In opening the union to Black men and (mainly) white women simultaneously in 1912, BTW delegates took two important egalitarian measures. It is possible that taking the first paved the way for taking the second in ways beyond the simple contagion of freedom at the convention. Bringing in (white) women balanced the voting power of Black men and removed the possible objection of wives that Black men were making decisions that affected white families while white women could not participate. The logic of stomach equality and the grounding of antiracism in appeals to white masculinity left little place for consideration of Black working class women. Their absence, amidst such full discussion of race and manhood on the one hand and of idealized Southern (white) womanhood on the other, was hardly accidental. In no Southern industry organized energetically by the IWW were Black females a significant enough part of the labor force to necessitate bringing them into the logic of biracial cooperation. African American women could hardly gain acceptance by proving their manhood and, since their role in the mythology of the white South was as valued 'Mothers of Dixie' only to the extent that they provided maternal care to *white* families, they would have fit uneasily into paeans to motherhood. As the important recent studies of Tera Hunter and others demonstrate, white workers, not just upper- and middle-class whites, sought and bought the services of African American cooks, child nurses and especially washerwomen for their families. This further complicated any possibility of seeing working class Black and white women as being victims of common oppression. When African American women did prominently appear in BTW publications it was as prostitutes serving the desires of scabs, in the improbable ratio of two women for every man. The exaggeration played on the images Black women as harlots, of libidinous 'nigger scabs' and of race-mixing 'white trash' strikebreakers. Black men not in the union were meanwhile said to have menaced white women. 'Nigger scabs go into the post office', *The Lumberjack* reported during the Merryville strike, 'and push the women around [while] the white trash laugh'. On at least one occasion the *Voice of the People* replied to the charge that BTW members were 'nigger lovers' by arguing that it was the anti-union workers who 'visit some colored lady's house in the wee small hours of the morning'.[113]

However, in considering Black men *in the union*, Hall sharply broke from Southern ideas that branded African American masculinity as pathological. He also abandoned the labor movement's general commitment to what Mary Ellen Freifeld has called the 'white man ethic', which equated whiteness and manliness. The 'manly' skilled worker, whom David Montgomery has rightly placed at the center of craft union campaigns to maintain and extend workers' control, autonomy and mutuality in the late nineteenth and early twentieth centuries, was ideally not only a man but a 'white man'.[114] Usages of 'white man' by skilled workers to describe their class and gender ideal did at times show a sharply limited awareness that biology was not destiny. White male workers could turn out not to have 'any manhood', if they 'turned nigger' by 'blackening themselves' as scabs. Conversely, class-conscious Black workers could, as the *National Labor Tribune*'s account of an 1882 iron and steel workers' strike had it, prove that 'They are white men.' However, just as the labor historian Patricia Cooper has argued that, *as a group*, 'Women could hardly be manly', in the estimation of male workers, neither were white workers likely to concede that, as a group, African Americans were 'white'.[115] Among other things, white skilled workers associated lack of manliness at work with slavery and slavery with race. Even in proclaiming that strikebreaking was 'slave-like' behavior, whether undertaken by whites or Blacks – indeed even when arguing that all workers were 'wage slaves' – whites could not lose sight of the historic link between race and slavery. Thus Jacob Stage, a white McKeesport, Pennsylvania strikebreaker was 'nothing more or less than a natural-born slave' according to the union press. Therefore to people around McKeesport he was 'better known as "the nigger"'.[116]

Whiteness, maleness and pride in craft joined in the fashioning of an identity. James J. Davis's autobiographical *The Iron Puddler*, partly set in Louisiana, combined craft and gender in writing of the 'man of iron' as the masculine ideal. But Davis, an inveterate performer in amateur minstrel shows and later a US congressman, added that he wanted to create specifically white 'men of iron' as 'civilization's shock troops grappling with tyrannous nature'. Davis added, 'Some races are pig-iron; Hottentots and Bushmen are pig-iron. They break at a blow.' Others, like the 'meek Chinese' let nature slowly 'whip [them] with cold, drought, flood, isolation and famine.' Only Davis's own race could take up the manly task of 'belting the world with railroads and bridging the seas with iron boats.'

The fierce resistance of craft unionists to entry of Blacks and of females into their trades reflected how widespread was Davis's conflation of craft, race and gender. Integration at work would not only make the manly skilled worker associate with the supposedly servile but also would associate his *craft* with degradation and weakness.[117]

The idea that Blacks threatened the dignity of skilled tradesmen often found its way into workers' language. Not only was *nigger work* generally synonymous with servile, *driven* labor, but individual crafts developed occupational slang that reinforced the point that Blacks would sully their trades. Thus, for electrical workers a *nigger* was an impurity fouling connections, for cowboys a *nigger brand* was a saddlesore and for railroaders *nigger locals* were especially burdensome short runs. In other cases, workers' language connected mechanization to 'niggers', with the logic probably built on the twin associations of Blacks with the hard work (especially lifting) being replaced by machines and with perception that both machines and Blacks posed a threat to whites' employment. Mississippi sawyers thus called devices to turn heavy logs *steam niggers* and in many trades powerful winches were *niggerheads*.[118] The combination of Blacks and machines was especially fearsome. The great Black writer James Weldon Johnson listened closely to white 'engineers, machinists, plumbers, electrical workers and helpers' in a shipboard smoking room. Their words convinced him of 'how lean a chance' the Black worker had 'with his white brothers of the proletariat'. He wrote, 'The expression which I heard at least a hundred times was, "Never let a nigger pick up a tool."'[119] Such language and such strictures suggest the extent to which the white manliness of skilled workers was not easily dissolved by deskilling. Rather than reacting to the loss of job control and status by seeing their interests as more like those of unskilled workers, including Blacks, semi-skilled and newly deskilled craft unionists often seized on racial or gender issues, reasserting their manhood and whiteness ever more insistently and taking the 'threat' to their skilled status posed by Blacks and women considerably more seriously than the threat posed by capital.[120]

Any attempt to build a biracial labor movement was bound to emphasize that Blacks had overcome, or at least could overcome, slavery and become men. But the chances for success in making this argument were slim, especially in craft unions. In the 1890s, when Samuel Gompers was still quite active in pressuring constituent the AFL unions not to bar qualified Blacks from membership, he stressed that 'colored brothers' were proving to 'white brothers' that the 'docility of slavery has passed'. To the hesitant-to-integrate white New Orleans union leader John M. Callaghan, he emphasized the manhood of workers of both races. He appealed to Callaghan to listen 'As a man whom I have every reason to believe you are.'[121] The great labor journalist John Swinton packed a short

1886 report on integration in the Knights of Labor with approving references to 'colored men' who were 'fraternizing' with white 'trades brothers'.[122] But retreats from biracial unity and from integration followed the
same pattern of appealing to manhood. Terence Powderly used a fully
patriarchal logic to reassure white Southerners that the Knights would
not push for 'social equality'. He promised never to violate 'the sanctity of
the fireside circle [since] every man has the right to say who shall enter
beneath his roof; who shall occupy the same bed ... or such other place as
he is master of.' Gompers, in his 1895 compromise with (or rather capitu-
lation to) the International Association of Machinists on the issue of racial
exclusion, agreed that so long as the union did not bar Blacks from membership through its constitution it could do so through its *fraternal* rituals.
The worst examples of labor's campaigning for color bars were, not coin-
cidentally, found among the all-white railway brotherhoods.[123]

The BTW was thus remarkable on several counts. Hall took its status
as a brotherhood seriously, styling it as a 'freemasonry of labor' and cred-
iting its use of fraternal rituals with much of its initial success. But the
BTW was a brotherhood that admitted women. Unlike the typical fraternal organizations of industrializing America, ones that Mary Ann Clawson
has aptly described as seeking 'mutuality in the lodge room even if this
were no longer feasible in the workplace', the BTW sought transformation at the point of production. Unlike most labor brotherhoods, it actively sought fraternity with Black workers. In a South and a nation in
which appeals to the manhood of whites usually caused African Americans
to suffer – where color bars were justified by invocations of the ideal of a
'white's man [mining] camp', a 'white man's country', a 'white man's town'
or a 'white man's union' – the BTW at least tried to turn manhood against
white supremacy.[124]

The BTW was relatively well-poised to challenge the idealization of
the 'white man' as the paragon of labor movement virtue. As a biracial
industrial union whose leadership considered the advent of the 'mass
worker' to signal the declining importance of craft skills, the BTW was
partially immunized against the 'white man ethic'. Like miners in organized, integrated pits in the South, Louisiana lumber workers had reason to
know that Black workers often proved both manly and 'white' in the
course of a strike or of a day's work. Skilled and recently deskilled craft
unionists tended to conceptualize manliness around issues of control, so-
briety, skill, responsibility, steady employment and moderation, and at
times to see performance of physically hard work as unmanly. In the lumber industry (and mining) danger and backbreaking work were facts of life
for most of the prospective union membership, Black and white. Manliness could thus be identified far more closely with strength and physical
courage – attributes which Black workers undeniably possessed – rather

than with characteristics which racial stereotypes reserved for the white race.[125]

Posing the question confronting workers as 'SLAVES OR MEN, WHICH?' *The Lumberjack* emphasized that slavery grew out of unmanly behavior, not out of racial characteristics. Black or white, any worker who failed to demand and collect the 'FULL PRODUCT' of his or her labor could be termed a 'laboring slave'. That it was servility which emasculated workers was brought home via definitions that made 'slave' synonymous with 'company sucker', a figure in turn connected to the 'eunuch'. That the slave was a 'nigger' or 'white trash' mattered, but so did the fact that he was less than a man.[126]

Hall's rhetorical strategy of disarming the racism of white workers through an appeal to the masculinity they were said to share with Blacks was both ingenuous and ingenious. It reflected his sincere belief, one shared by many of his readers, and grounded in the material reality of white Southern gender relations, in the importance of manhood and of paternalism in gender relations. It advanced the argument for biracial unity from the pragmatic, but problematic, terrain of (white) self-interest to the realm of natural rights conferred by manhood. However, because of its racelessness amidst racism and its fixation on being 'MEN', it raised perhaps as many problems as it solved in organizing Black and white workers.

As Barry Goldberg's penetrating recent work has demonstrated, emphasis on the 'slavery' common to the experience of Black and white workers often signalled a denial of the special oppression, historic and contemporary, of African Americans. Like many other white activists, North and South, Louisiana labor radicals argued at times that 'wage slavery' lacked the paternalism of chattel slavery and therefore featured much harsher oppression. H. G. Creel, a leading socialist orator who supported the BTW, went further, chiding white 'slaves' who objected that a lumber company had given 'Negro Emancipation Day' as a holiday but not the Fourth of July: 'The niggers used to be chattel slaves. Now they're only wage slaves. ... The niggers have something to celebrate, while you white men haven't. Wait till you're freed. Then you'll be as good as the niggers.'[127] On one level, Creel's humor undoubtedly provided a useful, mocking antidote to the 'niggers off our necks' radicalism of the Huey Long, Senior variety and made the apt suggestion that looking for emancipation in Southern history meant looking at the African American tradition. But on another level, Creel's joke came troublingly close to mocking Long in the sense of imitating him by playing to white fears that somehow Blacks were being treated better than they were, and that white manhood was under specific threat. Moreover, even in the relatively capable hands of Creel, the image of 'wage slavery' tended to lose track of the fact that African Americans had suffered slavery in reality and white workers in metaphor. It misconstrued the history of slavery by assuming that the slave shared the servility, and thus the moral taint, of the strikebreaker. Thus trade unionists spoke of scabs as 'white Sambos'.[128]

Also problematic was the extent to which Hall's publications tended to present the ideal unionist as a fighter eager for confrontations but, when discussing Black members, more often prized forbearance and 'feminine' virtues. One of the most sympathetic African American figures in BTW literature was, for example, a single father, evicted from his home by the company, and caring for two 'half-clothed children', the victims of meningitis.[129] Hall insisted that 'MIGHT IS RIGHT' and advised, 'Thou shalt not kill [but] if you must take life, take it easy.'[130] His editorials held that the only good 'gunman' (company policeman) was a dead one. He wrote of battles with such gunmen as tests of manhood. Nonetheless, he featured an account of the Merryville strike – indeed the same article that warned against 'nigger scabs' menacing white women – which praised a 'Negro fellow worker' who 'took it' when faced with humiliation by a gunman 'because he did not want to start a riot'. It is difficult to know whether such praise for passivity reflected a glimmer of recognition of the extra risks of attack and lynching faced by Black workers – the worker in question was ultimately shot despite his caution – or whether it illustrated Hall's holding a different standard of masculinity when speaking about Black men. In either case, questions are raised about how far a simple invocation of common manhood could go in transcending race.[131]

Likewise troublesome was the very attempt by (however well-intentioned) white unionists to act as arbiters of what constituted manly behavior among Black workers. In arguing that hesitancy to join the union signalled an absence of masculinity (and proof of slavish 'nigger' status) labor organizers may well have closed communications with workers who could have gradually been brought into the union. Black male workers who left the Southern countryside in the World War I era often defied vagrancy laws and Klan terror to do so. They weighed choices, as the recent work of James Grossman and Joe William Trotter shows, with a close eye to the welfare of their families. They considered family responsibility, job prospects, the record of labor's racism, and exploitation by the employer in making often provisional decisions about union membership. Some ultimately made compromises with the paternalism of mine and lumber management, hoping to manipulate such paternalism to their own advantage.[132] None faced the simple 'man or eunuch' choice the BTW press imagined. While the great Packinghouse Workers organizing drive on 1917 in Chicago achieved initial successes at biracial unionism around the slogan 'BE MEN – JOIN THE UNION', it also partly shifted the ground for considering the merits of unionism from a debate about class and race to non sequiturs regarding gender. William Tuttle's fine account of attempts to organizing packinghouse workers in Chicago captured the mood:

> 'Fuck the union, fuck you in the [union] button', raged a black worker. Knives and revolvers proliferated on both sides. 'If I catch you outside I will shoot you', a Negro warned an insulting committee man. ... 'Where is your button?' demanded an organizer. 'I ain't got none on', was the angry reply, 'but [if I did] I would put it on the end of my prick.'[133]

Of course, as the provocative recent work of Nancy Hewitt, Ava Baron, Dolores Janiewski, Patricia Cooper, Mary Ann Clawson, Elizabeth Faue and others has shown, class feeling was a thoroughly gendered phenomenon in the late nineteenth and early twentieth centuries. Hall may well have exhorted his followers to be 'mothers' and 'MEN' even if race had not been at issue in his union. But when 'manhood' was made to stand in for both class and racial identities, it surely tended to run through labor discourse with more frequency and shrillness. Therefore it is worth considering in conclusion whether Hall's creative and well-grounded efforts to disarm race through masculinity may have contributed to the union's having a short, if heroic, life. Hall later regarded the central problem of BTW organizers as their being placed consistently in the situation of having to rein in the desire to fight of 'rebel' Southern workers who had seen their region sold to 'alien exploiters' and lost their 'peace-loving character'. He hinted at regrets that with 'all Louisiana and the entire timber country ... on the verge of revolt', he joined other BTW leaders in 'work[ing] night and day to balk it.'[134]

However, it would be hard to support such a view of the BTW as counselling pacifism from the files of Hall's publications. His cultural magazine was called *Rebellion* and featured 'Dreams and Dynamite' in its subtitle. According to his memoirs, 'from the very first start of *The Lumberjack* there was much talk of guns'. His featuring in the BTW press of 'a cut showing two crossed rifles, with this caption, "The only argument a gunman understands"' hardly urged nonviolence. Neither did touting *The Lumberjack* as 'a machine gun of the revolution', nor the warning to deputies, 'We mean to slug and kill you, man for man, rank for rank.'[135] The leadership of the BTW may well have 'balked' armed revolt but its rhetoric also fostered expectations that such revolt was immanent.

Of course, violence was often initiated by the lumber companies, and the BTW plausibly maintained that its guns were simply for self-defense. 'No violence!' *The Lumberjack* held, 'We do not want violence and we are going to stop the masters' violent treatment of the workers.' However, to the extent that manliness came to be connected with gunplay, and with 'smiling' at the death of enemies of the unions, more subtle, and perhaps sustainable, methods of waging class conflict suffered. The BTW preached sabotage as a tactic perhaps more than any other IWW affiliate did. But it was possible to spell *sabotage* in two different ways. The first of these narrowly focussed on confrontation with strikebreakers:

> Scabs!
> Attention
> Brotherhood of Timber Workers
> On Strike at Merryville, La.
> Take Warning.
> American Lumber Co.
> Going crazy.
>
> Everybody's doin' it!
> Doin' what? Nawthin.

The second spelling suggested an ongoing strategy of creatively 'striking on the job':

> Soap stops water from making steam in boilers.
> Asafetida keeps patrons from struck theatres.
> By working slow profits are greatly reduced.
> Oil containing emery makes machinery strike.
> Telling trade secrets wins battles for workers.
> Accidents often are an aid in winning strikes.
> Guerrilla warfare always gets the bosses' goat.
> Ends that are revolutionary justify the means.[136]

However understandable the confrontational first approach to spelling *sabotage* may have been, it is hard to believe the zeal with which it was propagandized was not intensified by the tremendous emphasis on manhood, in part as a way to disarm race, in BTW thinking. And, of course, the fear of emasculation and the need to assert manhood applied with special force among white male workers because to be 'cringing' and 'servile' meant not only being unsexed, but less than white as well. Conversely the second, less confrontational 'spelling' of sabotage was relatively neglected. Hall's publications came to identify sabotage with the improbable image of the rattlesnake, not the black cat symbolizing the tactic elsewhere. When IWW leader Vincent St John argued that the rattlesnake's warning before attack made it an inapt symbol of sabotage, Hall replied that the warnings made it a manly, honorable symbol.[137]

A greater appreciation of African American patterns of resistance might have argued for using Brer Rabbit as the symbol for sustained, creative, gritty struggle. Instead the BTW not only sought confrontation but, like the rattlesnake, made noise about doing so. Since it preached to its members that they were slaves and eunuchs incapable of providing for their families, if they could not 'SEIZE and HOLD' power, the union needed speedy results in order to keep its hold on Southern members. Joy Parr's penetrating work on relatively skilled furniture workers, like that of Paul Tayblon on railway crafts, suggests that a manly 'breadwinner union-ism' was particularly compatible with craft-conscious, conservative union-ism as members sought recognition as men and increases in compensation from employers. When less skilled miners, factory workers and timber workers organized around masculinity and 'breadwinner's' issues, a mili-tant industrial unionism was, as the BTW demonstrated, among the pos-sible outcomes. However, industrial breadwinner unionism could also tend toward tactical brittleness, despair and a willingness to 'be mollified with a managerial apology rather than structural change'. Failing quick victories, the logic of the union itself led workers to accept that they were beaten and degraded. Paternalist employers were ready with strong argu-ments that avoiding unions, staying on the job and securing a family home was the more viable way for a 'man' to defend 'his good wife and the little ones who toddle'. Within two years after its heroic 1912 convention, the BTW, once armed with as many as 20,000 members and with a strategy of using class and manhood to smother race, had gone down fighting. The road to class solidarity did not plow under and pave over consciousness of race and of gender. Instead all three roads – of class, gender and race – were made to intersect for a time in the cause of biracial labor unity. But each road continued to run, and all could easily diverge.[138]

Notes

1. Covington Hall, 'Labor Struggles in the Deep South', 189–90 (typescript, Labadie Collection, University of Michigan, Ann Arbor, 1951). Much of this article was written and revised in England and in Ghana. The generosity of Steven Watts, LeeAnn Whites, Franklin Rosemont and Patrick Huber in sending important materials made this writing possible. Also helpful was the microfilming of *The Lumberjack* and *Voice of the People* by the Western His-torical Manuscripts Collection at University of Missouri-Columbia. The quotations intro-ducing Part II are from Charles Neider, ed. *The Outrageous Mark Twain*, New York 1977, 6, and Terry Eagleton, *Nationalism, Irony and Commitment*, Derry 1988, 6. Thanks to Jean All-man, Susan Porter Benson, Randy McBee, James Barrett, LeeAnn Whites, James Stodder, Julie Rose, Brett Rogers, Abra Quinn, Franklin Rosemont, Donald Winters, Kristine Stilwell, Robin D. G. Kelley, Bonnie Stepenoff, Caroline Waldron, Patricia Cooper, Dana Frank, Eric Arnesen, Paul Taillon and Patrick Huber for criticism and ideas on this research.

2. Hall, 'Labor Struggles', 190; *Census of the United States, 1910*, vol. 9 (Manufactures), 416, and vol. 4 (Population and Occupation Statistics), 465–6.

3. *The Lumberjack* [hereafter *LJ*], 6 March 1913. On membership, see Merl E. Reed, 'Lumberjacks and Longshoremen: The I.W.W. in Louisiana', *Labor History* 13 (Winter 1972): 45n10.

4. *LJ*, 27 March 1913. See also 19 June and 3 and 10 July 1913; *Voice of the People*

[hereafter *VP*], 5 and 12 March 1913.

5. Anthony Dunbar, *Against the Grain*, Charlottesville, Va. 1981, 107; Herbert Shapiro, *White Violence and Black Response from Reconstruction to Montgomery*, Amherst, Mass. 1988, 244; 'Jeff Sutter Interviews H. L. Mitchell', in Dave R. Roeidiger and Don Fitz, eds, *In the Shell of the Old: Essays on Workers' Self-Organization*, Chicago 1990, 23; Franklin Rosemont, 'The IWW and the STFU: An Interview with H.L. Mitchell', *Industrial Worker*, April 1988; Raymond and Charlotte Koch, *Educational Commune: The Story of Commonwealth College*, New York 1972, 65–6.

6. Dunbar, *Against the Grain*, 107; Shapiro, *White Violence*, 244; James R. Green, *Grass-Roots Socialism: Radical Movements in the Southwest, 1895–1943*, Baton Rouge, La. 1978, 211–12; Thomas Becnel, 'Louisiana Senator Allen J. Ellender and IWW Leader Covington Hall: An Agrarian Dichotomy', *Louisiana History* 23 (Summer 1982): 270; David R. Roediger, 'An Injury to One: IWW Organizing in the Deep South', *Industrial Worker* (April 1988): 5.

7. Joyce Kornbluh, ed., *Rebel Voices: An IWW Anthology*, Chicago 1988, esp. 14, 52 and 56; Franklin Rosemont's introduction to *Juice Is Stranger Than Friction: The Writings of T-Bone Slim*, Chicago 1992, is an important study of the IWW and language, esp. at 22–33.

8. Archie Green, *Wobblies, Pile Butts and Other Heroes: Labor Explorations*, forthcoming from University of Illinois Press, collects Green's marvelous work. See esp. 'The Name "Wobbly" Holds Steady'; Stewart Holbrook, 'Wobbly Talk', *American Mercury* 7 (January 1926): 62–5; Mencken, *The American Language*, 4th edn, New York 1937, 175, and the many IWW references in the Peter Tamony Collection, Western Historical Manuscript Collection, University of Missouri-Columbia. See also Franklin Rosemont, 'Gadfly vs. Gasbag', *Industrial Worker* (September 1978): 8.

9. Rosemont, ed., *Juice Is Stranger*, 22–3; David R. Roediger, ed., *Fellow Worker: The Memoirs of Fred W. Thompson*, Chicago 1993, Chapters 1 and 2.

10. Esther Dolgoff, 'Covington Hall in Stelton' (typescript in possession of the author, 1985), 1–2.

11. Rosemont, ed., *Juice Is Stranger*, 22–3; Hall, 'Labor Struggles', 200–202; *LJ*, 27 March 1913; *VP*, 14 August 1913 and 25 November 1914; Covington Hall, *Dreams and Dynamite: Selected Poems*, David R. Roediger, ed., Chicago 1985, 17; Roediger, 'Covington Hall: The Republic of the Imagination', in Paul Buhle et al., eds, *Free Spirits*, San Francisco 1982, 178–81. Hall's fullest 'defense of dreaming' is in *Industrial Solidarity*, 8 July 1925.

12. Thompson to Roediger, 16 October 1981.

13. *LJ*, 12 March and 10 April 1913; *VP*, 4 December 1913.

14. Quoted in Philip S. Foner, *Organized Labor and the Black Worker, 1619–1973*, New York 1974, 109. See also Eastman, 'The Southern Negro and One Big Union', *International Socialist Review* 13 (June 1913): 890–91. For an example of a correspondent who does follow Eastman's suggestion, see *LJ*, 31 April 1913 (misdated by Hall), where 'Wat Tyler' uses 'negro' even in naming African American strikebreakers. See also the pre-IWW BTW's leaflet 'TO THE COLORED WAGE WORKERS OF LOUISIANA AND TEXAS'. Reprinted in M. L. Alexander to Fleishel, 26 December 1911, in Louisiana Lumber Company Records, Western Historical Manuscript Collections, University of Missouri-Columbia. Merl E. Reed's, 'The IWW and Individual Freedom in Western Louisiana, 1913', *Louisiana History* 10 (Winter 1969): 64n3, which observes that 'IWW accounts always referred to black strikebreakers as "niggers" and to black union men as "Negro Fellow Workers"', does not take Eastman into account, but is near to the mark on Louisiana IWW practice generally.

15. For a populist/pragmatist view, laced with concern for issues of language, see Michael Kazin, 'A People Not a Class: Rethinking the Political Language of the Modern US Labor Movement', in Mike Davis and Michael Sprinker, eds, *Reshaping the US Left: Popular Struggles in the 1980s*, London 1986, 257–86; for a distinctive mixture of acute insights regarding race and class and a too urgent desire to restrict discussion of race as a causative factor in US history, see Barbara Fields, 'Slavery, Race and Ideology in the United States of America', *New Left Review*, no. 181 (May-June 1990): esp. 118.

16. See James Stodder's fine unpublished introduction to his projected publication of Hall's 'Labor Struggles', 22, in my possession and cited with permission. The 'shell of the old' image is from the 1908 preamble to the IWW's constitution, reprinted in Kornbluh, ed., *Rebel Voices*, 13; Tera Hunter, *Contesting the New South: The Politics and Culture of Wage House-*

hold Labor in Atlanta, 1861–1920, forthcoming.

17. Biographical material on Hall comes from Hall, 'Labor Struggles'; Koch and Koch, *Educational Commune*, 65–6; St Louis *Post-Dispatch*, 17 April 1922; Stodder, 'Life and Values', 1–22 and 43; and Roediger, 'Covington Hall: The Poetry and Politics of Labor Radicalism and Southern Nationalism', *History Workshop Journal*, no. 19 (Spring 1985): 162–8; Thompson to Roediger, 16 October 1981; Dolgoff, 'Hall in Stelton', 1–2, and a two-sided mimeo tribute to Hall (1975?) issued by the long-time Wobbly Alvin Stalcup and in possession of the author. Hall's salary as editor of *The Lumberjack* was apparently $18 weekly. See Louisiana Central Lumber Company Records, F-830, for a reprint of BTW proceedings from 15 December 1912 to that effect. For context, see Green, *Grass Roots Socialism*, esp. 211–15; Green, 'The Brotherhood of Timber Workers, 1910–1913: A Radical Response to Industrial Capitalism in the Southern USA', *Past and Present* 60 (August 1973): 161–200; Reed, 'Lumberjacks', 41–59; Hall, 'The Victory of the Lumber Jacks', *ISR* 13 (December 1912): 470–71; Jeff Ferrell and Kevin Ryan, 'The Brotherhood of Timber Workers and the Southern Trust: Legal Repression and Worker Response', *Radical America* 19 (July-August 1985): 55–74; Bernard Cook, 'Covington Hall and Radical Rural Unionization in Louisiana', *Louisiana History* 18 (1977): 227–38; James Fickle, 'Race, Class and Radicalism', in Joseph Conlin, ed., *At the Point of Production: The Local History of the IWW*, Westport, Conn. 1981, esp. 101–5; Donald Winters, 'Covington Hall: The Utopian Vision of a "Wobbly" Poet', *Labor's Heritage* (Summer 1992): 54–63.

18. Still valuable on racial paternalism as a late-nineteenth-century alternative to Jim Crow is C. Vann Woodward, *The Strange Career of Jim Crow*, New York 1974.

19. Hall, 'Labor Struggles', 30–45; William Ivy Hair, *Bourbonism and Agrarian, Protest* Baton Rouge, La. 1969, 176–85; Foner, *Organized Labor and the Black Worker*, 60–61; Jeffrey Gould, 'Sugar War', *Southern Exposure* 12 (November-December 1984): 45–55. The exposure to extreme racist brutality, with family members or townspeople responsible for the violence, was a factor in the radicalization of other white Southern dissenters as well. See Mitchell, *Mean Things*, 1–3, and John de Graaf and Alan H. Stein, 'Stetson Kennedy: A Klandestine Man', *In These Times*, 11–17 December 1991, 4–5.

20. Hall, *Dreams and Dynamite*, 16; Hall in *ISR* 5 (December 1904): 347; Oscar Ameringer, *If You Don't Weaken*, New York 1940, 209. See also Uncle Covamy, 'Advice to Boys', *One Big Union Monthly* [*OBUM*], 2nd ser., 2 (June 1938): 31; Hall, 'For Instance' and 'The Wisdom of Onc' Pierre', *OBUM*, 2nd ser., 2 (May 1938): 17.

21. See, among a growing number of fine works, Joy Parr, *The Gender of Breadwinners: Women, Men and Change in Two Industrial Towns, 1880–1950*, Toronto 1990, 142–50, with the quotation from p. 149; Alice Kessler-Harris, *A Woman's Wage: Historical Meanings and Social Consequences*, Lexington, Ky. 1990; Elizabeth Faue, *Community of Suffering and Struggle: Women, Men, and the Labor Movement in Minneapolis, 1915–1945*, Chapel Hill, N.C. 1991; and Whites, 'DeGraffenreid Controversy'. Whites' important soon-to-be-published work on gender in the postbellum South enriched this study greatly, as did her acute criticisms of a draft of this chapter. bell hooks offers especially acute commentary on the redefinition of patriarchy in her *Black Looks: Race and Representation*, London 1992, 93–4.

22 Covington Hall, *Songs of Rebellion*, New Orleans 1915, 39; Hall, *Battle Hymns of Toil*, Oklahoma City, Okla. 1946, 60 and 84–5; Koch and Koch, *Educational Commune*, 66. Lamentably, Slufoot Sam also found a place in the culture of the later Southern Tenant Farmers' Union. See H. L. Mitchell, *Mean Things Happening in This Land*, Montclair, N.J. 1979, 20. The critic is James Weldon Johnson, as quoted in Sterling Stuckey's introduction to Sterling Brown, *Southern Road*, Boston 1974, *xxxiii*.

23. Hall, *Songs of Love and Rebellion*, as quoted in Stodder, 'Introduction', 19; the 'Aryan' references, not surprisingly, were removed from Hall's 1946 collection, *Battle Hymns of Toil*, 68–9; *Solidarity*, 8 May 1915.

24. Hall, *Songs of Rebellion*, dedication; *OBUM*, 1st ser., 1 (August 1919): 15; Hall, *Battle Hymns of Toil*, 78.

25. Harold M. Baron, 'The Demand for Black Labor: Historical Notes on the Political Economy of Racism', in James Green ed., *Workers' Struggles, Past and Present*, Philadelphia 1983, 39; on the North and the 'white worker', see David R. Roediger, *The Wages of Whiteness: Race and the Making of the American Working Class*, London 1991. Fittingly, the literature on

postbellum biracial unionism and its limits in the South is the best at studying race and labor in the US: see, e.g. W. E. B. Du Bois, *The Negro Artisan*, Atlanta 1902, 110–20 and 173–5; Herbert Gutman, 'Black Coal Miners and the Greenback-Labor Party in Redeemer, Alabama: 1878–1879', *Labor History* 10 (Summer 1969): 506–35; Eric Arnesen, *Waterfront Workers of New Orleans: Race, Class and Politics, 1863–1923*, Oxford 1991; Daniel Rosenberg, *New Orleans Dockworkers: Race, Labor, and Unionism, 1892–1923*, Albany, N.Y. 1988; Ronald Lewis, *Black Coal Miners in America: Race, Class and Community Conflict, 1780–1980*, Lexington, Ky. 1987; Richard Straw, 'Birmingham Miners Struggle for Power, 1894–1908' (Ph.D. dissertation, University of Missouri, 1980); Peter Rachleff, *Black Labor in Richmond, 1865–1900*, Urbana, Ill. 1989; Green, *Grass-Roots Socialism*; Joe William Trotter, *Coal, Class and Color: Blacks in Southern West Virginia, 1915–1932*, Urbana, Ill. 1990. Paul Worthman, 'Black Labor and Labor Unions in Birmingham, Alabama, 1897–1904', in Milton Cantor, ed., *Black Labor in America*, Westport, Conn. 1969; Arnesen, 'Longshore Workers in the Gulf Ports: The Evolution of Biracial Unionism in the Early Twentieth Century' (paper presented to the Organization of American Historians meeting, St Louis 1989); Jonathan W. McLeod, *Workers and Workplace Dynamics in Reconstruction-Era Atlanta: A Case Study*, Los Angeles, 1989.

26. See Lawrence Goodwyn, *The Populist Moment*, New York 1976.

27. Du Bois, *Negro Artisan*, 173–5; Worthman, 'Black Labor in Birmingham', 59; Baron, 'Historical Notes', 39; John Michael Matthews, 'The Georgia "Race Strike" of 1909', *Journal of Southern History* 40 (November 1974): 613–30; Hugh B. Hammett, 'Labor and Race: The Georgia Railroad Strike of 1909', *Labor History* 16 (Fall 1975): 470–84; Worthman, 'Black Labor in Birmingham', 59; Gerald David Jaynes, *Branches without Roots: Genesis of the Black Working Class in the American South, 1862–1882*, New York 1986, 263–4; Foner, *Organized Labor and the Black Worker*, 18–39; George Fredrickson, 'Antislavery Racist: Hinton Rowan Helper', in *The Arrogance of Race: Historical Perspectives on Slavery, Racism and Social Inequality*, Middletown, Conn. 1988, 51.

28. Philip S. Foner and Ronald L. Lewis, eds, *The Black Worker: A Documentary History*, Philadelphia 1978–84, 3:282–3.

29. Arnesen, *Waterfront Workers*, 114 and 126–45.

30. *Oxford English Dictionary*, 2nd edn [hereafter *OED2*], Oxford 1989, 13:422; Billy Bowles and Remer Tyson, *They Love a Man in the Country*, Memphis and Atlanta 1989, 47; Albert D. Kirwan, *Revolt of the Rednecks: Mississippi Politics, 1876–1925*, Lexington, Ky. 1951, 212; *American Dialect Dictionary*, New York 1944. C. Vann Woodward, *Tom Watson: Agrarian Rebel*, New York 1938; Barton Shaw, *The Wool Hat Boys: Georgia's Populist Party*, Baton Rouge, La. 1984, 1 and 10–11.

31. David W. Maurer, 'The Lingo of Good People', *American Speech* 10 (February 1935): 19; McAlister Coleman and Stephen Raushenbush, *Red Neck*, New York 1936; George G. Korson, *Coal Dust on the Fiddle*, Philadelphia 1943, 327 and 430; for a continuation of this practice see the photo of the Pittston miners' strike, in New York, *Workers' Vanguard*, 26 January 1990; on the National Miners' Union and 'red necks', see Malcolm Cowley, 'Kentucky Coal Town', *New Republic* 70 (2 March 1932); Theodore Dreiser and others, *Harlan Miners Speak: Report on Terrorism in the Kentucky Coal Fields*, New York 1932, 108–9 and 293; David Corbin, *Life, Work and Rebellion in the Coal Fields: The Southern West Virginia Miners, 1880–1922*, Urbana, Ill. 1981, 198; *OED*, 20:519–20; and note 30 above. Patrick Huber's superb 'Rednecks and Wool Hats, Hoosiers and Hillbillies: Working Class Southern Whites, Language and Definition of Identity' (MA thesis, University of Missouri-Columbia, 1992), esp. 112–19, has fully guided my work on both the first two terms in its title. Corbin, in correspondence with Huber, also has unearthed another 'redneck versus scabs' song, 'West Virginia Hills', reprinted in Edith Fowke and Joe Glazer, eds, *Songs of Work and Protest*, New York 1973, 56–7. Useful on the racism, but not on the tensions within the racism, of *rednecks* is Julian B. Roebuck and Mark Hickson III, eds, *The Southern Redneck: A Phenomenological Class Study*, New York 1982, 76–80 and 174–6. Some of their evidence, especially at p. 106, speaks powerfully to that tension, however.

32. *A Dictionary of American English, On Historical Principles* [hereafter *DAE*], Sir William A. Craigie and James R. Hulbert, eds, Chicago 1938, 4:2479; *Dictionary of Americanism, On Historical Principles* [hereafter *DA*], M. M. Mathews, ed., Chicago 1951, 2:1120; W. E. B. Du Bois, *Black Reconstruction in the United States, 1860–1880*, New York 1977 (1935), 727 and

passim; Neil R. McMillen, *Dark Journey: Black Mississippians in the Age of Jim Crow*, Urbana, Ill. 1989, 159; Dolores Janiewski, 'Seeking "A New Day and a New Way": Black Women and Unions in the Southern Tobacco Industry', in Carol Groneman and Mary Beth Norton, eds, '*To Toil the Livelong Day*': *America's Women at Work, 1780–1980*, Ithaca, N.Y. 1987, 162–3; H. L. Mencken, 'Designations for Colored Folk', *American Speech* 19 (October 1944): 169.

33. Garry Boulard, 'Blacks, Italians and the Making of New Orleans Jazz', *Journal of Ethnic Studies* 16 (Spring 1988): esp. 54; George Cunningham, 'The Italian: A Hindrance to White Solidarity in Louisiana, 1890–1893', *Journal of Negro History* 50 (January 1965): 24–6 and 34; Dominguez, *White by Definition: Social Classification in Creole Louisiana*, New Brunswick, N.J. 1986, 234; on *coonass*, see *Dictionary of American Regional English*, Frederic Cassidy, ed., Cambridge, Mass. 1987, 1:764; Alan I. Marcus, 'Physicians Open a Can of Worms: American Nationality and Hookworm in the United States, 1893–1909', *American Studies* 30 (Fall 1989): 103–21. Huber's 'Rednecks and Wool Hats' is indispensable on these matters. On *redbones*, see Otis Dunbar Richardson, 'Fullerton, Louisiana: An American Monument', *Journal of Forest History* 27 (October 1983): 200; Bernice Larson Webb, 'Company Town – Louisiana Style', *Louisiana History* 9 (Fall 1968): 326; Green, 'Brotherhood', 164; and Calvin L. Beale, 'An Overview of the Phenomenon of Mixed Racial Isolates in the United States', *American Anthropologist* 74 (June 1972): 706, 708.

34. *People's Party Paper*, 26 August 1892.

35. David Carlton, *Mill and Town in South Carolina, 1880–1920*, Baton Rouge, La. 1982; W. J. Cash, *The Mind of the South*, Garden City, N.Y. 1954 (1941), 311.

36. Baron, 'Historical Notes', 42; Janiewski, 'Tobacco Industry', 162–63.

37. Julian Symons, 'Conan the Logician', (London) *Sunday Times*, 8 September 1991; *OED*, 1:1009; *DAE*, 1:288; M. Schele DeVere, *Americanisms: The English of the New World*, New York 1872, 91–2. For a discussion of the evolution of *boss* before 1870, see Roediger, *Wages of Whiteness*, 54. For elite attempts to undermine biracial unity on the New Orleans docks by proclaiming 'THE NIGGER IS THE BOSS' among longshoremen, see Arnesen, *Waterfront Workers*, 182.

38. Lillian Smith, *Killers of the Dream*, New York 1963 (1949), 160–61.

39. Hall, 'Labor Struggles', 238; Q.T.H. to Mr C. E. Slagle, 19 December 1912: Louisiana Center Lumber Company Collection, F-832, Western Historical Manuscript Collection, University of Missouri-Columbia; Glen Jeansonne, 'Longism: Mainstream Politics or Aberration?' *Mid America* 71 (April-July 1989): 93, for the Long quote.

40. Green, *Grass-Roots Socialism*, 212; Hall, 'Labor Struggles', 147; for use of *redneck* to mean 'laborer' among East Texas sawmill workers, see Edward Berry, 'Sawmill Talk', *American Speech* 3 (October 1927): 25.

41. Hall, 'Labor Struggles', 191.

42. *LJ*, 10 April 1913.

43. Green, *Grass-Roots Socialism*, 210–11; Hall, 'Labor Struggles'; Ferrell and Ryan, 'Brotherhood of Timber Workers', 59; *LJ*, 6 March 1913; William D. Haywood, *Big Bill Haywood's Book*, New York 1929, 241–2.

44. Boston *Daily Evening Voice*, 21 May 1866; Foner, *Organized Labor and the Black Worker*, 23n; (Chicago) *Workingman's Advocate*, 31 August 1867; James C. Sylvis, ed., *The Life, Speeches, and Essays of William H. Sylvis*, Philadelphia 1872, 339–46. Cf. Du Bois, *Black Reconstruction*, 354.

45. Powderly, *Thirty Years of Labor*, Columbus, Oh. 1889, 656–9; Rachleff, *Black Labor in Richmond*, 172–8; Foner, *Organized Labor and the Black Worker*, 55; Kenneth Kann, 'The Knights of Labor and Southern Black Workers', *Labor History* 17 (1976); Melton McLaurin, *The Knights of Labor in the South*, Westport, Conn. 1978.

46. Quotes from Rayford W. Logan, *The Betrayal of the Negro from Rutherford B. Hayes to Woodrow Wilson*, New York 1972, 155; Foner, *Organized Labor and the Black Worker*, 76–7. See also Herbert Hill, 'In the Age of Gompers and After: Racial Practices of Organized Labor', *New Politics* 4 (Spring 1965): 26–46.

47. Worthman, 'Black Labor in Birmingham', 63–85; Foner, *Organized Labor and the Black Worker*, 91 and 64–102 passim; Logan, *Betrayal of the Negro*, 152–7. Herbert Hill, 'Mythmaking as Labor History: Herbert Gutman and the United Mine Workers of America', *International Journal of Politics, Culture and Society* 2 (Winter 1988): esp. 177–83. For other

biracial labor celebrations, see Arnesen, *Waterfront Workers*, 183; George Brown Tindall, *South Carolina Negroes, 1877–1900*, Baton Rouge, La. 1966 (1952), 139–40. On colonization, see Will H. Winn, 'The Negro: His Relation to Southern Industry', *American Federationist* 4 (February 1898): 269–71.

48. Gompers as quoted in Logan, *Betrayal of the Negro*, 155; Worthman, 'Black Labor in Birmingham', 69; Atlanta quote from Herbert Gutman, 'The Negro and the United Mine Workers of America', in Julius Jacobson, ed., *The Negro and the American Labor Movement*, Garden City, N.Y. 1968, 119–20; Noel Ignatiev, '*Matewan:* The Film and History', *Red Balloon* (Spring 1988): 60.

49. Ameringer, *If You Don't Weaken*, 218–19; Arnesen, *Waterfront Workers*, 184–5. The AFL unions' tendency to attack 'few of the presumptions of white superiority' even while advocating biracialism, is brilliantly discussed in Barry H. Goldberg, 'Beyond Free Labor: Labor, Socialism and the Idea of Wage Slavery, 1890–1920' (Ph.D. dissertation, Columbia University, 1979), 419–22.

50. Quoted in Worthman, 'Black Labor in Birmingham', 63; Matthews, 'Race Strike', 613–30, esp. 615; Claude McKay, *The Negroes in America*, Alan L. McLeod, ed. and Robert J. Winter trans. from Russian edn, Port Washington, N.Y. 1979, 38; BTW Second Convention, *Proceedings* (1912) in Louisiana Central Lumber Company Records, Western Historical Manuscripts, University of Missouri, 16–17.

51. Quotes in Marc Karson, *American Labor Union and Politics*, Carbondale, Ill. 1958, 139; Logan, *Betrayal of the Negro*, 156.

52. McKay, *Negroes in America*, 29; Rosenberg, *New Orleans Dockworkers*, 151; the very important debates over Gastonia and the wisdom of injecting the race issue into labor struggles may be followed in volumes 8 and 9 (1928–29) of *The Communist*, esp. 8:324–391 and 541 and 9:46, 52, 154–5, 159, 239ff and 296. See also Abram L. Harris, 'Black Communists in Dixie', *Opportunity* 3 (July 1925): 200. On Black support for separate locals, and on the reasoning behind such support, see Earl Lewis, *In Their Own Interest: Race, Class and Power in Twentieth-Century Norfolk, Virginia*, Berkeley, Calif. 1991, 15–17 and passim; and Eric Arnesen, 'Rethinking the Historical Relationship between Black Workers and the Labor Movement', forthcoming in *Radical History Review*. On the BTW case, see Green, 'Brotherhood', 184–90.

53. Stetson Kennedy, *Southern Exposure*, Garden City, N.Y. 1946, 305; cf. Shubel Morgan, 'The Negro and the Union: A Dialogue', in Bert Cochran, ed., *American Labor in Midpassage*, New York 1959, 149. For Gompers's use of the same argument, see Samuel Gompers to George L. Norton, 17 May 1892, reprinted in Foner and Lewis, eds, *The Black Worker*, 4:42.

54. Debs, 'The Negro in the Class Struggle', *International Socialist Review* (November 1903): 257–60.

55. Quoted in Rosenberg, *New Orleans Dockworkers*, 97; Philip S. Foner, *American Socialism and Black Americans*, Westport, Conn. 1977, 1311–38; Grady McWhiney, 'Louisiana Socialists in the Early Twentieth Century: A Study of Rustic Radicalism', *Journal of Southern History* 20 (August 1954): 315–36; James Weinstein, *The Decline of Socialism in America, 1912–1925*, New York 1969, 67. When looking at the South, it is hard to agree with Erik Olssen that the 'SP's record is undoubtedly better on issues of race ... than that ... of the AFL'. See Olssen, 'The Case of the Socialist Party That Failed', *Labor History* 29 (Fall 1988): 434.

56. Weinstein, *Decline of Socialism*, 67–9; Green, *Grass-Roots Socialism*, 224; P. Allen, *Reluctant Reformers: Racism and Social Reform Movements in the United States*, Washington, D.C. 1974, 213–16; Manning Marable, *African and Caribbean Politics from Kwame Nkrumah to Maurice Bishop*, London 1987, 33. A still valuable critique of American Socialism's reductionist view of race is Mark Naison, 'Marxism and Black Radicalism in America: Notes on a Long (and Continuing) Journey', *Radical America* 5 (May-June 1971): 3–26. Opposition to political socialism was, however, hardly proof against racism for labor radicals. Earl C. Ford and William Z. Foster, *Syndicalism*, Chicago 1912, 26, raked the Socialist Party over the coals for its alleged leading of workers into the cul-de-sac of electoral reformism – and they titled their polemic 'The Nigger in the Woodpile'. For a critique of the racial exclusivism of Texas Socialists, see Neil F. Foley, 'The New South in the Southwest: Anglos, Blacks and Mexicans in Central Texas, 1880–1930' (Ph.D. dissertation, University of Michigan, 1990).

57. Allen, *Reluctant Reformers*, 213; Marable, *African Politics*, 33; Philip S. Foner and Sally M. Miller, eds, *Kate Richards O'Hare: Selected Writings and Speeches*, Baton Rouge, La. 1982, 7–8, and 46–7 for the quotes from the pamphlets, reprinted in full on 44–9; Green, *Grass-Roots Socialism*, 214–15; See also O'Hare's 'Only a Nigger' in *The National Rip-Saw* (February 1913): 3 and 7; and Sally M. Miller, 'The Socialist Party and the Negro, 1901–1920', *Journal of Negro History* 56 (July 1971).

58. Covington Ami [Hall], 'A Letter to the Editor', *OBUM* 1 (November 1919): 49.

59. *Industrial Worker*, 26 December 1912.

60. Hall, 'Labor Struggles', 141.

61. Ibid., 146; *LJ*, 23 January 1913; Green, 'Brotherhood', 187.

62. On the syndicalism of the BTW, see Stodder, 'Covington Hall, Life and Values', 10–17.

63. John R. Commons and Associates, *A Documentary History of American Industrial Society*, Cleveland 1910, 9:157–60.

64. Rosenberg, *New Orleans Dockworkers*, 149; Janiewski, 'Tobacco Industry', 169; The cartoons are from Ernest Riebe, *Mr. Block*, Franklin Rosemont, ed., Chicago 1984 (1913), unpaged and from *LJ*, 27 March 1913; on the attempts of unskilled workers in this period to exert control over their work, see David Montgomery, *The Fall of the House of Labor: The Workplace, the State, and American Labor Activism, 1865–1925*, New York 1987, 90–96.

65. *LJ*, 3 and 10 April 1913. See also Fickle, 'Race, Class and Radicalism', 101.

66. Hall, 'Labor Struggles', 138, on the 'white Chinese'; Stodder's typescript of 'Labor Struggles' includes at p. 60 a photocopy of the account in the Alexandria *Town Talk* giving a lengthy report of Hall's speech at the convention, from which all the other quotes are taken. For the AFL on the need to end 'white slavery' in textiles, see Goldberg, 'Beyond Free Labor', 275–7. Compare also LeeAnn Whites, 'The DeGraffenreid Controversy: Class, Race, and Gender in the New South', *Journal of Southern History* 54 (August 1988): 468–78.

67. Quoted in Janiewski, 'Tobacco Industry', 171. Cf. Lillian Smith, *Killers of the Dream*, 166.

68. Barbara S. Griffith, *The Crisis of American Labor: Operation Dixie and the Defeat of the CIO*, Philadelphia 1988, 66–7.

69. Robin D. G Kelley, *Hammer and Hoe: Alabama Communists during the Great Depression*, Chapel Hill, N.C. 1990, 137 and 28.

70. Quoted in Ignatiev, 'Matewan', 60.

71. Priscilla Long, *Where the Sun Never Shines: A History of America's Bloody Coal Industry*, New York 1989, 161–2; Kelley, *Hammer and Hoe*, 29; Eric Arnesen, 'To Rule or Ruin: New Orleans Dock Workers' Struggle for Control, 1902–1903', *Labor History* 28 (Spring 1987): 165–6. On *nigger lover* as a term of contempt, see John Dollard, *Caste and Class in a Southern Town*, Garden City, N.Y. 1949 (1937), 45–6; Lewis M. Killian, *White Southerners*, Amherst, Mass. 1985, 31; Janiewski, 'Tobacco Industry', 165.

72. *LJ*, March and 3 July 1913; *VP*, 12 March and 14 July 1914; *Rebellion* 1 (April 1916): 22–3. On *white trash*, see *OED2*, 18:439; *DAE*, 4:2482. On *Negroes* and *niggers* as a Southern distinction, see e.g. Boonville (Missouri) *Advertiser*, 19 January 1903, and, for a reactionary quote from a Louisiana AFL leader that eerily echoes Hall in some ways, Fisk University Social Science Documents, *Racial Attitudes: Interviews Revealing Attitudes of Northern and Southern White Persons of a Wide Range of Occupational and Educational Levels, Toward Negroes*, no. 3, Nashville, Tenn. 1946, 251; Andre Jackson and Bill Smith, 'Separate: Races Keep to Themselves in Most Areas of Daily Life', St Louis *Post-Dispatch*, 11 December 1988.

73. New Orleans *Tribune*, 22 April 1866; *LJ*, 9 January 1913.

74. Hall, 'Labor Struggles', 122, 138 and 183; *VP*, 5 March 1914.

75. Hall, 'Labor Struggles', 147–8; Arnesen, *Waterfront Workers*, 213, notes that United Fruit's dock employed mostly Blacks and Sicilians at the time. Hall may have seen Italians as part of a 'Latin' race. On Mexican support for the BTW, see Ferrell and Ryan, 'Brotherhood of Timber Workers', 55.

76. *VP*, 17 July 1913; *LJ*, 27 March 1913.

77. Hall, 'Labor Struggles', 148.

78. *LJ*, 10 July 1913; Donald Winters, 'Dreams and Dynamite: Covington Hall and the Wobblies' (paper presented to the North American Labor History Conference, 1990), 2.

79. Baron, 'Historical Notes', 39; William Tuttle, 'Labor Conflict and Racial Violence: The Black Worker in Chicago, 1894–1919', in Cantor, ed., *Black Labor in America*, 92. Cf. Gompers in Weinstein, *Decline of Socialism*, 64.

80. Tuttle, 'Labor Conflict', 89–95; James Grossman, *Land of Hope: Chicago Black Southerners and the Great Migration, 1916–1925*, Chicago 1989, 218; Elliott M. Rudwick, *Race Riot at East St Louis, July 2, 1917*, Carbondale, Ill. 1964, 19–26; Peter Gottlieb, *Making Their Own Way: Southern Blacks' Migration to Pittsburgh, 1916–1930*, Urbana, Ill. 1987, 166–7; Mary Ellen Freifeld, 'The Emergence of the American Working Classes: The Roots of Division, 1865–1885' (Ph.D. dissertation, New York University, 1980), 514–24. For examples of Southern unions as largely Black institutions, attacked by whites, see Eric Foner, *Nothing But Freedom: Emancipation and Its Legacy*, Baton Rouge, La. 1983, 101 and 106; Jerrell H. Shofner, 'Militant Negro Laborers in Reconstruction Florida, *Journal of Southern History* 39 (1973): 397–408; McLeod, *Workplace Dynamics*, 35; Gould, 'Sugar War', 45–55; Worthman, 'Black Workers in Birmingham', 83; Tindall, *South Carolina Negroes*, 138; *Minutes of the General Council of the First International, 1870–1871*, Moscow, n.d., 228.

81. On 'unorganizable whites', see Long, *Sun Never Shines*, 160; Trotter, *Coal, Class and Color*, 3, and 'Interview with Sam Griggs, and Others' (1919) in David Saposs Collection, State Historical Society of Wisconsin – Madison, File 4.

82. Nicholas Klein, 'Hobo Lingo', *American Speech* 1 (September 1926): 651. Reference from the Peter Tamony Collection, Western Historical Manuscripts Collection, University of Missouri-Columbia.

83. Freifeld, 'American Working Classes', 520–24; Goldberg, 'Beyond Free Labor', 406–20; Herbert Gutman, 'Black Coal Miners', 522; Quote from Lewis, *Black Coal Miners*, 42. For the fascinating context of the *Labor Advocate* correspondent's remarks, see Hill, 'Myth-Making', 156n.

84. See Goldberg, 'Beyond Free Labor', 420–24; cf. Foner and Lewis, eds, *The Black Worker*, 3:243; Gottlieb, *Making Their Own Way*, 167, for union attempts to brand Black strikebreakers as race-mixers, bootleggers and drug addicts, and to recruit them into the union nonetheless.

85. *LJ*, 10 July 1913. For a comparison of AFL and IWW/BTW policies on race, see Foner, *Organized Labor and the Black Worker*, 64–102, 107–19 and 136–43.

86. See Jay Smith, *An Appeal to the Timber and Lumber Workers*, Alexandria, La. 1912, which concludes that in the case of exclusionary white unions 'it is hardly up to the whites to damn the "niggers"' for replacing striking workers.

87. *LJ*, 10 July 1913: Du Bois, as quoted in Thomas C. Holt, 'The Political Uses of Alienation: W. E. B. Du Bois on Politics, Race and Culture, *American Quarterly* 42 (June 1990): 313. On migration and the support of kin, see Green, 'Brotherhood', 165.

88. Hall, 'Labor Struggles', 43, 86, 112–13 and 186. The clearest expression of Hall's own syndicalism is his 'The Force That Rules the world', in the (Clinton, Illinois) *Strike Bulletin*, 23 September 1913. Thanks to Caroline Waldron for this reference.

89. For fascinating evidence of how, even in partially integrated industries like mining, Jim Crow workplaces limited options of Black workers and enhanced the power of blacklisting, see Herbert G. Gutman, *Power and Culture: Essays on the American Working Class*, Ira Berlin, ed., New York 1987, 204. See also Stodder's note on p. 82 of his typescript of Hall's 'Labor Struggles', where he observes that Hall's description of blacklisted timber workers going to the oil fields to lay the basis for industrial unionism ignores the fact that the fields were more or less closed to Black employment.

90. Quoted from BTW leader Jay Smith in Foner, *Organized Labor and the Black Worker*, 116; *VP*, 21 August 1913; Stodder, 'Covington Hall, Life and Values', 22. On color bars, see Ruth A. Allen, *East Texas Lumber Workers: An Economic and Social Picture, 1870–1950*, Austin, Tex. 1961, 54, 58 and (for farmers' seeking to bar all Black workers on leased land), 186–7; Kristine Stilwell, 'The Louisiana Central Lumber Company and Benevolent Paternalism' (seminar paper, University of Missouri, 1990); McMillen, *Dark Journey*, 159; Robert Norrell, 'Caste in Steel: Jim Crow Careers in Birmingham, Alabama, ' *Journal of American History* 73 (December 1986): 691. For Hall on the 'abolition of the skilled worker', see *VP*, 19 February 1914.

91. Covington Ami [Hall], 'Southern Conditions', *OBUM*, 1st ser., 1 (September 1919):

45; 'All about Civilizing the Uncivilized', *OBUM*, 2nd ser., 2 (January 1938): 31; *LJ*, 17 April 1913; Hall, *Battle Hymns of Toil*, 103.

92. C. Vann Woodward, *Origins of the New South*, Baton Rouge, La. 1971; Patrick J. Hearden, *Independence and Empire: The New South's Cotton Mill Campaign, 1865–1901*, Dekalb, Ill. 1982.

93. Worthman, 'Black Labor in Birmingham', 83; Rachleff, *Black Labor in Richmond*, 139.

94. Rosenberg, *New Orleans Dockworkers*, 97; *LJ*, 27 February 1913; *VP*, 26 November 1914; Stodder, 'Covington Hall, Life and Values', 22.

95. *LJ*, 23 January, 27 February and 6 March 1913; Hall, 'Labor Struggles', 128 and 200–207; *Industrial Worker*, 30 May 1912, as extracted from Louisiana Central Lumber Company records, Western Historical Manuscripts, University of Missouri, F-768. In 1947, the prolabor writer and Klan infiltrator Stetson Kennedy set up a 'mock Klan' in Chicago, bringing together African American, Japanese, and native American and white members in a fraternal order 'open to all believers in democracy regardless of race, creed or national origin'. The plan was not to build a multiracial Klan, however, but to incorporate under the name Knights of the Ku Klux Klan in order to prevent the real Klan from using that name. See Alan Harris Stein and John de Graaf, 'Southern Exposure: Unmasking the Klan', (Chicago) *Heartland Journal* 37 (March-April 1992): 19.

96. *VP*, 16 April 1914; *Rebellion* 1 (December 1915).

97. Cited from *Rebellion* (1914) in Stodder, 'Introduction', 20; *VP*, 26 November 1914.

98. Thomas Cripps, *Slow Fade to Black: The Negro in American Film, 1900–1942*, Oxford 1977, 51; Hall, 'Labor Struggles'. Late in his life, Hall delightfully referred to the KKK as the Koo Koo Klan. See *Industrial Worker*, 10 May 1947. Thanks to Franklin Rosemont for the reference.

99. Hall in (Hallettsville, Texas) *The Rebel*, 21 December 1912; Hall, 'Labor Struggles', 220; Roediger, 'Covington Hall', 166.

100. Gerald David Jaynes, *Branches without Roots: Genesis of the Black Working Class in the American South, 1862–1882*, New York 1986, 255–8; George Rable, *But There Was No Peace: The Role of Violence in the Politics of Reconstruction*, Athens, Ga. 1984.

101. Cripps, *Slow Fade to Black*, 41–2 and 47–8; William L. Van Deburg, *Slavery and Race in American Popular Culture*, Madison, Wis. 1984, 67–85; Oscar Ameringer, *Life and Deeds of Uncle Sam*, Chicago 1985 (1909), 36–7. Hall's view of Reconstruction was also very largely shared by the leading historian connected with the Socialist Party. See Algie M. Simons, *Social Forces in American History*, New York 1911, 285–303.

102. *Solidarity*, 25 May 1912; *Industrial Worker*, 30 May 1912; Hall, 'Labor Struggles', 202; Jaynes, *Branches without Roots*, 280–96; Edward Magdol, *A Right to Land*, Westport, Conn. 1977, passim.

103. Hall, 'Labor Struggles', 32 and 130–45; Gould, 'Sugar War', 45–55 and note 19 above; on Elaine, Hall, 'A Letter to the Editor', *OBUM*, 1st ser., 1 (November 1919): 49; and Richard C. Cortner, *A Mob Intent on Death*, Middletown, Conn. 1988.

104. Oscar Ameringer as quoted in Arnesen, *Waterfront Workers*, 326n111; on Hall's primitivism, see Roediger, 'Covington Hall', 163–5. Cf. the John Sloan cartoon reprinted in Leslie Fishbein's introduction to Rebecca Zurier, *Art for the Masses: A Radical Magazine and Its Graphics, 1911–1917*, Philadelphia 1988, 17, and originally in *International Socialist Review* 14 (January 1914): 419. On the African American critique of alienation under industrial capitalism, see W. E. B. Du Bois, *The Gift of Black Folk*, Millwood, N.Y. 1975 (1924), 53–4; see also Green, *Grass-Roots Socialism*, 207. Du Bois's *Black Reconstruction* clearly casts Black workers as the leading edge of the broadly defined Southern labor movement. Historians have been slow to evaluate that idea and to assess its validity after Reconstruction. See, however, notes 25, 80 and 102 above and Leon F. Litwack, *Been in the Storm So Long: The Aftermath of Slavery*, New York 1979, 416–17, 433–43; Eric Foner, 'Black Labor Conventions during Reconstruction' (unpublished paper forthcoming in a collection in tribute to Philip S. Foner). For an interesting, if romantic, argument on white racism, 'nigger work' and the implications of a loss of contact with land by whites, see Wendell Berry, *The Hidden Wound*, Boston 1970, 102–8.

105. *LJ*, 6 and 27 March, 23 April, and 26 June 1913; Hall, 'A Dirty Lay', *The Rebel*, 14 December 1912, cited in Jeff Ferrell, 'The Song the Capitalist Never Sings: The Brotherhood

of Timber Workers and the Culture of Conflict', *Labor History* 32 (Summer 1991): 430.

106. *LJ*, 7 and 23 April and 26 June 1913; Hall, 'I, the Working Man' and 'Forward', *OBUM*, 1st ser., 1 (August 1919): 15; Hall, 'Little Mother', in *Battle Hymns of Toil*, 78; 'Mother, Mother of Christ', in *LJ*, 3 April 1913; Hall, 'Why I Am a Socialist', *International Socialist Review* 5 (December 1904): 347.

107. Committee of Defense-BTW, 'Impartial Justice' undated leaflet issued in Alexandria and in Louisiana Central Lumber Company records, Western Historical Manuscripts, University of Missouri, F-821. On the 'black brute rapist', see Nell Irvin Painter, 'Social Equality, Miscegenation, Labor and Power', in Numan V. Bartley, ed., *The Evolution of Southern Culture*, Athens, Ga. 1988, esp. 50–51; Joel Williamson, *The Crucible of Race: Black–White Relations in the American South since Emancipation*, New York 1984, 115 and 119–24. On single/married ratios, see Allen, *East Texas Lumber Workers*, 197; Vernon Jensen, *Lumber and Labor*, New York 1945, 77. On 'homeguards' and family, see Green, 'Brotherhood', 164–75. Note, however, that according to Big Bill Haywood's reminiscences some Louisiana lumber companies 'kept women who lived in little shacks [and] stayed and took the newcomers as husbands for the duration' when men changed camps. See Haywood, *Haywood's Book*, 243, and compare Luise White, *The Comforts of Home: Prostitution in Colonial Nairobi*, Chicago 1990.

108. Hall, 'Labor Struggles', 138–9; *LJ*, 17 April 1913; Stodder, 'Covington Hall, Life and Values', 24.

109. Hall, *Dreams and Dynamite*, 17; *LJ*, 6 March and 17 April 1913; *Rebellion* 1 (April 1916): 22–3.

110. Hall, 'Labor Struggles', 138–9.

111. Nancy Hewitt, '"The Voice of Virile Labor": Labor Militancy, Community Solidarity; and Gender Identity among Tampa's Latin Workers, 1880–1921', in Ava Baron, ed., *Work Engendered: Toward a New History of American Labor*, Ithaca, N.Y. 1991, 159; Hall, 'Labor Struggles'; *VP*, 4 December 1913 and 26 March 1914; *LJ*, 20 and 27 February, 6 and 20 March, and esp. 17 April 1913; Committee of Defense, 'Impartial Justice', as cited in note 107 above.

112. Quoted in Herbert G. Gutman's preface to Sterling Spero and Abram Harris, *The Black Worker: The Negro in the Labor Movement*, New York 1969, xiii; 'Mississippi', from 'Meridian Notes', *Machinists' Monthly Journal* (April 1894): 119, with thanks to Paul Taillon for the citation. On the segregated, women-employing industries of textile and tobacco production, the leading studies are Jacqueline Dowd Hall et al., *Like a Family: The Making of a Southern Cotton Mill World*, Chapel Hill, N.C. 1987, and Dolores E. Janiewski, *Sisterhood Denied: Race, Gender, and Class in a New South Community*, Philadelphia 1985. See also Whites, 'DeGraffenried Controversy', 476–7, and, for an acute comparison of textiles and tobacco, Dolores Janiewski, 'Southern Honor, Southern Dishonor: Managerial Ideology and the Construction of Gender, Race, and Class Relations in Southern Industry', in Baron, ed., *Work Engendered*, 82–8. Conversations with Caroline Waldron much deepened my understanding of these points.

113. *LJ*, 27 February 1913, and *VP*, 21 August 1913, as quoted in Green, 'Brotherhood', 1984. See, however, *VP*, 16 April 1914, for a bitter denunciation of the lynching of a Black woman. For suggestive evidence on marriage and family among Black workers in the region's lumber industry, see Allen, *East Texas Lumber Workers*, 58–62; Green, 'Brotherhood', 165 and 173, and, esp. Delia Crutchfield Cook's excellent 'They Served Three Masters: Black Workers at the Louisiana Central Lumber Company, 1902 to 1923' (unpublished paper, University of Missouri, 1992), 10–14. On white workers employing Black domestics, see Tera Hunter, 'The Politics of Paid Household Labor in Atlanta and the New South (paper presented at the April 1991 meeting of the Organization of American Historians, Louisville), 18–19; Trotter, *Coal, Class and Color*, 91; Janiewski, *Sisterhood Denied*, 127–9; Whites, 'DeGraffenreid Controversy', 477–8 and 478n82; and David R. Roediger, 'Race and the Working Class Past', forthcoming in *International Review of Social History*.

114. Freifeld, 'American Working Classes', 514–22; Montgomery, 'Workers Control of Machine Production in the Nineteenth Century', *Labor History* 17 (1976): 491–2.

115. Freifeld, 'American Working Classes', 520 and 522; Goldberg, 'Beyond Free Labor', 407–12; Patricia Cooper, *Once a Cigarmaker: Men, Women and Work Culture in American Cigar Factories, 1900–1919*, Urbana, Ill. 1987, 220.

116. Freifeld, 'American Working Classes', 522; Barry Goldberg, 'Slavery, Race and the Languages of Class: "Wage Slaves" and White "Niggers"', *New Politics* 11 (Summer 1991): 64–83; Alexandria *Town Talk*, as cited in note 66 above. On the connection of the hatred of 'white niggers' with real fears of the extent of race-mixing and of 'invisible blackness', see Joel Williamson, *New People: Miscegenation and Mulattoes in the United States*, New York 1980, 98 and 103–8.

117. James J. Davis, *The Iron Puddler: My Life in the Rolling Mills and What Came of It*, New York 1922, 72, 108–9 and 158–9; Michael Denning, *Mechanic Accents: Dime Novels and Working-Class Culture in America*, London 1987, 175–7; William M. Tuttle, Jr, *Race Riot: Chicago in the Red Summer of 1919*, New York 1984 (1970), 142–3. See also Colin J. Davis, 'The Railroad Shopmen's Strike in the Southeast', in Robert H. Zieger, ed., *Organized Labor in the Twentieth Century South*, Knoxville, Tenn. 1991, 113–34, on honor and segregation in the shop crafts. For an academic endorsement of the white craft unions' questioning of African American manliness, see John R. Commons, *Races and Immigrants in America*, New York 1913, 48–9.

118. *The American Thesaurus of Slang*, 2nd edn, Lester V. Berrey and Melvin Van Den Bark, eds, New York 1962, 724 and 850; *A Dictionary of American Slang*, Maurice H. Weseen, ed., New York 1934, 73 and 82; H. L. Mencken, 'Designations for Colored Folk', *American Speech* 19 (October 1944): 169; A. A. Roback, ed., *A Dictionary of International Slurs (Ethnophaulisms)*, Cambridge Mass. 1944, 55; for *niggerhead* as a white miners' term for impure, worthless coal, see Trotter, *Coal, Class and Color*, 115; on Mississippi, see McMillen, *Dark Journey*, 157; *OED2*, 10:403; *DA*, 2:1117; Roediger, *Wages of Whiteness*, 15.

119. James Weldon Johnson, *Along This Way*, New York 1933, 355; see also *DAE*, 3:1601.

120. See Ava Baron's superb 'Questions of Gender: Deskilling and Demasculinization in the US Printing Industry, 1830–1915', *Gender and History* 1 (Summer 1989): 178–99, and the important recent research of Paul Taillon, esp., '"By Every Tradition and Every Right": Fraternalism and Racism in the Railway Brotherhoods, 1880–1910' (unpublished paper presented at the American Studies Association annual meeting, Baltimore, 1991).

121. Foner and Lewis, eds, *The Black Worker*, 4:38–40, 42; Cf. Gutman, 'Black Coal Miners', 528.

122. Foner, *Organized Labor and the Black Worker*, 50–51, quotes Swinton.

123. See Rachleff, *Black Labor in Richmond*, 175; Stuart B. Kaufman and others, *The Samuel Gompers Papers: The Early Years of the American Federation of Labor, 1887–90*, Urbana, Ill. 1987, 297; Foner, *Organized Labor and the Black Worker*, 71 and 103–7.

124. *LJ*, 6 March 1913, contains injunctions to 'Be a MAN, a UNION MAN, an I.W.W.' from three different correspondents and the 'free masonry of labor' reference. Cf. (New Orleans) *Union Advocate*, 16 February 1903, with thanks to Eric Arnesen for the reference; Clawson, *Constructing Brotherhood: Class, Gender and Fraternalism*, Princeton, N.J. 1989, 17; and James R. Orr and Scott G. McNall, 'Fraternal Orders and Working-Class Formation in Nineteenth-Century Kansas' in McNall, Rhonda F. Levine and Rick Fantasia, eds, *Bringing Class Back In*, Boulder, Colo. 1991, 101–17. On the various 'white man's' usages, see Matthews, 'Race Strike', 615; A. Yvette Huginnie, 'Mexicans in "American Towns": Race and Work in the Arizona Mining Industry' (unpublished paper, 1989); Rudwick, *Race Riot*, 28; Lawrence Goodwyn, 'Populist Dreams and Negro Rights: East Texas as a Case Study', *American Historical Review* 46 (December 1971): 1439–51; Grossman, *Land of Hope*, 241.

125. *LJ*, 17 April 1913; *VP*, 4 December 1913 and 19 February 1914; Goldberg, 'Beyond Free Labor', 417–20; William E. Forbath, *Law and the Shaping of the American Labor Movement*, Cambridge, Mass. 1991, 136–9. On the sober, responsible, manly skilled (and semi-skilled) worker, see Taillon, '"By Every Right"', and Nick Salvatore, *Eugene V. Debs: Citizen and Socialist*, Urbana, Ill. 1982, 23. See also Paul Willis, 'Shop Floor Culture, Masculinity and the Wage Form', in John Clarke, Chas Crichter and Richard Johnson, eds, *Working-Class Culture: Studies in History and Theory*, New York 1979, 185–98.

126. *LJ*, 6 March and 17 April 1913; *VP*, 4 December 1913 and 5 March 1914.

127. Goldberg, 'Beyond Free Labor', 281–2 and 265–86, passim; Goldberg, 'Slavery, Race and the Languages of Class', 64–83; *Industrial Worker*, 28 November 1912. See also Stodder, 'Introduction', 22–3, and David R. Roediger, 'Strange Legacies: The Black International and Black America', in Roediger and Franklin Rosemont, eds, *Haymarket Scrapbook*, Chicago 1986, 94.

128. Goldberg, 'Beyond Free Labor', 412; Foner and Lewis, eds, *The Black Worker*, 3:75.

129. *LJ*, 23 January 1913. The best ideas in this paragraph come from Abra Quinn.

130. *VP*, 19 February and 26 November 1914.

131. *LJ*, 27 February and 10 July 1913.

132. Trotter, *Coal, Class and Color*, esp. 114–15; Grossman, *Land of Hope*, 1–35 and 210–44; Hall, 'Labor Struggles', 204. Indeed among white workers as well those not joining unions at times claimed a superior manliness. See James N. Gregory, *American Exodus: The Dust Bowl Migration and Okie Culture in California*, New York 1989, 162–3; and Mike Yarrow, 'The Gender-Specific Class Consciousness of Appalachian Coal Miners: Structure and Change', in McNall, Levine and Fantasia, eds, *Bringing Class Back In*, esp. 304. Randy McBee and Julie Rose developed this point acutely in seminar discussions of gender and labor.

133. Tuttle, 'Black Worker in Chicago', 97 and 109.

134. Hewitt, '"Virile Labor"', 142–67; Janiewski, *Sisterhood Denied*; Cooper, *Once a Cigarmaker*; Clawson, *Constructing Brotherhood*; Elizabeth Faue, *Community of Suffering and Struggle: Women, Men and the Labor in Minneapolis, 1915–1945*, Chapel Hill, N.C. 1991; Hall, 'Labor Struggles', 199.

135. Hall, 'Labor Struggles', 199–200; *Industrial Worker*, 23 January 1913.

136. *LJ*, 10 April 1913; *VP*, 26 November 1914; *Industrial Worker*, 26 December 1912. Ferrell, 'Song the Capitalist Never Sings', 426–7, discusses the important issue of sabotage in the BTW and also reproduces both spellings of the word. On employer- and state-initiated antilabor violence in the industrializing South, see David Montgomery, 'Violence and the Struggle for Unionism in the South, 1880–1930', in Merle Black and John Shelton Reed, eds, *Perspectives on the American South: An Annual Review of Society, Politics and Culture*, New York 1981, 35–48, esp. 42–3.

137. *Industrial Worker*, 12 June 1913. Hall avowed support for sabotage very early. See *Industrial Worker*, 16 November 1911. For the rattler, see *VP*, 5 March 1914, and Hall, 'Labor Struggles', 229; *VP*, 7 August 1913, converts the sabotage cat into a lion in a striking cartoon. On the language and symbolism of sabotage, see Archie Green, *Wobblies, Pile Butts and Other Heroes*, forthcoming; Kelley, *Hammer and Hoe*, 101, notes the reliance of Black Communists in Alabama on 'evasive, cunning forms of resistance' and their avoidance of 'revolutionary martyrdom'. He connects these choices with a heritage of resistance dating from slavery. Informal resistance through sabotage was not, of course, the same thing as sloppy work. Trotter, *Class, Coal and Color*, 65 and 214–65, and Kelley, '"We Are Not What We Seem": Toward a Black Working-Class Infrapolitics in the Twentieth-Century South (paper presented to the Southern Labor Studies Conference, Atlanta, October 1991), 25–6, emphasize that efficient work was not only required to keep Black jobs but a source of pride among Black workers. Kelley argues that sabotage and foot-dragging were nevertheless practiced by Black Southern workers but that since 'strategies of resistance are determined by the character of subordination' (p. 26), the dynamics leading to sabotage were different for white and Black workers.

138. *VP*, 26 November 1914; Foner, *Organized Labor and the Black Worker*, 119; Reed, 'Lumberjacks', 45n10. On employers' arguments regarding paternalism, homes and manhood, see Allen, *East Texas Lumber Workers*, 186–7, and Kristine Stilwell, 'Benevolent Paternalism;' Parr, *Gender of Breadwinners*, 142–50; Taillon, '"By Every Right"'; Willis, 'Shop Floor Culture;' and Yarrow, 'Gender-Specific Class Consciousness', 301, for the final quotation.

11

Whiteness and Ethnicity
in the History of 'White Ethnics'
in the United States

Barbara Fields has recently argued that the absence of the term *white people* in the United States Constitution 'is not surprising [since] in a legal document ... slang of that kind would be hopelessly imprecise.' Nonetheless, the first Congress convened under that Constitution voted in 1790 to require that a person be 'white' in order to become a naturalized citizen of the US. Predictably enough, the hopeless imprecision of the term left the courts with impossible problems of interpretation that stretched well into the twentieth century. As Robert T. Devlin, United States Attorney at San Francisco, understated it in 1907: 'There is considerable uncertainty as to just what nationalities come within the term "white person."' The courts thus discovered in the early part of this century what historians have belatedly learned in its latter stages: that the social fiction of race defies rigorous definition. If science were to determine whiteness, problems proliferated because ethnological wisdom constantly changed. In particular, modern ethnology shunned the word *white* and used instead terms like *caucasian* and *Aryan*, which were not current when the legislation was passed in 1790. Moreover, science tended to classify Syrians and Asian Indians as caucasians, a view that clashed with the commonsense view of federal naturalization officials and of some judges bent on excluding them as nonwhites.

If the ground were shifted to culture and geography as determinants of who was white, the inconvenient fact was that these standards too had evolved messily over time. The Pennsylvania jurist Oliver B. Dickinson acutely noted, 'Although the original 1790 statute probably was not intended to include the Latin races ... later immigration expanded the term to cover Latin Europeans', and still later southeastern Europeans came to be included. Color differences were so varied within so-called 'races' as to

181

preclude the possibility that whiteness could have literally been measured by (absence of) pigmentation. The 1923 Supreme Court decision to deny naturalization to Bhagat Singh Thind marked the culmination of a process by which the legal system, in the words of Joan M. Jensen, 'rejected science, history, legal precedent and logic to put the Constitution at the disposal of a legal fiction called "the common man"' – an invented figure who knew that Asian Indians were not white. Between 1923 and 1927, sixty-five Asian Indians suffered denaturalization in the wake of the Thind decision. Lower courts had naturalized them as white immigrants, but the under the test of 'common understanding' they had become nonwhite.[1]

If the legal and social history of Jim Crow often turned on the question 'Who was Black?' the legal and social history of immigration often turned on the question 'Who was white?' And yet, amidst the large and sophisticated literature on ethnic consciousness and Americanization among immigrants, we know very little about how the Irish and Italians, for example, became white; about how the Chinese and Japanese became nonwhite; or about how groups like Asian Indians and Mexican Americans were at least partly identified as white before becoming nonwhite.[2]

The recent outpouring of historical writing on the social construction of whiteness as a racial category and as an identity opens the possibility of closing this gap in the historical literature and of undertaking a full reconsideration of the relationship between race and ethnicity in US history.[3] Until now, most objections to the conflation of the category of race with that of ethnicity have turned on the quite reasonable point that, historically, civilly and structurally, racial minorities have not been treated in a relevantly similar way to those immigrants who came to be identified as 'white ethnics'. Richard Williams's elegant *Hierarchical Structures and Social Value* has recently pushed this argument to the fascinating conclusion that in the US ethnicity is made possible by race – that ethnicity is a social status assigned to those immigrants who, though slotted into low-wage jobs, were *not* reduced to the slavery or systematic civil discrimination that 'racial' minorities suffered. But however compelling the case that racial oppression has not equalled ethnic oppression, another challenge deserves to be made to analyses that do not sharply differentiate between race and ethnicity as ideological categories. *Among whites*, racial identity (whiteness) and ethnic identity are distinct, and this article will argue, often counterposed, forms of consciousness.[4]

This latter distinction, and its importance, becomes clearer as we look at a recent passage from the distinguished legal historian William Forbath's *Law and the Shaping of the American Labor Movement*. Forbath aptly summarizes the position of the 'new labor history' on why US labor is not so 'exceptional' by world standards in its historical lack of class consciousness. He writes, 'Ethnic division is the other principle factor in the traditional exceptionalism story. In any revised account, ethnic and racial cleavages will surely remain central. However, the new labor historians have discovered that ethnic identities and affiliations were not as corrosive of class-based identities and actions as we tend to assume.'[5] The sliding here from an argument about ethnicity to one about race and ethnicity and back to one about ethnicity is significant. Surely, as the work of Wayne Broehl, Earl Lewis, Vicki Ruiz, Victor Greene, Robin D. G. Kelley and others shows, specific white ethnic (that is, Polish American, Irish American, and so on), African American and Mexican American cultural forms and institutions often undergirded class mobilization in the US past.[6] But what happens when we remember that racial identity also means *whiteness*? The central point of much of the recent writing on the instances of attempts to organize specifically as white workers – in hate strikes and campaigns for Oriental exclusionism, for example – is how fully such mobilization played into the emergence of a narrow, brittle and at best craft-conscious labor movement.[7] Ethnicity is one thing in this case, and whiteness quite another.

'Racial identities are not only Black, Latino, Asian, Native American and so on', Coco Fusco has written, 'they are also white. To ignore white ethnicity is to redouble its hegemony by naturalizing it.' Fusco's comment is breathtakingly clear in its recognition of the need to explore the social construction of white identities, but her use of the term *white ethnicity* introduces interesting complications with regard to how white Americans have historically come to think of themselves as white. Fusco uses white ethnicity in the same sense as one might use *white racial identity*, illustrating a long tendency in US scholarship to conflate race and ethnicity. But *white ethnicity* has also meant, at least for the last forty years, the consciousness of a distinct identity among usually second- or third-generation immigrants who both see themselves and are seen as racially white and as belonging to definable ethnic groups. And the complications do not end there. As Barry Goldberg and Colin Greer have observed, this 'white ethnicity', which gained force in major cities from the 1950s onwards in opposition to racial integration of neighborhoods, was not just a heading grouping together specific ethnic identities (Greek American, Polish American, Italian American and so on) but a 'pan-ethnic' ideology that 'did not emphasize cultural distinction but the shared values of a white immigrant heritage.' Thus it was possible to become more self-consciously 'white ethnic', but less self-consciously Greek, Polish or Italian at the same time.[8]

Though the phrase *white ethnic* trips off the tongue easily today, the relationship between whiteness and ethnicity is in no sense simple, not now and certainly not historically. This essay attempts to survey some of the historical complexities of the interplay of racial and ethnic consciousness among whites in the US. Its very preliminary nature qualifies it as less a survey of what we know about this understudied topic than as a survey of what we do not know. Although we badly need studies of how 'nonwhite' ethnic groups became so defined – indeed, in effect became 'races' – the focus here is on the process of 'becoming white' with material on nonwhiteness largely included to illuminate that process.[9]

The Not-Yet-White Ethnic

Alex Haley's epilogue to Malcolm X's *Autobiography* features a rivetting scene in which Malcolm admires European children newly arrived at a US airport and predicts that they are soon to use their first English word: *nigger*. The force of the passage lies in its dramatic rendering of the extent to which European immigrants became not just Americans but specifically *white* Americans and of the apparent ease with which they did so.[10] As important as the telescoped, long-range historical truth in the passage is, it also leads us to miss – as most historians have missed – the dramatic, tortuous subplots of immigration history via which, as James Baldwin has written, arriving Europeans 'became white'.[11]

The history of what John Bukowczyk has called the 'not-yet-white eth-nic' remains to be written.[12] Its writing will sharply focus our attention on the fact that immigrants could be Irish, Italian, Hungarian and Jewish, for example, without being white. Many groups now commonly termed part of the 'white' or 'white ethnic' population were in fact historically re-garded as nonwhite, or of debatable racial heritage, by the host American citizenry. In the mid nineteenth century, the racial status of Catholic Irish incomers became the object of fierce, extended debate. The 'simian' and 'savage' Irish only gradually fought, worked and voted their ways into the white race in the US. Well into the twentieth century, Blacks were counted as 'smoked Irishmen' in racist and anti-Irish US slang.[13] Later, sometimes darker, migrants from Southern and Eastern Europe were similarly cast as nonwhite. The nativist folk wisdom that held that an Irishman was a Black, inside out, became transposed to the reckoning that the turning inside out of Jews produced 'niggers'. Factory managers spoke of employees distinctly as Jews and as 'white men', though the 'good Jew' was sometimes counted as white. Poorer Jews were slurred as Black with special frequency. Indeed a 1987 Supreme Court decision used the record of Jews having been seen as a distinct race in the nineteenth century as precedent to allow a Jewish group to sue under *racial* discrimination stat-utes. Stock anti-Black humor was pressed into service as anti-Semitic, anti-Czech and, later, anti-Polish humor.[14] Slavic 'Hunkies' were non-white in steel towns.[15] Among 'white' miners defending their 'American towns' in Arizona mining areas, not only the Chinese and Mexicans, but also Eastern and Southern Europeans, were termed nonwhite. As the leading scholar of nativism, John Higham, has observed, 'In all sections [of the US] native-born and northern European laborers called themselves "white men" to distinguish themselves from the southern Europeans whom they worked beside.'[16]

Of course none of this implies, as the modern white ethnics' historical memories and invented traditions often do, that the immigrant experience was parallel to that of African Americans, except for the more successful outcome, arising from determination and effort. Not-yet-white immigrants consistently had a more secure claim to citizenship, to civil rights and political power, and a greater opportunity to choose to pass as whites, especially in seeking jobs.[17] The duration of 'not-yet-whiteness', as measured against that of racial oppression in the US, was quite short. In Joe Eszterhaus's much-better-than-the-movie labor novel, *F.I.S.T.*, set in and after the 1930s, the Afro-Polish freight-handler Lincoln Dombrowsky is plagued by a boss who 'kept after him, hitting his buzzer. Calling him "polack" as if he were saying "nigger".'[18] Readers understand that the implied use of the latter term greatly added to the sting of the former. It is, as Lawrence Joseph's withering review of the recent collection *Devil's Night* by the Michigan-raised Israeli writer Ze'ev Chafets, maintains, 'silly' for Chafets to portray himself as a 'nonwhite' in writing about Detroit. Chafets's self-described 'bad hair' and 'swarthy skin' notwithstanding, Joseph argues, 'In America, blacks cannot choose which racial side they're on; in America, Chafets can.'[19] To write the history of the whitening of the not-yet-white ethnic thus requires close attention to change over time. In reconstructing that history we may, for example, not only develop an appreciation for why the pioneer labor researcher David Saposs consistently referred to anti-Slavic and anti-Southern European prejudice as 'race prejudice' as late as the 1920s but also a sense of the problems raised by his and others doing so.[20] Further complexity arises when we cease to regard racial and ethnic identities as categories into which individuals simply are 'slotted', as Williams's *Hierarchical Structures* has it, and begin to see whiteness as in part a category into which people place themselves.[21] James Baldwin's point that Europeans arrived in the US and became white – 'by deciding they were white' powerfully directs our attention to the fact that white ethnics, while they lived under conditions not of their own choosing, by and large chose whiteness, and even struggled to be recognized as white.[22]

We urgently need studies of how and why this choice was made by specific immigrant groups. It is not strictly true that, as Baldwin argues, 'no one was white before he or she came to America.' In a few cities providing significant numbers of migrants, such as London, there was a significant Black population and a developing sense of whiteness within the working class before immigration.[23] White Cuban immigrants brought to the US a sense of the importance of race, though one not nearly as finely honed as that present in the US.[24] We need also to know far more about folk beliefs regarding Blacks in areas like Ireland, Germany and Slavic Europe. The extent to which, as Williams argues, English anti-Irish oppression was racism rather than ethnic prejudice – or to which anti-Sicilian oppression in Italy or anti-Gypsy and anti-Semitic oppression in Europe involved a kind of race-thinking – deserves consideration in accounting for the development of a sense of whiteness among immigrants to the US. Robbie McVeigh's astute comments on 'anti-traveller' ideas as a source of racism in Ireland begin such studies penetratingly.[25] Nonetheless, in its broad outline Baldwin's point is hardly assailable. Norwegians, for example, did not spend a great deal of time and energy in Norway thinking of themselves as white. As the great Irish nationalist and antiracist Daniel O'Connell thundered to Irish Americans who increasingly asserted their whiteness in the 1840s, 'It was not in Ireland you learned this cruelty.'[26]

But neither was whiteness *immediately* learned in the United States. At times a strong sense of ethnic identity could cut *against* the development of a white identity. Thus Poles in the Chicago stockyards community initially saw the post–World War I race riots there as an affair between the whites and the Blacks, with Poles separate and uninvolved.[27] The huge numbers of 'birds of passage' – migrants working for a time in the US and then returning home – were probably less than consumed by a desire to build a white American identity.[28] That the native population questioned their whiteness may also have led immigrants to a sense of apartness from white America and occasionally to a willingness to sympathize and fraternize with African Americans. The best-studied example of the dynamics of such solidarity and mixing is that of the Italian (and especially Sicilian) immigrant population in the late nineteenth and early twentieth centuries, especially in Louisiana – a 'not-yet-white' population both in the view of white Louisianans, and in its self-perception. Many Black Louisianans, according to Hodding Carter, Sr's *Southern Legacy*, 'made unabashed distinctions between Dagoes and white folks and treated [Italians] with a friendly, first-name familiarity.' White natives also made such distinctions, counting 'black dagoes' as neither Black nor white. If Paolo Giordano exaggerated in treating Italian Louisianans unequivocally as a group that 'associated freely with the Blacks, going clearly against the accepted social order', he did so only slightly. The associations of Blacks and Italians took place at peddlers' carts, in the cane fields, in the timber camps and in the halls and bars where jazz was made.[29] Italian–Black solidarity was also strikingly present, albeit alongside its opposite, in New York City and, from Buffalo to California, Italians suffered from racial typing and what Micaela di Leonardo calls 'racist oppression'.[30]

The Italian and Polish examples are far from isolated ones of mixing and solidarity. However vexed the record of relations between African Americans and Jews, the history record of solidarity with Black civil rights causes by radical and mainstream Jewish organizations and individuals is clear.[31] The important Ukrainian American paper *Svoboda Cbob' OAA* included militant antilynching articles and even homages to John Brown. Roger Horowitz's work on interracial unionism in meatpacking identifies Croatian American workers in Kansas City as 'among white packinghouse workers' the group most clearly committed to interracialism. He attributes this commitment to the Croats sharing oppression with Blacks as they worked 'at the bottom end of the employment ladder [and] chafed under mistreatment by German foremen who called them "Hunky" rather than their ... name.'[32] Raymond Mohl's and Neil Betten's research on Gary, Indiana shows examples of positive Black–Greek associations. In Houston, such interracial contacts were not pronounced, as Greek Americans quickly learned Jim Crow. But the Greek community also long continued to differentiate itself from *i aspri* (that is, 'the whites') a term often used disparagingly.[33] The Mississippi Chinese, whose racial status was the object of contention over decades but who arguably eventually became accepted as white, also frequently socially mixed with and married Blacks in the early years after migrating. Even some Irish were 'not yet white' in their own eyes, and not just in the eyes of nativists, in the 1820s and 1830s and mixed considerably with free Blacks.[34]

As the term *not-yet-white ethnic* implies, many of these patterns of association of immigrants and Blacks were ephemeral. Moreover, it was quite possible for immigrants and African Americans not to see their interactions in Black–white terms but nonetheless to regard each other with suspicion and even hatred, much as rival immigrant groups did at times. Still the patterns are important in that they signal that the 'white ethnic' developed historically and that he or she was certainly not white because of his or her ethnicity. Indeed at times of great identification with homeland and ethnicity, immigrants' identification with whiteness was often minimal.

Americanization or Whitening?

Malcolm X therefore had a great deal of the story right when he argued that in the process of Americanizing European immigrants acquired a sense of whiteness and of white supremacy. As groups made the transition from Irish in America or Poles in America to Irish Americans or Polish Americans, they also became white Americans. In doing so they became white ethnics but also became less specifically ethnic, not only because they sought to assimilate into the broad category of American but also because they sought to be accepted as white rather than as Irish or Polish. In the Irish case this seeking of whiteness involved constructing a pan-white identity in which Irish Americans struggled to join even the *English* in the same racial category. In Ireland, it goes without saying, there was little talk of the common whiteness uniting Anglo-Saxon and Celtic peoples.

Nonetheless the precise relationships among Americanization, whiteness and loss of specific ethnicity are extremely complex. One complicating factor is that immigrants at times developed significant contacts with Black culture, and through those contacts maintained elements of their own ethnic cultures that resonated with Black culture, even as they embraced whiteness. The haunting example of the blacked-up Irish minstrel, singing songs of lost land and exile, is, as Leni Sloan has tellingly observed, an extreme case of the phenomenon. The essence of minstrelsy was the whiteness – not specific ethnicity – beneath the mask, but elements of Irish memory and culture were perversely maintained in blackface. Alexander Saxton's fine World War II labor novel *Bright Web in the Darkness* provides a more modest and modern example. Its hero, the young union militant Tom O'Regan, notices that his wife-to-be is standing with a Black student when he picks her up from a welding class. 'So', O'Regan asks, 'who's the smoked Irishman?' Sensing disapproval, he adds, 'Oh, it's only a joke, Sally, don't act so huffy. After all, I'm an Irishman … like you're all the time telling me.' Saxton here picks up on the combination of racism, defensiveness and a certain desire to keep alive comparisons of Black and Irish that runs through Irish American retellings of 'Paddy and the Slave' jokes.[35] Still more recently, as Donald Tricarico has shown, the most self-consciously 'proud because we're Italian' segment of New York City youth culture has 'generously appropriated' African American styles in forming a 'guido' subculture. Deriding assimilationist 'wannabes', Guidos, sometimes called B-boys, have adopted the anti-Italian slur 'Guinea' – a term perfectly illustrative of the 'not-yet-white' period of Italian American history, as their preferred form of address. They have become able hiphop musicians. Nonetheless, Tricarico adds, Guidos on other levels 'resist identification with Black youth' and 'bite the hand that feeds them style.'[36]

Moreover, partial identification with African American culture cannot simply be connected to a defense of specific ethnicity against the cultural homogeneity or the emptiness of white American culture. It may well be that, as the music historian Ronald Morris has argued, Sicilians playing jazz in New Orleans embraced Black music because 'Sicilians were like black people in seeing music as a highly personalized affair … born of collective experience.' But in the playing, Sicilians not only retained this sensibility but contributed to creating a new American art form, though far from a white American one. Louis Prima, the second-generation Italian American jazz great, may have rebelled out of some sense of ethnic pride when forced to learn to play the violin in the classical tradition 'as a means of cultural assimilation'. But when he picked up the horn and discovered Louis Armstrong, he moved into a wide and great Black and American tradition in a career that took him to the most famous 'white' clubs in New York City, to the Apollo in Harlem, the Howard in Washington, D.C., and the palatial hotels of Las Vegas, but, out of principle, not to segregated Southern venues.[37] The same might be said of Chicago's ethnic jazzmen, especially those in and around the Austin High Gang, who fled the homogenizing influences of suburban culture and assimilationism and preserved much of the best of immigrant resistance to routinization via an identification with African American culture, even as they helped innovate within an American music. The best modern example is undoubtedly Johnny Otis, the important bluesman and West Coast music promoter. Otis, born of Greek immigrant parents who ran small stores in Black neighborhoods, chose the vibrancy of African American life over what he saw as the relative stagnation of white American mass culture and then pioneered in forms of rock and roll, which much changed US culture and the world's.[38]

The examples of Prima and Otis suggest that it was at least possible to become an American, rather than to become a white American, and that through participation in an 'incontestably mulatto' American culture a greater part of that which was vital in immigrant culture was capable of being preserved and developed than by assimilating to white Americanism. However, such glorious subplots in immigration history remain subplots. In particular, political mobilization around the claiming of white Americanism by immigrants was far more constant and powerful than the episodic claiming of a nonracial Americanism – as perhaps in the case of the early CIO or the Knights of Columbus's response to the resurgence of Anglo-Saxonism after World War I with the antiracist 'Gifts of American peoples' initiatives.[39] The very claiming of a place in the US legally involved, as the Asian Indian example shows, a claiming of whiteness.

But more than that, immigrants often were moved to struggle to equate whiteness with Americanism in order to turn arguments over immigration from the question of who was foreign to the question of who was white. Nativists frequently favorably compared the long-established Black population with the newcoming immigrant one as an argument to curtail the rights of the latter. Abolitionists made the same comparison to buttress the case for African American freedom.[40] Blacks at times used their long-established tenure in America to argue that they should be protected against 'invading' Italians or Chinese or at least placed on a par with the immigrants.[41]

Immigrants could not win on the question of who was foreign. They lost as long as the issue was whether, as Jack London put it, 'Japs' and 'Dagoes' would usurp the jobs and privileges of 'real Americans'.[42] The new immigrant was often viewed by the host population as a threat to 'our [American] jobs'. But if the issue somehow became defending 'white man's jobs' or a 'white man's government', the not-yet-white ethnic could gain space by deflecting debate from nativity, a hopeless issue, to race, an ambiguous one. The first dramatic example of this phenomenon was the embrace of Democratic Party appeals to an 'American race' of 'white men' by the huge masses of Catholic Irish arriving in the antebellum US. If whiteness made for Americanity and if the Irish could qualify as white, nativist arguments suffered greatly. It was even possible for the Irish to campaign for an Irish monopoly of New York City longshore jobs under the cover of agitation for an 'all-white waterfront'.[43] After the Civil War, the newcoming Irish would help lead the movement to bar the relatively established Chinese from California, with their agitation for a 'white man's government' serving to make race, and not nativity, the center of the debate and to prove the Irish white. 'What business has the likes of him over here?' a recent Irish settler in California asked regarding resident Chinese. The question made sense only if whiteness conferred a right to settle.[44] Sixty years later, the despised newcoming internal migrants, the 'Okies', would similarly seek to establish their claims as more fit to be Californian than long-established Californians by turning to questions of race. One new arrival from Oklahoma asked, 'Just who built California?' before misanswering his own question: 'Certainly not the Chinese, Japanese, Hindus, etc.'[45]

'Shared' Oppression and the Claiming of Whiteness

The process by which 'not yet' and 'not quite' white ethnics, whose own status as white Americans was sharply questioned, came to stress that their whiteness made them Americans shows how fraught with problems are those interpretations that posit that 'shared' oppression should have caused new immigrants to ally with African Americans. It was not just that the oppression of new working class immigrants differed from that of African Americans but that even very similar experiences of oppression could cause new immigrants to grasp for the whiteness at the margins of their experiences rather than concentrating on the ways in which they shared much in daily life with African Americans. It seems to me worth investigating whether the immigrant groups with sufficient numbers of small businessmen to be identified as 'trading minorities' – for example, Jews, New Orleans Italians, Syrians, the Mississippi Chinese and Greeks – had greater opportunity to develop a positive sense of non-white identity, and even to cross over into African American culture, than did more overwhelmingly proletarian new immigrant groups. Certainly, as the tragedy of African American relations with Korean merchants today suggests, trading minorities with businesses in the Black community often have developed a sense of distance from, or hostility towards, the neighborhoods in which they trade, and vice versa. But it is also precisely those 'trading minorities' that have produced some of the nation's best transgressors of the color line and race traitors, from Louis Prima to Johnny Otis. Of course, proximity to the Black community at his family's store mattered in the case of Otis, but more broadly the very distance between the ways trading minorities were stereotyped and the ways wageworking ethnic groups were stereotyped afforded a certain assurance that, however much they might be termed nonwhite, trading minorities were not in danger of being branded 'niggers'. As Carey McWilliams noted, the trading minority was usually seen as 'not ... lazy but ... too industrious' as 'not ... incapable of learning but ... too knowing'.[46] If members of such minorities (like the broader middle class today) often developed superficial or even exploitative relations with African American culture, they also may have been able to borrow more confidently from Blacks without fearing that they would be cast as 'white niggers' and their jobs as 'nigger work' – an anxiety that the white working poor seldom escaped.[47]

Different dynamics characterized proletarian new immigrants' relations to African Americans, producing at once greater social proximity and a greater desire for distance. In his 1914 volume *The Old World and the New*, the nativist sociologist E. A. Ross approvingly quoted expert testimony from a physician who held that 'the Slavs are immune to certain kinds of dirt. They can stand what would kill a white man.' Slavs had excellent reasons to want out from under such a stereotype, which not only declared them nonwhite but gave free rein to employers hiring them as laborers (and to native-born skilled workers hiring them as helpers) to place them in the dirtiest and most unhealthy jobs. In such positions Slavic workers would be said to be 'working like niggers' and would, like the most exploited Jews, Sicilians, or Louisiana creoles elsewhere, face further questioning of their whiteness based on the very fact of their hard and driven labor. Such sharing of oppression with Blacks doubtless made many Slavs question whether they wanted to be white Americans, but at the same time bitter knowledge of how Blacks fared made whiteness that much more attractive. In the case of working class Italian Americans in and around Harlem, *proximity* of position, language, culture and appearance made for an especially sharp need to establish that Puerto Rican migrants were of another race while cultural and color *differences* allowed for more tolerance toward Haitians, and even to the perception that Haitians were 'not black'.[48]

Thus the logic of class propelled Slavs and other not-yet-white ethnics at once in both of the direction of appreciating that which they had in common with African Americans *and* of denying the same. At times, it may simply have been that job competition made Slavs conscious of the potentialities of their possible whiteness. However, much more subtle processes could also be at play, as is illustrated by the rich testimony regarding both the possibility of rejecting whiteness and the attractions of claiming it from a Slovak woman from Bridgeport, Connecticut interviewed by the Federal Writers Project in the 1930s:

> I always tell my children not [to] play with the nigger-people's children, but they always play with them just the same. I tell them that the nigger children are dirty and that they will get sick if they play. I tell them they could find some other friends that are Slovaks just the same. This place now is all spoiled, and all the people live like pigs because the niggers they come and live here with the decent white people and they want to raise up their children with our children. If we had some place for the children to play I'm sure that the white children they would not play with the nigger children. ... All people are alike – that's what God says – but just the same it's no good to make our children play with the nigger children because they are too dirty.

Ivan Greenberg, whose fine dissertation includes this important passage, observes that the very '"dirty" stereotype' long used to abuse immigrants was turned by Slovak and Italian Bridgeport residents against Blacks and criticism of white ethnics was thus deflected if not defused.[49]

It would of course be simplistic to suppose that whiteness and white supremacy were embraced and forwarded by not-yet-white ethnics simply as a public relations ploy to shore up their own group image. What gave force, poignancy and pathos to the process of choosing whiteness was that it not only enabled the not-yet-white ethnics to live more easily with the white American population but to live more easily with themselves and with the vast changes industrial capitalist America required of them. I have argued this case in some detail with regard to Irish Americans in my book *Wages of Whiteness*, but other later-coming groups also came to grips with their own (forced) acceptance of time discipline, loss of contact with nature and regimented work by projecting 'primitive' values onto 'carefree' African Americans. Thus a resident in the Italian-Slavic enclave studied by Greenberg combined racism and envy in holding that Blacks had it easier than 'white' workers:

... the nigger people can stay up to 3 o'clock in the morning playing and dancing and they don't have to worry about going to work. ... We [white] poor people can't even have a good time one time a week. ... The nigger people have a holiday every day in the week.

The tremendously conflicted emotional decision of white ethnics to abandon urban neighborhoods – and, as Robert Orsi observes, often to abandon parents and grandparents in the city – was similarly softened by the development of a historical memory emphasizing that 'black crime' moved white ethnics to the suburbs by 'driving them out' of the center city, though the timing of mass suburbanization hardly fits such a pattern.[50]

Other dimensions of the ways in which whiteness was constructed among immigrants remain so shrouded by mystery and inattention from historians as to be perfectly illustrative of the fact that at this stage we are much better placed to report on our ignorance rather than our knowledge of the history of white ethnic consciousness. In closing, it is worth evoking a particularly rich passage in William Attaway's great 1941 proletarian novel *Blood on the Forge*, which suggests not only how far we have to go in understanding that history but also how well worth the effort developing such an understanding can be. Attaway describes the reaction of Irish workers in a foundry after a Black worker, Big Mat, had knocked out a 'hayseed' before he could hit an Irishman. Mat was 'the hero of the morning' and drew praise for being both a model 'colored worker' and for being more than Black. The boss melter, a 'big Irishman' in charge of five furnaces, took the former line of praise: 'Never had a colored helper work better on the hearth ... do everythin' the melter tell him to do and take care of the work of a whole crew if he ain't held back.' Other Irish workers on the gang conferred the title 'Black Irish' on Mat. One 'grinned' that 'Lots of black fellas have Irish guts.' Another added, 'That black fella make a whole lot better Irisher than a hunky or a ginny. They been over here twenty years and still eatin' garlic like it's as good as stew meat and potatoes', before 'glanc[ing] sharply around to see if any of the foreigners had heard him.' But Big Mat did not celebrate his newfound acceptance. He made no answer when called Black Irish but instead 'full of savage pressure', took refuge in the 'pleasant thought' of animals 'tearing at each other' and hurried away to the dogfights.[51] Some of this arresting scene is familiar: the social construction of race; the question of whether 'foreigners' merit inclusion over African Americans; the combination of a commitment to specific (Irish) ethnicity and a lack of reference to whiteness; and the importance of timing, in that the Irish are by now natives, not newcomers.

But much is also unsettling. There is little grandeur in the breaking down of race lines here, in part because the break is a superficial and momentary one, based on Mat's temporary status a model 'colored worker'. Moreover, the very thing that makes Mat such a model to the more privileged Irish workers and bosses – a supposed loyal willingness to do anything for his superiors if not 'held back' – are bound to define him as a 'nigger' in the eyes of the 'hunkies and ginnies' on the gang. In this scene at least, Attaway shows us a workplace that does not bridge distinctions between African Americans and white ethnics but tragically recasts such distinctions. What should perhaps be most unsettling to us as historians is how little prepared we are to judge how typical this scene was at the shopfloor level and how it was experienced by the 'colored workers', the not-yet-white ethnics, and the white ethnics who built America. Until we follow the example of the recent and brilliant work on Italian Americans by Robert Orsi and develop a history of American immigration that 'puts the issues and contests of racial identity and difference at its center', we are likely to remain puzzled.[52]

Notes

1. Barbara Fields, 'Slavery, Race and Ideology in the United States of America', *New Left Review*, no. 181 (May-June 1990): 99; Joan M. Jensen, *Passage from India: Asian Indian Immigrants in North America*, New Haven, Conn. 1988, 246–69, with the Devlin quote on p. 248, the summary of Dickinson on p. 258 and the quote from Jensen on p. 255. For a thorough survey of the legal history of a variety of ethnic groups declared nonwhite in the US, see Stanford Lyman, 'The Race Question and Liberalism: Casuistries in American Constitutional Law', *International Journal of Politics, Culture and Society* 5 (Winter 1991): 203–25.

2. Sarah Deutsch, *No Separate Refuge: Culture, Class, and Gender on an Anglo-Hispanic Frontier in the American Southwest, 1880–1940*, New York 1987.

3. On whiteness, see Vron Ware, *Beyond the Pale: White Women, Racism and History*, London 1992; David R. Roediger, *The Wages of Whiteness: Race and the Making of the American Working Class*, London 1991; Alexander Saxton, *The Rise and Fall of the White Republic: Class Politics and Mass Culture in Nineteenth-Century America*, London 1991. For prominent and otherwise useful studies continuing the conflation (and confusion) of race and ethnicity, see Werner Sollors, *Beyond Ethnicity: Consent and Descent in American Culture*, New York 1986, and Orlando Patterson, *Ethnic Chauvinism: The Reactionary Impulse*, New York 1977.

4. Richard Williams, *Hierarchical Structures and Social Value: The Creation of Black and Irish Identities in the United States*, New York 1990, 2. My views here are much influenced by the perceptive comments on race and ethnicity in Barry Goldberg and Colin Greer, 'American Visions, Ethnic Dreams: Public Ethnicity and the Sociological Imagination', in Louis Kushnick, ed., *Sage Race Relations Abstracts* 15 (1990): 29–31. On the differences between the prospects of 'white' immigrants and African Americans, see Suzanne Model, 'Work and Family: Blacks and Immigrants from South and East Europe', in Virginia Yans McLaughlin, ed., *Immigration Reconsidered: History, Sociology and Politics*, New York 1990, 130–59; Stanley Lieberson, *A Piece of the Pie: Blacks and White Immigrants since 1880*, Berkeley, Calif. 1980, 308ff.

5. William Forbath, *Law and the Shaping of the American Labor Movement*, Cambridge, Mass. 1991, 23.

6. Victor Greene, *The Slavic Community on Strike: Immigrant Labor in Pennsylvania Anthracite*, South Bend, Ind. 1968; Earl Lewis, *In Their Own Interests: Race, Class and Power in Twentieth-Century Norfolk, Virginia*, Berkeley, Calif. 1991; Robin D. G. Kelley, *Hammer and*

Hoe: Alabama Communists during the Great Depression, Chapel Hill, N.C. 1990; Wayne Broehl, Jr, *The Molly Maguires*, London 1968; Vicki L. Ruiz, *Cannery Workers, Cannery Lives: Mexican Women, Unionization and the California Processing Industry, 1930–1950*, Albuquerque, N.M. 1987.

7. Roediger, *Wages of Whiteness*; Alexander Saxton, *The Indispensable Enemy: Labor and the Anti–Chinese Movement in California*, Berkeley, Calif. 1971; Gwendolyn Mink, *Old Labor and New Immigrants in American Political Development*, Ithaca, N.Y. 1986; Dolores Janiewski, *Sisterhood Denied: Race, Gender and Class in a New South Community*, Philadelphia 1985.

8. Coco Fusco, as quoted in bell hooks, 'Representing Whiteness: Seeing Wings of Desire', *Z* 2 (March 1989): 39; Goldberg and Greer, 'American Visions, Ethnic Dreams', 30. See also Mary C. Waters, *Ethnic Options: Choosing Identities in America*, Berkeley, Calif. 1990, 160.

9. Recent work on Asian immigrants is especially promising in this regard. See esp. John Kuo Wei Tchen, 'Quimbo Appo's Fear of Fenians: Chinese-Irish-Anglo Relations in New York City' (1993) and Donna Gabaccia, 'The "Yellow Peril" and the "Chinese of Europe": Italian and Chinese Laborers in an International Labor Market, 1815–1930' (1993), both unpublished papers.

10. Malcolm X with Alex Haley, *The Autobiography of Malcolm X*, New York 1984, 399. I first became aware of this source on reading a manuscript version of what became Noel Ignatiev's '"Whiteness" and American Character: An Essay', *Konch* 1 (Winter 1990): 36–9. This excellent article also sent me back to the works of John Higham and David Brody, cited below, and stimulated me to think about whiteness and Americanization. For a Richard Pryor joke echoing Malcolm's 'nigger' remark, see John A. Williams and Dennis A. Williams, *If I Stop I'll Die: The Comedy and Tragedy of Richard Pryor*, New York 1991, 94.

11. James Baldwin, 'On Being "White" ... And Other Lies', *Essence* (April 1984): 90, 92.

12. John Bukowczyk, as cited in Barry Goldberg, 'Historical Reflections on Transnationalism, Race, and the American Immigrant Saga' (unpublished paper delivered at the Rethinking Migration, Race, Ethnicity, and Nationalism in Historical Perspective Conference, New York Academy of Sciences, May 1990).

13. For extended discussions of the Irish and race in the US, see Roediger, *Wages of Whiteness*, 133–63; Williams, *Hierarchical Structures*, and esp. Dale T. Knobel, *Paddy and the Republic: Ethnicity and Nationality in Antebellum America*, Middletown, Conn. 1986, 82–99.

14. G. Legman, *The Horn Book: Studies in Erotic Folklore and Bibliography*, New Hyde Park, N.Y. 1964, 486–7; *Anecdota Americana: Five Hundred Stories for the Amusement of the Five Hundred Nations That Comprise America*, New York 1933, 98; Nathan Hurvitz, 'Blacks and Jews in American Folklore', *Western Folklore* 33 (October 1974): 304–7; Fields, 'Slavery, Race and Ideology', 97; W. Lloyd Warner and J. O. Low, *The Social System of the Modern Factory: The Strike*, New Haven 1947, 140; Baldwin, 'On Being "White"', 90–92.

15. A. Yvette Huginnie, 'Mexicans in "American Towns": Race and Work in the Arizona Mining Industry' (unpublished paper, 1990); David Brody, *Steelworkers in America: The Nonunion Era*, New York 1969, 120.

16. John Higham, *Strangers in the Land: Patterns of American Nativism, 1860–1925*, New York 1963, 173. See also p. 66 and Saxton, *Indispensable Enemy*, 281; Lieberson, *A Piece of the Pie*, 25, and, generally, Gwendolyn Mink's provocative *Old Labor and New Immigrants*.

17. Lieberson, *Piece of the Pie*, 31 and passim; Waters, *Ethnic Options*, 160; Goldberg and Greer, 'American Visions, Ethnic Dreams', 29–31.

18. Joe Eszterhaus, *F.I.S.T.*, New York 1978, 88.

19. Lawrence Joseph, 'Can't Forget the Motor City', *Nation*, 17 December 1990, 775–6. The same point is more generally made in Louis Harap, *Dramatic Encounters: The Jewish Presence in Twentieth-Century American Drama, Poetry, Humor and the Black–Jewish Literary Relationship*, New York 1987, 4–5.

20. See David Saposs Papers, State Historical Society of Wisconsin-Madison, esp. Series 4, and, for context, Bari Watkins, 'The Professors and the Unions: American Academic Social Theory and Labor Reform, 1883–1915', (Ph.D. dissertation, Yale University, 1976).

21. Certainly many African Americans have chosen and choose to be Black as well, but in doing so they identify at least as much with African American national culture as with racial ideology. One would be hard pressed to find such a specifically white American *culture*. Indeed,

in its extreme forms identification with whiteness represents a cutting off of oneself from what Albert Murray calls America's 'incontestably mulatto' culture. In its production of identity through negation ('We are not Black'): and in the record of behavior it has called forth, whiteness in the US is best regarded as an *absence* of culture. In this it fundamentally differs from African Americanity and from specific 'white' ethnicities. See Murray, *The Omni Americans* New York 1983, and James Baldwin, 'On Being "White" ... and Other Lies', *Essence* (April 1984): 90–92.

22. Cf. Williams, *Hierarchical Structures*, and Baldwin, 'On Being "White"', 90–92. On race as, in part, a '(self-)constitution', see David Theo Goldberg, 'The Semantics of Race', *Ethnic and Racial Studies* 15 (October 1992): 561–5.

23. Baldwin, 'On Being "White"', 90; Peter Linebaugh, *The London Hanged: Crime and Civil Society in the Eighteenth Century*, London 1991, 349; Peter Fryer, *The History of Black People in Britain*, London 1984.

24. See Stephan Palmié, 'Spics or Spades? Racial Classification and Ethnic Conflict in Miami', *Amerika Studien/American Studies* 34 (1989): 211–21; Heriberto Dixon, 'The Cuban-American Counterpoint: Black Cubans in the United States', *Dialectical Anthropology* 13 (1988), esp. 222–6.

25. Williams, *Hierarchical Structures*, McVeigh, 'The Specificity of Irish Racism', *Race and Class* 33 (April-June, 1992), 40–43; on anti–Southern Italian 'racism' in Italy, see Robert Orsi, 'The Religious Boundaries of an Inbetween People: Street *Feste* and the Problem of the Dark-Skinned Other in Italian Harlem, 1920–1990', *American Quarterly* 44 (September 1992): 315; see also John D. Brewer, 'Sectarianism and Racism, and Their Parallels and Differences', *Ethnic and Racial Studies* 15 (July 1992): 352–64.

26. Quoted in George Potter, *To the Golden Door: The Story of the Irish in Ireland and America*, Boston 1960, 372.

27. Thaddeus Radzialowski, 'The Competition for Jobs and Racial Stereotypes: Poles and Blacks in Chicago', *Polish-American Studies* 33 (Autumn 1976): 16–17; Niles Carpenter with Daniel Katz, 'The Cultural Adjmustment of the Polish Group in the City of Buffalo', *Social Forces* 6 (September 1927): 81–2. Radzialowski's work suggests a history of sometimes bitter job competition among African Americans and Poles in the Chicago area prior to 1919, however.

28. Michael J. Piore, *Birds of Passage: Migrant Labor and Industrial Societies*, Ann Arbor, Mich. 1978.

29. Carter, *Southern Legacy*, Baton Rouge, La. 1950, 105–6; Paola Giordano 'Italian Immigration in the State of Louisiana', *Italian Americana* (Fall-Winter 1977): 172; George Cunningham, 'The Italian: A Hindrance to White Solidarity in Louisiana, 1890–1893', *Journal of Negro History* 50 (January 1965): esp. 24–6; Jean Scarpaci and Garry Boulard, 'Blacks, Italians and the Making of New Orleans Jazz', *Journal of Ethnic Studies* 16 (Spring 1988): 53–66. Compare, however, Arnold Shankman, 'This Menacing Influx: Afro Americans on Italian Immigration in the South, 1880–1915', *Mississippi Quarterly* (Winter 1977–78); Orsi, 'Inbetween People', 314–18 and 342n3.

30. Virginia Yans-McLaughlin, *Family and Community: Italian Immigrants in Buffalo, 1880–1930*, Ithaca, N.Y. 1971, 113–14; Micaela di Leonardo, *The Varieties of Ethnic Experience*, Ithaca, N.Y. 1984, 24n16. Orsi, 'Inbetween People', 316 and 346n62; Gerald Meyer, *Vito Marcantonio: Radical Politician, 1902–1954*, New York 1989.

31. See especially Harold David Brackman, 'The Ebb and Flow of Conflict: A History of Black–Jewish Relations Through 1900', (Ph.D. dissertation, University of California, Los Angeles, 1977; Hasia Diner, *In the Almost Promised Land: American Jews and Blacks, 1915–1935*, Westport, Conn. 1977, and Lenwood G. Davis, *Black–Jewish Relations in the United States, 1752–1984: A Selected Bibliography*, Westport, Conn. 1984.

32. See the superb index to *Svoboda Cbob' OAA* at the Immigration History Research Center in Saint Paul and Horowitz, '"Without a Union, We're All Lost": Ethnicity, Race and Unionism among Kansas City Packinghouse Workers, 1930–1941' (paper delivered to the Reworking American Labor History Conference, State Historical Society of Wisconsin, Madison, April 1992).

33. Raymond Mohl and Neil Betten, 'The Evolution of Racism in an Industrial City, 1906–1940: A Case Study of Gary, Indiana', in Theodore Kornweibel, ed., *In Search of the*

Promised Land: Essays in Black Urban History, Port Washington, N.Y. 1981, 150; Donna Misner Collins, *Ethnic Identification: The Greek Americans of Houston, Texas*, New York 1991, 210–11.

34. Maria de los Angeles Torres, 'Working against the Miami Myth', *Nation*, 23 October 1988, 392; James W. Loewen, *The Mississippi Chinese: Between Black and White*, Cambridge, Mass. 1971; F. James Davis, *Who Is Black? One Nation's Definition*, University Park, Penn. 1991, 114–16; Roediger, *Wages of Whiteness*, 134. Randall M. Miller, introduction to Miller, ed., *States of Progress: Germans and Blacks in America over 300 Years*, Philadelphia 1989, 17, treats German–Black solidarity extending into the twentieth century.

35. 'Irish Mornings and African Days on the Old Minstrel Stage: An Interview with Leni Sloan', *Callahan's Irish Quarterly* 2 (Spring 1982): 49–53; Saxton, *Bright Web*, 24–5. A letter from Jim Barrett first made me begin to think about this point.

36. Donald Tricarico, 'Guido: Fashioning an Italian-American Youth Style', *Journal of Ethnic Studies* 19 (Spring 1991): esp. 56–7. Orsi, 'Inbetween People', 341. The portrayals of Italian Americans in Spike Lee's *Do the Right Thing* and *Jungle Fever* are fascinating in this regard. While in *Jungle Fever* love relationships between Italian Americans and African Americans are connected in part with desires on the part of members of the former group to escape confining aspects of Italian American culture, Lee also shows, with uncommon clarity and no romanticizing, the ways in which a sense of Italian Americanity depends, in inner New York City at least, on imitating African American culture and exploring ethnicity specifically in counterpoint to African Americanity.

37. Boulard, 'Making of New Orleans Jazz', 55, quotes Morris, and treats Prima on 59–64, with the quote on 'assimilation' coming on 60.

38. Burton W. Peretti, 'White Hot Jazz', *Chicago History* (Fall-Winter 1988–89): 26–41; George Lipsitz, 'Interview with Johnny Otis' (Rock and Roll History Project, 14 December 1986), in possession of the author; and Lipsitz, 'Land of a Thousand Dances: Youth, Minorities, and the Rise of Rock and Roll', in Lary May, ed., *Recasting America: Culture and Politics in the Age of Cold War*, Chicago, 1989, 273–4.

39. On the attempts by the Knights of Columbus to portray 'the racial contributions' of Black as well as 'white' immigrants, see Herbert Aptheker's fine introduction to W. E. B. Du Bois, *The Gift of Black Folk*, Millwood, N.Y. 1975 (1924), esp. 7–8; John B. Kennedy, 'The Knights of Columbus History Movement', *Current History* 15 (December 1921): 441–3, and Edw. F. McSweeney, LL.D., 'The Racial Contributions to the United States', which introduces *The Gift of Black Folk*, 1–29.

40. Kerby A. Miller, 'Green over Black: The Origins of Irish American Racism' (unpublished seminar paper, Univeristy of California, Berkeley, 1969), esp. 79–81; David Hellwig, 'The Afro American and the Immigrant, 1880–1930' (Ph.D. dissertation, Syracuse University, 1973).

41. Shankman, '"This Menacing Influx"'; Hellwig, 'The Afro American and the Immigrant'.

42. London, as quoted in Saxton, *Indispensable Enemy*, 211.

43. See Roediger, *Wages of Whiteness*, 140–44.

44. Forrest G. Wood, *Black Scare: The Racist Response to Emancipation and Reconstruction*, Berkeley, Calif. 1970, 98; Ralph Mann, 'Community Change and Caucasian Attitudes toward the Chinese', in Milton Cantor, ed., *American Workingclass Culture: Explorations in American Labor and Social History*, Westport, Conn. 1976, 410 and 416–17. See also Saxton, *Indispensable Enemy*, 14.

45. James N. Gregory, *American Exodus: The Dust Bowl Migration and Okie Culture in California*, New York 1989, 164–9, with the quote from 165.

46. Carey McWilliams, *A Mask for Privilege: Anti-Semitism in America*, Westport, Conn. 1979 (1948), 163–9, esp. 164; Davis, *Who Is Black?*, 114–16; K. Hugh Kim, 'Blacks against Korean Merchants: An Interpretation of Contributory Factors', *Migration World* 18 (1990), passim.

47. On *nigger work* and *white niggers*, see Roediger, *Wages of Whiteness*, 129–30, and 68 and 145 respectively.

48. Quoted in Lieberson, *Piece of the Pie*, 25; Orsi, 'Inbetween People', 331–5.

49. Ivan Greenberg, 'Class Culture and Generational Change: Immigrant Families in Two Connecticut Industrial Cities during the 1930s' (Ph.D. dissertation, City University of

197

New York, 1990), 76–7, includes the quote. See also Lieberson, *Piece of the Pie*, 349, and Claudia L. Bushman, 'The Early History of Cleanliness in America', *Journal of American History* 74 (March 1988): 1228–32; on opportunities for promotion and mobility, see Lieberson, *Piece of the Pie*, esp. 31–5 and 308–37; on the 'love/hate' attitudes of Italian Americans toward African Americans, see di Leonardo, *Ethnic Experience*, 175; see also Martin Oppenheimer, The Sub-Proletariat: Dark Skins and Dirty Work', *Insurgent Sociologist* 4 (1974): 7–20.

50. Greenberg, 'Class Culture', 78, for the quote; Orsi, 'Inbetween People', 329; Terrence J. McDonald, 'The "White" Version: *Devil's Night* and Other Not So True Tales of Detroit', *Michigan Quarterly Review* 31 (Winter 1992): esp. 123–6.

51. William Attaway, *Blood on the Forge*, New York 1987 (1941), 122–3.

52. Orsi, 'Inbetween People', 335.

Index

THE HAYMARKET SERIES

Already Published